A CHILDHOOD LOST TO THE ARMENIAN GENOCIDE

Imagine being a young boy, barely fourteen, pulled from your home and forced by invaders to march with your family and neighbors across the desert. Imagine seeing the people you know and love removed, one by one, as you stand by, helpless. Imagine the atrocities committed with impunity before your eyes.

Why would you imagine that? Because it must not be forgotten.

And now there is no need to imagine; you can live it through the eyes of a survivor of the Armenian genocide.

Yet, far from a hand-wringing tale of woe, Zaven's Destiny is filled with hope, courage, honor and compassion. Walk with young Zaven as he follows a compelling force inside of him to sacrifice personal safety and comfort and avenge his people; his family, friends and countrymen.

Bedros Margosian's words, energized by his daughter, Liz, breathe life into a time long past and transport us into the genuine adventure that was his life. More than just a history and travelogue, Zaven's Destiny reveals the Armenian heart and mind. It reflects the nobility of a people persecuted as the world largely ignored their plight. It is a fascinating recounting of a momentous event too often overlooked.

While this life was not what Zaven would have chosen, it was most certainly one in which he magnificently fulfilled his destiny.

Bedros Margosian was born in Armenia and was fourteen years old when the atrocities of the Armenian genocide began. Through his intelligence and determination, he survived. Not much is known about what happened to him after the end of World War I. It's believed he was recruited by the French Armenian Legion, which was affiliated with the legendary French Foreign Legion, and he became a mercenary. After finding his way to America to join his sister, he became an American citizen, attended and graduated from Boston University, and joined the U.S. Army. During World War II, he was with the OSS (Office of Strategic Services), the wartime intelligence agency and a predecessor of the CIA. It was during the war that he met a British woman in London and fell in love. They married in England and then came to the United States.

Upon returning to the US, he began writing. The rough manuscript for what would become *Zaven's Destiny* remained unpublished until his daughter, Elizabeth, took on the project of completing it.

Bedros Margosian, a true hero, died in 1967.

Elizabeth Marks (Margosian) was born and grew up in an Armenian community in Watertown, Massachusetts, where she lived with her parents, brother, and her Armenian aunt and uncle. Most of her childhood friends were Armenian. With her Aunt Mary doing all the cooking, she learned to love the cuisine and would spend hours in the kitchen watching her aunt cook. Though she spent long periods of time in the UK with her mother and away from her father and the Armenian community, Elizabeth counts among her treasures early childhood memories of her father telling her fanciful bedtime stories of a heroic young man and his adventures.

Years after her father died, Elizabeth learned of an unpublished manuscript and determined it was largely the story of her father's life. Reading it, she realized the tales he had been telling her were real events he had lived through. She set out to validate what she read through family interviews and historical documentation. Completing the manuscript became a labor of love and a rediscovery of the father she hadn't really known but learned to respect and cherish.

Elizabeth lives with her husband in Los Angeles and is a principal in a global consulting firm.

ZAVEN'S DESTINY

Amid the atrocities of the Armenian genocide, a young boy survives to become a man of courage, compassion, and honor.

ZAVEN'S DESTINY

BEDROS MARGOSIAN
with ELIZABETH MARKS

CAPE WEST PUBLISHING
Toluca Lake, California

CAPE WEST PUBLISHING

10061 Riverside Drive, Suite 540
Toluca Lake, CA 91602-2560

First Edition

Printed in the United States of America

Library of Congress Control Number: 2015931930

Publisher's Cataloging-in-Publication

Margosian, Bedros., and Elizabeth Marks (Margosian)

Zaven's destiny : amid the atrocities of the Armenian genocide, a young boy survives to become a man of courage, compassion, and honor / Bedros Margosian with Elizabeth Marks. -- First edition. -- Toluca Lake [California] : Cape West Publishing, [2015]

pages ; cm.

ISBN: 978-0-9863358-0-8 (hardcover) ; 978-0-9863358-1-5 (soft cover) ;
978-0-9863358-2-2 (ebook)

Summary: A novel based on the author's own experiences of the Armenian genocide. Imagine being a young boy, barely 14, pulled from your home and forced by invaders to march with your family and neighbors across the desert, seeing the people you know and love murdered as you stand by, helpless. Walk with young Zaven as he follows a compelling force inside of him to sacrifice personal safety and comfort and avenge his people; magnificently fulfilling his destiny in a story of hope, courage, honor and compassion.--Publisher.

1. Armenian massacres, 1915-1923--Fiction. 2. Armenia--History--Revolution, 1917-1920--Fiction. 3. World War, 1914-1918--Atrocities--Fiction. 4. Georgian-Armenian War, 1918--Fiction. 5. Armenian massacres survivors--Fiction. 6. Armenians--Crimes against--Fiction. 7. Historical fiction, Armenian. I. Marks, Elizabeth (Elizabeth Hope) II. Title.

PS3525.M3375 Z38 2015 2015931930
813/.54--dc23 1503

Book consultant: Ellen Reid
Cover and book design: Patricia Bacall
Author photo: Starla Fortunato

FOREWORD

About one hundred years ago, the first genocide of the twentieth century was unfolding in Eastern Europe. My father was fourteen years old when, along with thousands of other Armenians, my family was forced to cross the desert in a group of caravans.

But he left behind a story. His sister, who also survived the genocide, verified many of the events in this book. He wrote the manuscript over sixty years ago. Typed on yellow carbon paper with a manual typewriter, there were over three hundred pages of it, with notes written in the margins and corrections throughout. He was never able to get it published, and it remained a forgotten work until now.

I learned of my father's unpublished manuscript many years after he died and realized that it was his story of survival. I became determined to honor his memory by getting the book published. Throughout that long process I learned something about my father that I never knew growing up—he was strong, fearless, and brave. He was a hero in his time. His story became my passion, and has made me feel closer to the Armenian community. My wish has been fulfilled, and I hope you enjoy reading the book as much as I learned to live it.

CHAPTER 1

It was a gloomy morning in Sivas, Armenia, in early May 1915. On the main street where the American Missionary School was located, there was a bustle of activity. Goods were piled on the side of the street. At first glance, it may have seemed like any normal day, but that was far from the truth. Instead, it was here that the deportation of Armenians began. The conflict between Turkey and Armenia, two countries with people of vastly different cultures and religion, had its roots centuries ago.

The dispute was being resolved by the forceful domination of the stronger power. A young boy stood among the crowd, dressed in the typical garb of that time—high black boots, tightly fitted breeches, brown cotton shirt, and a fur hat. He was preoccupied with a spirited black donkey, when his attention was distracted by the sound of greased, wooden axels announcing the arrival of forty ox carts. The Turkish government made them available to the Armenian families that were being deported.

The boy ran toward the carts, but hesitated when he heard a familiar voice. "Stop, stop, Little Destroyer. Don't pick any cart until I see it." It was his Uncle Kaspar, who stood beside their pile of family belongings and watched him. The young boy was accustomed to his nickname. If his uncle called him by his proper name, Zaven, he knew that he was in trouble.

"I won't pick any cart, uncle," said Zaven, looking back, "but everyone is rushing to pick one. If we don't hurry, the best ones will be taken."

"All right, go ahead," mumbled the old man. "But don't pick one by its looks as you did with your donkey."

The long train of ox carts filled the entire street. Zaven walked by slowly, searching for one suitable for his family. His eyes rested on a Turkish peasant dressed in dark brown loose pants and a black handmade vest. His beard was neglected and yellowed in spots. Zaven caught the peasant's sympathetic eyes, which lent him an air of honesty. The peasant stepped in front of Zaven, partly blocking his way.

"Looking for a cart, son?" he asked with a suppressed smile.

"Yes, sir," replied Zaven hesitatingly.

"Will mine do?"

Zaven quickly examined the cart. It was not new or flashy, like some others, but the two wheels balancing the heavy flat top appeared solid. He looked at the oxen. The black one with a tiny white spot on his forehead jerked its head. It was a strong, healthy-looking ox. The other half of the team, a light brown ox, seemed just as strong.

"Yes, sir," said Zaven. "We would be grateful to travel with you."

Just then Zaven saw his uncle approaching. "Here comes my uncle. Will you speak to him?"

The peasant nodded, then turned to Zaven to ask, "How many in your family, son?"

"Just the four of us—me, my mother, my sister, and her baby."

"Well, you know that two families must share a cart. Who will be the other family?" asked the peasant.

"My uncle's, sir."

"And how many in his family?"

"Only three—my uncle, my aunt, and their daughter."

Uncle Kasper walked up in time to hear Zaven's last comment. "It looks like you've already picked the cart," he said softly.

"Your nephew is a bright boy," remarked the peasant. "I think we will get along just fine."

"You are very kind," said Uncle Kasper as he apparised the cart and ox team. "My name is Kasper Hagopian. I had a haberdashery store in the bazaar. How far is your village from the city?"

"I remember your store," said the peasant, "and have bought things from you. My name is Hussien. I'm from the village of Black Water."

"Well, we'll try to make the best of this. We have several donkeys to ride, and a cow," remarked Kasper.

The peasant moved closer to him and whispered, "Carry food, and lots of it. There may be times when money won't buy it."

"Thank you for your advice," said Uncle Kasper. Then, turning to Zaven, he said, "You did well, Little Destroyer."

Zaven ran back to the courtyard and soon reappeared carrying a heavy trunk on his back. He laid the trunk on the cart and stopped to watch the sergeant, riding a high-stepping black stallion, take charge of supervising the deportation activities. How Zaven had wished his mother had bought a horse for him instead of the donkey! But Uncle Kasper had overruled him. "It would invite thieves and blackmailers," he had reasoned.

Zaven closely observed the sergeant and was impressed. His skin was dark and he had a tough, but not vicious, appearance. His jacket was covered with cartridge belts, and his cutlass was suspended by the side of his saddle. He moved toward Hussien's cart.

"Did you engage your cart?" he asked Hussien.

"Yes, sir," Hussien replied. They were distracted by a quarrel taking place between a fat, ill-tempered peasant and an elderly woman.

"What's the trouble here?" asked the sergeant.

"I won't let her overload my cart," answered the peasant with a scowl. "These are the only oxen I have, and I'm not going lose them. I want to bring them back alive."

The sergeant turned to the woman. "It's for your own good to not overload the cart. Leave things here that are not absolutely necessary. You may come back someday and find them."

Zaven, his uncle, and Hussien finished loading the cart with all the belongings they could fit into three trunks. Hussien took an elegant prayer rug and neatly spread it over the trunks and mattresses. Zaven's mother and sister sat cross-legged on the cart, covering themselves in black shawls, with only the top portion of their faces visible. His mother was about forty and quite attractive, despite the shawl. Her soft, brown eyes focused on Zaven, who stood beside the cart with his donkey, Chalo.

Unexpectedly, an impressive-looking officer in black military dress with shining gold epaulets appeared on the street. With a measured and deliberate pace, he approached the cart and stood in front of Zaven's mother.

"I'm asking you again, Noami," said the commissar, "it's not too late. We grew up together. You know I admired your husband, even though he was part of the Armenian opposition. But with me, you and your family would be safe. Although you would need to conform for outward appearances, you would not need to change your beliefs. Will you stay, Noami?"

Zaven was about to tell the man what he thought, but his mother's stern look stopped him. She held her head high, and her soft brown eyes peered through the shawl. "You have always been good to me and my husband, when he was alive," she responded in a calm, unemotional voice, "but I cannot detach myself from my people's fate. Nothing could make me leave my sister and all those who are with us. I know you are kind, but I need to live the remaining days of my life with a clear conscience."

"But Noami," the commissar pleaded, "if you have no concern for your life, think of your daughter and her baby—think of your son."

"God will protect them."

The commissar nervously tapped his baton against his thigh and said, "You know, I can force you to the leave the baby with me."

"I know that, and I also know that you would not do it. You should not think badly of me. No one could have prevented what is happening today."

"But Noami, let me take the baby. I promise in the name of Allah that he will be yours and your daughter's any time you want him."

"Could you give him up if he were yours?"

The commissar, rejected, slowly turned away.

From a distant doorway down the street, the commissar's son, an officer in the Turkish army, had observed the discussion. He walked into the commissar's house, the largest on the street. Next to it was a modest two-story dwelling with closed shutters and a padlocked gate. It was the house where Noami had lived. The only one aware of the officer's movement was Margarette, the baby's mother and Noami's daughter. She watched from a position where the officer couldn't see her. Margarette thought of her childhood and how she and the officer had spied on each other through door cracks and curtain openings. What would have been their fate if there had been no insurmountable barriers between them? Had her mother weakened and stayed, could she have avoided becoming the officer's wife?

The commissar handed a sealed envelope to a sergeant who was standing at attention. "This is my order, sergeant," he said. "It concerns Noami Minassian, the one you saw me speaking to, and her family. This order authorizes you to bring her back, if she wishes, when you return."

The Minassians were one of the wealthier families in the city. The elder Minassian, Zaven's grandfather, was a shrewd businessman. He had established an import business, which was still operating. But his son, Zaven's father, turned out to be more of an idealist than a businessman. He graduated from the local college and devoted most of his time to writing. He later was a recognized figure in the Armenian liberation movement. With the 1908 revolution that established the constitutional government, David Minassian became a state representative.

Turkey joined the Central Powers three months after the start of World War I. Until that time Turkey's role in the war was uncertain. The Armenians' fate hung in the balance. There was some hope that Turkey would take the side of the Allies. This might have happened if Britain had delivered the two battleships that it had just completed for Turkey, instead of arguing over payment. Germany seized the opportunity and offered two of its ships that were bottled up in the Sea of Marmora. This convinced Turkey to ally with Germany. This allegiance was against the interests of the Armenian minority.

In the early spring it was reported that a whole Armenian regiment fighting under the Turkish flag had gone over to the enemy's side, and that several Armenian towns near the Russian border were in open revolt. David Minassian and a dozen leaders were arrested and presumably sent to Constantinople (now called Istanbul). In truth, no one knew if they reached Constantinople. A few weeks later, Margarette's husband, a young engineer, was taken from his office, along with all the Armenian men in the city. They were kept in prison for about a week and then mysteriously began to disappear—to where, no one knew.

Zaven was a bright student and normally quiet, but when angered he was capable of getting into serious trouble. On one occasion, a neighborhood bully—a Turkish boy several years older—had beaten Zaven because he resented being called "karfour" (infidel).

The following Sunday, Zaven, pretending to be ill, was allowed to stay home from church. He methodically planned his revenge. He went to his father's study, opened a drawer, and took out a short, pearl-handled dagger. He tucked the dagger into his vest. He knew where to find the bully—in the playground behind the Turkish school. He entered the playground and spotted his target among a noisy group. Zaven ground his teeth, clenched his fists, and marched forward. The bully saw him and began heading toward him, shouting and swearing. Zaven kept moving forward until he was close enough to reach him. The dagger flashed out. A shrill scream followed. Blood flowed from the top of the bully's leg. He ran away, his playmates fleeing in terror ahead of him. News of the event spread and the Turks were alarmed. His father had to pay the school a large sum of money to quell the incident.

These early indicators of Zaven's bravery, forthrightness, and resourcefulness were to stand him in good stead on the arduous journey that lay before him and his family.

CHAPTER 2

As the clock from a distant church tower struck noon, the long parade of ox carts and pack animals rumbled along the main street. Women and children rode on the carts, while boys were astride their donkeys and men walked alongside. Mohammedans crowded along the side of the street—some bade farewell to neighbors they knew; others watched in silence. Despite the grim aspect of their upcoming journey, this group started out with some degree of optimism. Miss Blake, a respected American missioner in charge of the girls' school, was allowed to join her students. This fact gave the Armenians a level of comfort, however misguided.

The first day was short and comfortable enough. The caravan crossed the Kizil river and camped on its bank. After his family finished their evening meal, Zaven brushed the donkeys and filled the water containers. Hussien was conscientious about his responsibilities and sat on top of the cart where he could keep an eye on the family. The caravan was settling into a quiet evening.

Zaven stretched down on his quilt beside his mother. He was tired but couldn't sleep because of the thoughts whirling in his head. He felt a gentle pressure on his arm.

"Can't you sleep, son?" whispered his mother. Zaven remained silent. "Talk to me," she implored, stroking his forehead.

Zaven raised himself up. "Mother, do you think we will ever see father and Margarette's husband again?"

She took a very long time to answer but finally said simply, "God knows."

Zaven heaved a great sigh and said, "I should have gone with the boys from school when they went into the mountains."

"What would you have done?"

"Fight, Mother! We must fight for our rights. Father did not have that chance, but I see that the day will come."

Noami rested her hand on the fiery-eyed youth's shoulder. "You're so young, and I want you to know that your father and the others did not use violence so that they could save us. Do you understand that, son?

"I do, Mother, but I still wish I were the one carrying a rifle instead the person I gave it to."

"Aren't you glad that you are with me and our family? We need you with us, Zaven."

"Can't you understand, Mother, I'm not thinking of myself. Yes, I want to help, but can I—"

Noami didn't let him finish, but drew him close to her and kissed him, whispering, "To have you close to me and safe is all that I want."

The next ten days went fairly smoothly, although not without incident. One night bandits attached the caravan, and the commissar's sergeant and his guards engaged them in a gun battle. Zaven watched the skirmish in grim fascination from behind the wheels of the ox cart, his hair standing on end at the frightened cries of women and children. The bandits were eventually chased away, much to the fervent thanks of the Armenians. The good feelings would be short-lived, however.

The caravan reached a small Kurdish village, and met up with two other caravans from Sivas that had started several days before and were still there. It was here that they learned the Turkish sergeant and his men would return to Sivas. The journey so far under their protection did not prepare the Armenians for what lay ahead.

The next morning, while Noami baked bread on an open fire, the sergeant approached her. "My authority ends here, Mrs. Minassian," he said respectfully, "but I have an order to take you back to Sivas."

Noami was surprised by his words. She looked at her sister, and then caught her son's eyes, which were bitter and resolute. She was going to choose between life and an unknown fate. Her eyes rested on Miss Blake, the American missioner who did not have to be on the journey but had chosen to cast her lot with them.

"Thank you, sergeant," said Noami, "but I cannot leave my sister."

The sergeant cautioned her, "I want to remind you that the journey from here on out won't be the same. Hardship and peril await you."

"I realize that, and am grateful for what you have already done. We all are."

The sergeant shook his head. "As you wish, madam. Godspeed."

The bad news came quickly. Since there were not enough remaining guards, the three caravans were combined. All males fifteen and older were separated from their families and were to remain in the village. The group included Zaven's Uncle Kaspar and others, including the minister of his church and some of his teachers. Zaven watched the proceedings and fear gnawed at him. Any hopes he had of a safe place to settle down disappeared. A guard noticed his expression and looked away. Uncle Kaspar hobbled away with the helpless men and looked back at Zaven again and again. Zaven wanted to rush toward his uncle and hold onto him. The thought that he was the only man left in the family held him back. Zaven shed a single tear, and it would be his last.

The next day the caravan left the Kurdish village to continue its hazardous journey, with fewer guards than they had previously. The sergeant in command was a cruel-looking Kurd. His men carried rifles, but were not in uniform. The black strips of cloth on their sleeves were the only indications of their office. Things looked bad. The caravan had not gone far when the guards carried off several women and girls. A young boy, who stood up against a Kurd trying to drag away his sister, was shot in cold blood. Miss Blake confronted the sergeant, whose harsh answer was, "Things like that are bound to happen."

The caravan continued to creep slowly along. The guards' abduction of women and children and killing of any who opposed them became a chilling routine. The guards were no longer protectors, but predators.

Fortunately for Zaven's family, Hussien's vigilant watch and revolver kept the Kurds away from his cart.

On one occasion, Zaven and several others about his age rode their donkeys ahead of the caravan. An armed Kurd approached them from the opposite direction. He dismounted and the boys became suspicious of him, but they didn't see a reason to run back. When two of the boys were close to the Kurd, he made a sudden leap, dragged one of them down, and drove his saber though the midsection of the boy, who fell with a sharp scream. Horrified, Zaven jumped off his donkey and ran. When he looked back, he saw the Kurd chasing the other boy. He stopped looking back and kept running until he realized that he was behind the last cart of the caravan.

After the horrible experience with the Kurd, Zaven—contrary to Hussien's advice—on occasion found himself at the head of the caravan. His donkey was fast, and Hussien kept his cart in the middle of the caravan, which he considered the safest place. Zaven became aware that an elderly Kurd on a mule, carrying a rifle and wearing a black piece of cloth on his sleeve, had been following him for some time.

"Wait, son!" shouted the Kurd. "I want to talk to you."

Zaven stopped. The Kurd dismounted. Zaven was alarmed, but a look at the Kurd's weather-beaten face temporarily dispelled his fears. The boy got down from his donkey.

"I want to save you and your mother, boy," announced the Kurd. "This evening I'm returning back to my village. I want to take you along with me. Ahead is certain death for you both. I have a large flock of sheep. You can be very helpful to me, and your mother can be useful around the house."

"Oh, thank you, sir!" said Zaven gratefully. "That's very kind of you. My grandmother and I will be so grateful."

"Your grandmother..." frowned the Kurd in obvious distaste. "Tell me, son, who is that good-looking woman in black, whom I've seen with you?"

"Oh, she's one of the teachers of the school," replied Zaven indifferently. "My grandmother and I share the cart with her."

"What's your family name, and what was your father's business?"

"My family name is Sarkissian, but I haven't a father or mother. I am one of the orphans of the school. The American lady looks after us."

"Your grandmother hasn't any money, then?"

"No, sir. She is very poor. She worked in the kitchen of the orphanage."

Zaven observed the disappointed expression of the Kurd, who spat in the dirt, got back on his mule, and took off without further comment in search of things we wanted most: a strong boy to attend his flock, and a rich, attractive woman to cook his meals and provide moments of pleasure—even though he may have one or two more wives around the house.

For the rest of the day Zaven did not get close to their cart, fearing that the Kurd might be spying on him. When it was time to camp and he was sure that the Kurd wasn't there, and likely on his way back to his village with the loot he sought, Zaven joined his family. Noami's grim face brightened when she saw her son.

"Where have you been all day?" she inquired.

"Just around. I almost got a Kurd husband for you."

"Son—!"

"Don't be alarmed. He is gone—I told him you were my grandmother to scare him off. But I wish you didn't look so pretty."

Noami smiled. "We will fix that. And in the meantime, I want you to stay close to the cart from now on. Change your donkey with Margarette's. He will keep you with the rest of us. By the way, you look as though you could stand a little change, too."

The next morning, with mud-smeared face, Zaven appeared in a dirty nightshirt, with a red handkerchief tied around his head. Noami gazed at him with mixed emotions. She too looked different—old, haggard, and dressed in rags.

The ragged and weary deportees were unusually active that evening. Every family was dipping deeply into its scanty supply of cash to buy goatskin sacks to be used as water containers. The custodian officer, anxious to be helpful, was making exorbitant profits. Their nonstop journey through the desert meant long hours through the burning sand, in the unrelenting sun. Water alone could save them and goatskin sacks were the most practical containers, used by the desert-dwellers. Noami bought three of the sacks. Hussien filled them and very carefully tied them on the cart.

They began the journey shortly after midnight. The night was cool and fresh, giving no hint of the disaster that would soon follow. All went quietly until the sun was high upon the horizon. Then, they witnessed grayish, half-naked corpses, partially buried in the sand, scattered along the trail. The rags, the broken fragments of brightly shining bones, and the awful stench completed this preview of hell.

As the day went on, the desert continued its ravages, adding fresh victims to its toll of death. Water was their lifeblood, but it was very scarce. Zaven saw a woman barely clinging to life, her lips shriveled and dry as parchment. Terrified, he retreated, looking back repeatedly, unable to tear his eyes from the ghastly sight. "She died," he muttered to himself, "the poor woman died."

The owners of the carts issued an order that no one would ride in the carts, making the journey more miserable. They made matters even worse by lightening their own carts, even throwing away precious food. Hussien was not one of these.

Half dazed, Zaven trudged beside his donkey. He heard someone calling him and stopped. There was Anna, the daughter of the minister, sitting helplessly on the sand. Memories took him back to the days, which were not so far back but seemed like ages ago, when he waited for her after school. The sight of her had made him happy then. She was pretty and full of life. He associated her with a melody he had heard Miss Blake play on the phonograph at a school party, "Moonlight Serenade." Anna was calling him. She was exhausted and had fallen, unable to move. Her mother could not help. She had three younger ones to look after. He went to her.

"Don't leave me, Zaven," she sobbed.

"Of course not, Anna."

He opened his tiny canteen and moistened her dried lips. She drank a little, and then she pushed it away.

"You'll need it."

He soaked his handkerchief in water and patted her burning cheeks. She put her arms around him. When he looked at her, his heart filled with joy unknown to him. He pushed back her long, light brown curls. Her skin regained its normal brightness. Her lovely dark eyes looked brighter than ever. He helped her on the back of his donkey, and with one arm around her, walked along. What a beautiful moment, he thought, in the midst of a veritable hell.

Zaven had lost contact with his family, but he had no energy left to look for them. As the evening approached, the torrid heat gradually faded. A breeze from the river marking the boundary line of the desert brushed the parched faces, giving some relief. Then, unexpectedly, the river came in sight. The half-dead deportees who moments before could barely lift their feet began to run wildly to the water.

Zaven found his mother and sister on the bridge, where they waited anxiously for him. There was an ugly wound on Noami's cheek.

"What's that, Mother, how did your get it?" he asked anxiously.

"A Kurd wanted the donkey, and I was fool enough to refuse. Hussien got it back, though. I did not mind for the donkey as much as for the food that he carried."

Zaven examined the wound closely. "Thank heaven it isn't deep. Does it hurt, Mother?"

"No, son."

"Nonetheless, we must attend to it."

"Yes, son, as soon as we are settled down."

Rubbish, broken dishes, torn blankets, smoke-blackened stones, and half-burned fragments of scattered wood indicated that many caravans had camped here before. Looking over the devastated plain, which once had been a fertile grain field, one could see several other occupied camps. The usual procedure of forming the ox-cart circle was underway. Soon the confusion died down, and the family grouped around Noami, while her sister dressed the wound. Hussien, after attending the oxen and donkeys, had joined the group.

"I almost hate to leave you," he said with a note of sorrow in his voice. "But this is as far as we come. If it were possible to take you back with me..."

Hussien's words died unanswered in the dark. Where ... to what ... or to whom ... Could there be anything worse? To them, life had already stopped. They merely existed, biding time.

Hussien's eyes rested on Noami's bandaged head. "I would have killed that ruffian if he hadn't shown his heels," he said boastfully.

Noami replied, "We should thank God that he ran away when he saw you drawing your gun—"

"I'm a peace-loving man, madam, but when aroused..." Embarrassed by his own bravado, Hussien's voice trailed off.

Noami smiled at him. "We all are grateful to you for what you have done. God bless you."

Hussien shrugged. "I've done no more than any decent man would have done."

"Do you think this is as far as we come, Hussien?" asked Noami's sister.

"I wish I knew the answer," said Hussien. "My guess is that you will stay here for a while. Maybe they will allot places for you to settle. Malatia is not far—only a few hours' trip from here. They may let you get there to buy food, and if you should go down farther, the donkeys will be useful."

"Thank you for saving one of them, Hussien," said Noami. "You can take everything back with you that you want. We cannot carry it with us."

Early the next morning Hussien started back to Sivas with a large sum of money in his pocket, and his cart loaded, including Uncle Kaspar's valuable prayer rug.

Shortly afterward, several things began to happen in quick order.

First, Miss Blake, who had accompanied the deportees so far, was to return to Sivas by order of the Turkish government. They did not want to be responsible for the life of an American citizen, and had arranged a carriage and a gendarme escort for her. Losing her meant losing all hope. She had been their champion, their consoler. Her protests, her pleas, and her assurance that she would not hold the Turkish government responsible should anything happen to her, were ignored.

Second, the guards warned the deportees that anyone who left the camp circle would do so at his own risk. But their curiosity was stronger than fear. Communication with the nearest caravan was established. One of them had been there for weeks. Other information was very bad. There was to be another separation of males—this time, all those who were ten years of age or more. The Mohammedans were given the privilege of taking away any boy, girl, or woman if they cared to do so. They would be saving the life of whoever went with them.

Early that morning, a large group of civilians, merchants, peddlers, and peasants entered camp to sell and barter food for valuables. They milled around with eyes searching for bargains, advising the deportees to buy food and sell all their valuables. Their strong and convincing argument was that the government would search them before leaving and confiscate everything of value.

The members of Zaven's family hid him from sight of the roaming soldiers. Zaven didn't like that, nor did he think for a moment that he could evade being separated from his family. He wanted to stand up, walk up to the mean-looking guard standing nearby, and give himself away. But he thought of his mother and her feelings. Since she had heard of this final separation of males in the camp, she had become distressingly silent. She stared at her son in a strange way, as though she didn't know him.

Zaven peeked over the heads hiding him. He saw a guard leading off two boys younger than him. His cousin Rose violently pushed his head down. Was this the start of dragging away the boys? No, that can't be.

They don't do a job like that in such a haphazard way.

"Noami," whispered Zaven's aunt, breaking the grave silence. "If we are to save Zaven, there is only one way." She hesitated; all eyes were turned to her. "Let's dress him as a girl."

Zaven was shocked. His mother's staring eyes shifted toward him.

"Should they take him away as a girl...what then?" she whispered.

"You're right, Aunt," agreed Cousin Rose. "But, we can change him so that no one will want him. I mean her. I will scratch his face and plaster it with mud. We'll shave his hair; lots of women have done so to keep their heads clean. Don't worry, when I'm through with him he'll look so disgusting that even a Kurd wouldn't look at him twice."

Cousin Rose's wily remarks brought a spark to Noami's eyes. Zaven was dismayed. If his mother approved this fantastic scheme, it would be hard to disobey her. He had better say something.

"What are you talking about, Rose?" Zaven laughed. "Dressing me as a girl? How silly! Why, others have tried it already."

A shrill whistle was the cue for another announcement. They listened. A harsh voice bellowed, "The ox carts owned by the deportees have to be taken to Malatia. We want boys who can drive these carts."

"That's a trick," said Noami.

Trick or no trick, the request for volunteers to drive the carts had come at the right time, Zaven thought. At least he would leave his mother with the thought that he was alive somewhere. The carts were there, and someone had to drive them to the city.

"That's all right, Mother," said Zaven. "Why miss the opportunity that could keep me alive? Things may take a better turn there. Who knows, I may even find a way to get you there, too. After all, isn't it better for you to think that I'm alive?"

"Why, son," cried Noami, "you mean to give yourself up."

"Not to give myself up, Mother, but to give myself a chance."

"I'm not going to be selfish, son," she whispered. "I realize I can't save you, and I'm not going to tell you what to do. Do whatever you think is best."

Zaven was relieved, although he did not expect her to give in so readily. Anticipating that this would be their last meal together, Noami prepared the best dinner they had eaten since leaving home. The large, square, red-trimmed tablecloth was spread with food. The family gathered around it. There were three large copper plates—one for dried meat, one for the pilaf, and one for stewed prunes. Tea and cheese followed the meal. It was a real feast.

The setting sun painted the horizon with brilliant orange. Everything seemed to be quiet at the camp. How many volunteers had answered the call of driving the carts was purely conjecture. Apparently, though, the quota was not filled, because the camping attendant began picking up boys, who were led away.

There was not much time left; the time between reporting as a volunteer and saying goodbyes to families was very short. On the spur of the moment, however, Cousin Rose came up with a clever scheme. Her sudden inspiration was to have Zaven lie on the ground, then cover himself with blankets and mattresses. It sounded all right, and in the excitement of the moment Zaven weakened and allowed himself to be jammed flat under the huge pile. Thinking this was insufficient, two members of the family sat on top of the mass. It was a wonder that he survived those breathless moments!

He might not have, had his suffering not been cut short by a guard who had watched the ruse unfold. Within seconds the sergeant and two others were standing by the pile. Roughly, they tossed down those sitting on it. A heavy kick in his ribs let Zaven know that he was discovered. He rolled over, gasping for air. The look on the guard's face terrified him. Cousin Rose began crying. Tears rolled down his sister's cheek, but no sound came from her lips. No one said a word. He looked at the baby, his little nephew. He wasn't crying; he just looked puzzled. Zaven wanted to hold him. He made the attempt, but was rudely pushed away.

A few paces apart, his mother stood motionless and speechless. He wanted to say something, give her one last kiss, and tell her goodbye. But he couldn't. She was staring strangely at him, her face blank, stoical. He never thought that his mother, always so serene, could look that way. If he could only see tears in her eyes, he would have felt better. The guard led him away. Zaven kept looking back. His mother remained there, in the same position, with the same look, and in the same deathly silence. He moved on in a daze though the mob. In and out among the ugly heaps of rubbish for the last time, he caught a glimpse of her. She was still there, standing like a statue, staring ...

CHAPTER 3

Zaven hated the Turks, not as individuals, but as tyrants. His reading of patriotic Armenian literature and his father's talks might have influenced him. Until now, the idea of killing those he hated had never entered his mind. But now, killing that wretch of a guard, who had dragged him, laughed at his unhappiness, and given him painful blows while they shuffled along, suddenly became an obsession.

The boys were assembled at the bottom of a low hill. Zaven's captor turned him over with a caustic remark to the Kurd in charge and returned to the caravan. Zaven saw one of his friends, Vahan, from school and elbowed his way toward him.

"Why, Zaven, you too!" said Vahan. "I thought your mother would never let you—"

"I was picked up," said Zaven.

"So, taking the carts to Malatia is a hoax," muttered Vahan.

"Looks that way."

"Let's run away. We may never get this chance again."

"With all these guards swarming around us?" said Zaven, looking despairingly at the vigilant Kurd a dozen paces away.

"What of it? We might get shot. I'd rather die that way."

"Not yet. We may get to the town. The carts have to be taken there."

There were more than a hundred boys over ten years old. The soldier who had made the last delivery muttered something in the ear of the Kurd, who ordered the boys to fall in line, pair by pair, and start marching. From the top of the hill, the vast plain stretched below. The faint glitter of campfires in the dusky twilight presented a sad picture. Not far away, a village, nestled in the ravine of the towering mountain, was in view. It was a small, isolated Kurdish village. The boys, numbed of feeling, climbed the winding trail through vineyards. The dirty street was deserted. The procession ended at the gate of a large storage house. A civilian standing by the half-opened door came forward pompously.

"Young men," he said in an oratorical voice, "pray for the life and victory of the Sultan of Turkey. You are young and innocent. We'll take you to Malatia. Some of you will find good homes, become true Mussulmen, and condemn those who conspire against us."

The group of boys was then led into the storage house, and the gate was latched from outside. The atmosphere of the place was damp and nauseating. It was dark. The lone outlet for light and fresh air was an opening in the center of the ceiling. Zaven spotted his friend Vahan just before the gate was locked. He groped his way toward him.

"This is a jail. Do you believe what the man told us outside?" asked Vahan.

"No, but that's an old Turkish ruse," answered Zaven.

"Why didn't you run away then?"

"We'll still get that chance. They won't kill us in this hole."

"You hope," said his friend miserably.

Gradually the place was filled with more boys who had been separated from the caravans. Among them there were two dressed as girls who appeared more embarrassed than afraid. The room was packed; it was very difficult to move around. More than two hundred of them stood close, shoulder-to-shoulder, breathing the noxious air.

Finally, the door of this black hole opened. A gendarme shouted, "We want fifty of you to drive the carts." Almost a hundred squeezed out before the door was closed.

Half an hour later the door opened again, and the same announcement was made. No one rushed out this time; the guards used force to fill the required number, including Vahan, who was pushed outside along with a group of boys.

Less than fifty boys were left waiting in dejected silence for their turns, trying to guess where the others had been taken. The door opened sooner than expected. Two soldiers and four Kurds entered and closed the door behind them. At a command, roughly given, the boys assembled at one side of the space. The soldiers stood in the middle with a long rope. Two Kurds moved to the empty side. The other two went toward the boys huddled in the corner. Each seized one and dragged them to the soldiers in the center, where they took from them everything of value, even articles of their clothing. Then the two were tied together by their wrists. The process continued until all the captives were tied in a long line.

Outside, one of the guards walked ahead of the ghostly human string. Two Kurds walked on each side, and another guard followed in the rear.

The night was dark and quiet, except for the sound of marching feet and the occasional howl of jackals. The boys moved in a daze, dreading to look around. There was one thought in Zaven's mind: What sort of death should he face? To be shot—not bad; slaughtered—what of it? The monotonous tapping of feet pounded on his nerves. He couldn't stand it. He had to do something. Talking was one distraction. He turned to the boy tied to his wrist. He was younger than Zaven, and appeared small and weak. The frightened stranger practically dragged next to him.

"What's your name?" Zaven asked.

"Hampar," stuttered the boy.

"Mine's Zaven. Have you anything to cut the rope?" whispered Zaven in his ear.

"I had a jackknife, but they took it away."

The procession was climbing up the mountain. Zaven turned around. Far below he could see the dim lights of camping caravans. Which one was theirs? Was his mother still standing there with that inscrutable look on her pretty face? A nudge at his elbow interrupted his reverie.

"Look," cried Hampar, pointing to the ravine where heaps of rags were outlined by the rising moon.

Among the rags Zaven could see naked human forms. He fell down. It was not fear that weakened his knees. Perhaps his feet became tangled with a scrub, or his toes hit a rock. He was not badly hurt, but the tumble had temporarily halted the march. When he looked up, he found the Kurd standing above him.

"Get up, you son of an infidel! Get up!" The shout was accompanied by a kick in his side. "You only have a short way to go."

He had scarcely taken a dozen steps when he noticed that the knot holding his wrist with Hampar's had loosened a little. He could move his arm up and down. He began to jerk at the rope with all his strength, attempting to pull his hand free.

"What are you doing?" Hampar whispered.

"Hush! The knot is loose. I'm trying to free my hand, and then we can get yours loose. When I jump out of line you follow me, and run like hell!"

With a few moments of hard work, Zaven slipped his hand out. Hampar also had pulled his wrist out of the noose.

"Now what?" the confused boy whispered.

"Be ready, and follow me."

One of the boys behind them heard their whispers. "What's going on?" he asked.

"We've loosened our hands," replied Zaven, "and in a moment we're going to make a run for it. Loosen yours too—we'll wait."

One of the Kurds began moving toward them. There was no time to waste. Zaven pulled Hampar's arm and jumped out of the line, and the escapees began running wildly down the hill. Confusion followed. The bewildered guards were shouting and cursing. They could not chase the two runaways because there were fifty more attempting to break away. The best they could do was to fire after them. But the bullets whistled over their heads.

Without looking back, Zaven heard the gunshots and screams from the boys who had been tied together. The Kurds had killed them all.

After running for fifteen minutes, Zaven stopped and listened. Hampar stood beside him, breathless. Where did that small, frightened boy get so much courage and energy? Zaven felt glad that he was there. It was a good feeling to have cheated death. Standing side by side, they gazed at each other, wondering what to do next. It seemed that the thing they wanted most was to rest.

But where would they be safe? The reality was that they may not have gained much by escaping. They crossed a small stream running down the ravine. Then, for a long time, they climbed heedlessly, through the almost impassible brush, stumbling over stumps and falling into hidden ditches. Yet they did not feel any pain.

Finally they saw clear sky; the stars and the moon above inspired in them a strange sense of security. They threw themselves down on soft dry grass. No ailment, either mental or physical, could keep them awake.

The hot sun on his face woke Zaven. He got up with difficulty, and could hardly stand on his feet. The mountain proved to be uglier by daylight than it had looked at night. The ghastly memory of the boys' slaughter that darkness had hidden was now before him in the daylight.

Hampar still slept. He hated to wake up the tired, frail boy and make him aware again of his plight, but they couldn't stay here. They had to keep moving in order to survive. He kneeled down over him, brushed his head gently and whispered his name. Hampar opened his eyes, bewildered, and jumped up. He felt better when he caught Zaven's smile. For a long time they sat side by side in silence. Then they decided they'd better get moving. The sun was high in the sky when they reached a wide valley. Here they found a small, clean stream. They washed their faces and drank a little, watching a vulture soaring over their heads with some trepidation until it disappeared.

"Now, let's see if we can find something to eat," said Zaven.

The sight of a green corn and wheat field below sharpened their hunger. They looked longingly in that direction, but didn't dare go out into the open. So they turned back to the mountain slope. Zaven looked up at the massive branches of a wild chestnut tree. There were nuts but they were too green to eat. He looked over some berry bushes, but their fruits, too, were green.

"Maybe we can find some mushrooms," suggested Hampar.

"Yes, but some mushrooms are poisonous," cautioned Zaven.

"I know the kind that is eatable."

"All right, let's look for them."

"I'm hungry, but I don't want to wander around in the open where it's not safe, " said Hampar. He pointed to a cave. "There is a nice place where we can hide."

"A cave," mumbled Zaven. "No, we'll be safer in the open and can see what's around us. After dark we'll look for something to eat."

Gradually, they became used to their surroundings and, thanks to Hampar's expertise, found mushrooms growing in abundance under the shady canopy of a little copse of oak trees. The following night they ventured to the fields and found fresh vegetables and corn. For three days they lived in the mountains, sleeping most of the day and coming out in the darkness in search of food. Once they dared to enter a Kurdish village, hoping to steal something more palatable, but were chased away by dogs.

On the fifth night, while wandering in the valley, they came across a road that Zaven recognized. Their caravan had passed that way. Far across the field they saw the lights of a camp.

"Here's our chance, Zaven," said Hampar. "Let's sneak into that caravan."

"No," said Zaven firmly. "I'll never return to a caravan. This road will take us to Malatia, and I want to go there. It is not far. We can reach there before daylight."

Hampar did not answer. They stood in silence, gazing at each other like strangers. They had reached a crossroads. Choice depended on each one's convictions and foresight. One path was dark and adventurous, the other fairly open and short.

"No, I'm going to join that caravan. I'm sure I'll find my mother on the road somewhere, some day," concluded Hampar.

Zaven could not argue with him. They shook hands and wished each other good luck.

As a fugitive walking alone on the road to Malatia, Zaven suddenly felt that he had grown up. With a full moon gleaming overhead, the night was clear and bright. He could see the ground around him. That gave him courage. He stopped for a moment to make sure that he was going the right way.

Yes, he was on this way to the city. Those willow trees, and the crystal stream below them, were familiar. Their caravan had stopped there once for the midday rest. He walked to the stream and stood on the same spot where he had offered drinks to his mother and sister and his little nephew. How sweet that was.

But, now was not the time to reflect. He started back on the road and came to a small village. To avoid running into anyone, he made a wide circle around it. It would be morning soon. Fearful that he would not reach the town under cover of darkness, he doubled his speed. Soon, from the summit of a hill he had just climbed, he saw the glittering minarets rising above the trees.

He hurried toward the village and was about to enter a street bordered by low walls, when he noticed a small guardhouse and a soldier standing along the wall. Zaven circled around the wall, climbed over it, and found himself in a garden surrounding a house. He hesitated, looking and listening for a watchdog. Luckily, there was no sign of one.

He tiptoed carefully through the garden and approached the gate. It was latched from the inside. He unfastened the latch and found himself in an empty street. A few moments later he was in a square, walking toward the open gate of an inn.

Near the gate a man stood in front of a lighted charcoal stove. There was a huge kettle on the stove and a table beside it set with bowls and glasses.

The smell of steamed milk stimulated Zaven's appetite. He walked directly toward the man, a milk vendor.

"Good morning to you," the milk vendor greeted him, examining the filthy young outcast with a worldly eye. "Where on earth did you come from?"

Zaven's pleading eyes said more than words could.

"You're an Armenian, I take it. A fugitive?" the man conjectured.

"Yes, our caravan is camping near the town. Last night I ran away and came here with the hope of finding someone who could use me as a servant. I'll work hard. And I can do anything. I can read and write, and I'm good at numbers."

The milk vendor stroked his chin thoughtfully and said, "Mine isn't exactly a business where I can use a smart boy like you, and I certainly can't keep a servant. I have six young mouths to feed, which is difficult enough without adding another. But you may be useful to someone else. Don't stay here. Go inside and see the innkeeper. He is a good man."

He filled a bowl with warm milk and gave it to him.

"Thank you, sir, but I haven't any money," said Zaven.

"I don't want your money, but don't stay here," repeated the milk vendor. "If the soldiers see you, they'll take you away."

Zaven grasped the bowl of warm milk and gulped it down ravenously.

"You poor thing, you must be starving," said the milk vendor, and gave him a few pieces of toasted bread.

Zaven thanked him again.

"See the innkeeper," the man repeated. "He might be able to help."

The inn was typical of those found in every small Turkish town. It had two stories, built around a rectangular courtyard, with a fountain in the center. The ground floor was a stable. The second floor had rooms with doors that opened onto the iron-fenced balcony. The stone stairways ascended from the courtyard where wagons and carriages were parked haphazardly. As Zaven entered the courtyard, he noticed a wagon driver watering two pairs of horses at the fountain, and he was having some difficulty in handling them.

Zaven saw this as his chance. He approached the man and said, "Can I help you, sir?"

The man turned and looked at Zaven with surprise. He was young, and his rough appearance was typical of a wagon driver. He had about him a cocky, devil-may-care air.

"Why, sure," said the wagon driver. "Are you one of those Armenian fugitives?"

"Yes, sir."

"How long have you been here?"

"Just arrived."

"Do you know anyone?"

"No."

"Watch out, they'll send you back to the caravan."

"I know that."

The wagon driver clapped Zaven hard on the back and said, "Well, come on then and lend a hand."

Zaven assisted the man with his horses, impressing him with his gentle way with the beasts. After the horses were in the stable, Zaven turned to leave.

"Where are you going now?" asked the wagon driver.

"I don't know. I haven't any place to go."

"Can you drive a wagon? Or take care of horses? It's not hard. I suppose you can learn."

"Yes, I know. I mean, I can—"

"Sulliman is looking for someone like you. Come on, I'll take you to him," said the wagon driver, grasping Zaven's arm.

They climbed the stairway, walked along the balcony, and stood in front of a half-opened door. In the corner of a candlelit room sat a one-armed, rough-looking Turk whose skin was a sickly yellow. He was dressed conventionally in woolen tights, a colorful shawl around his waist, and the familiar silk turban on his head. His legs were crossed under him and he sat on a mattress, contentedly smoking a hookah. He looked up at his visitors, his eyes a trifle bloodshot from the activity. The monotonous gargle of the pipe filled the room.

"Sulliman," said the wagon driver, "here's an Armenian runaway. I think he'll do. Lucky for him, he met me. Says he knows how to drive a wagon. He helped me with the horses, knows how to handle them. You don't want to make this next trip. Why not let him drive your team?"

While his new benefactor made Zaven's case and boasted of his unknown qualities, the smug, hard-looking Turk, Sulliman, scrutinized Zaven. The moments that passed were agonizing for Zaven. Would he measure up to the Turk's standards?

At length, Sulliman straightened up, took another long pull at his pipe, and said in a voice that sounded harsh to Zaven, "He'll do, Ghalil." Then, he turned to Zaven. "From now on your name is Mustafa. You're a Charkas. Do you understand?"

Zaven bowed his head in agreement.

"Are you hungry?"

"I just had some milk and toast," answered Zaven.

"That won't do; if you're to work for me, you must eat. Eat hard, drink hard, work hard, and be hard. Do you understand?"

Zaven nodded.

"Ghalil, go out and order some shish kebab, fresh bread, and cheese. And tell the innkeeper to bring some coffee," demanded Sulliman.

Ghalil walked out, closing the door behind him.

"Sit down, boy, sit," said Sulliman in a soft, sympathetic voice that surprised Zaven.

He looked for a suitable place to sit. There were two mattresses used for all-around purposes. Sulliman was sitting on one of them; the other must belong to Ghalil. He kneeled down on the carpet close to the door.

"Not there, boy, here," said Sulliman, patting the unoccupied portion of his mattress invitingly with his single hand.

To Zaven this was a premature familiarity, but he accepted it.

"Now," said Sulliman, looking straight into Zaven's eyes. "You don't have to tell me everything, my boy, just the truth so that I can help you."

Zaven felt awkward. Sulliman was a Turk; he held the power of life and death over him. Should he tell him the truth or make up a story not quite so violent? But what difference could it make? This one-armed, hard-looking wagonman's personality seemed different from what he showed on the surface.

"You know how things are without me telling about them," said Zaven calmly.

"Yes, my boy, I do. It's bad, worse than bad."

"Then you don't want to hear what I have been through."

"No, but I want to know about you."

"Very well then," said Zaven, straightening up and looking directly at Sulliman. "They were going to kill me, but I ran away."

The one hand holding the twisted velvet cord of the narghile (hookah) patted Zaven's shoulder.

"The moment I saw you, I knew that you were a fighter. Keep on fighting, my boy. I'll stand behind you."

Ghalil returned with the food. The roasted mutton was delicious. Sulliman watched Zaven with contentment while the hungry runaway voraciously chewed the spicy meat. After the meal was over, Sulliman suggested that Mustafa, the future wagonman, have a good rest.

"We have some errands to do," said Sulliman, "but we won't be long. I'm going to lock the door from the outside, so no one will disturb you."

Zaven heard the click of the key from the outside. For the first time since he left home, he felt safe. Sulliman's soft mattress a welcome change from the grass and rocks he had slept on recently. He stretched, lay down, and was soon in a deep sleep.

When he woke up he found fresh clothing fit for a wagonman beside him. Sulliman and Ghalil were not there. The clothes must be his, but he thought he should wait until Sulliman returned. The place needed a little cleaning. This was as good a time as any to show his appreciation and willingness to work. He was still at it when he heard the key in the lock again.

"Why didn't you put those clothes on?" asked Sulliman through the half-opened door.

Zaven just looked at him.

"Go on, then, get dressed," he ordered. "You'll look like a wagonman."

CHAPTER 4

Dressed in his new clothes with tights, shawl, red shoes with turned-up toes, and silk turban, Zaven—newly dubbed Mustafa—looked like a Charkas and a wagonman. He stood in front of the dirty, frameless mirror hung on the wall. How his appearance contrasted with his true personality! He was already learning how to blend in with whatever life dealt him.

That afternoon, feeling safe because of how he looked, Mustafa went out with his master, Sulliman, who had strictly instructed him not to answer any strangers' questions. The narrow streets and the crowded bazaars were flooded with goods taken from the Armenian deportees. Everything was cheap. The Mohammedans were getting bargains on things they had not dreamed of having. Mustafa and Sulliman dined in a high-class restaurant, and then went to a cafe. Sulliman ordered a large bottle of liquor. It was crystal clear, but Mustafa knew how potent it was. He squirmed when his master pushed a full glass in front of him.

"Three for one, and one for three," was Sulliman's toast. Mustafa grasped his glass; he had to drink it. He squinched his eyes shut tight and quickly drank it in one swallow. It almost choked him, but he forced himself to smile. A chunk of soured pickle, and then a ripe olive helped him to breathe. He hoped that his glass would not be filled again. But Sulliman filled it halfway and pushed it in front of him with the remark, "Drink if you can take it, son—only fools drink more than they can handle."

Mustafa felt better. The place was lively, the customers interesting, and for the moment he forgot about his situation until a soldier passed by their table. A chill ran down his spine.

"You rogue, and I thought you still believed that your mother had found you by the gate of a mosque," shouted Sulliman, slapping Mustafa's shoulder.

It surprised the young wagonman, who hadn't said a word, but was pleased when the soldier smiled at him and went away.

Sulliman did most of the talking and drinking. Now and then his mood changed. He would be melancholy one minute, a lively jester the next. Mustafa learned to humor him and stay in his good graces. At one point, a beggar stood by the table with open palms and pleading eyes. He was skeletally thin and clad in rags, and he stank.

"Listen, you fakir," Sulliman shouted. "Answer right, and I'll put a silver piece in that clay pot of yours."

"I will try, master," said the beggar with a bow.

"Tell me then, if you were to be born again, what you want to be?"

After a pretended hesitation, he mused, "A wagonman, master, for a wagonman's life is carefree."

"You lie," Sulliman cried, "for I know you ... you would be a beggar! But you've earned your baksheesh. We're wagonmen." With these words Sulliman slammed the silver piece on the table.

"And you're Charkas, a gallant clan, both of you. And the young one is of noble blood," said the beggar in a friendly voice.

"You're a dog in spite of your wit. Mustafa is of noble birth but a wagonman at heart," shouted Sulliman. "Here's another piece." The beggar slyly changed his countenance and left, looking at the youthful wagonman from the corner of his eye.

They returned early to the inn. Mustafa was fully indoctrinated as a wagonman in the stable. Sulliman fondly stroked the neck of a healthy-looking chestnut stallion.

"Be careful, Mustafa," he said, "when grooming this one. Alosh is his name. Go easy at his flanks. He gets playful and bites. He did that to me once, and for two weeks I couldn't use that arm."

Mustafa knew how to handle high-strung animals. With confidence he went up to the big chestnut, whispered softly, and rubbed him gently behind the ears. Then he began brushing him with the heavy iron comb. Several times the chestnut tossed his head nervously, but calmed itself by rubbing its nose against the boy.

"I do believe you've charmed the beast," said Sulliman with a pleased smile, and left.

"You're catching on fast, Mustafa," said Ghalil, who was in the next stall. "Sulliman likes you. He has a kind heart, but he is tough when people cross him."

"I owe it all to you, Ghalil," said Mustafa.

"I only did it so that I wouldn't have Sulliman on my back all the time. From now on the two of us will make the trips."

They finished their jobs at the stable and returned to their room. A third mattress lay along the wall between the other two that belonged to Sulliman and Ghalil. Mustafa didn't expect that kind of luxury, but neither did he question it.

"Did you give them double rations?" Sulliman asked, looking directly at Ghalil.

"Of course," answered Ghalil lazily, "and Mustafa groomed your wild beasts, such as they never have been."

"Good for you, Mustafa," said the master. "It's care more than the barley that keeps the horses fit. All these years I've failed to get this idea in Ghalil's thick head. You two better go to sleep. I'll check the loads on the wagon. Then I might drop into the coffee house for a cup of coffee."

Around daybreak two mounted soldiers appeared in the courtyard. They were very different from the ones Mustafa had encountered before. They didn't frighten him now that he was in disguise as a Turk. Twelve wagons, including Sulliman's two, were loaded with ammunition to leave for Karput. The courtyard of the inn became a hive of activity.

"Let's go," said Ghalil.

Mustafa followed him to the stable, untied his team, holding them close to their bits, and let them out. The horses were skittish, but Mustafa was determined to show who was in control, and managed to bring them beside the wagon. He then realized that he had no idea how to harness them, and he didn't want to show his ignorance with Sulliman watching him.

"Wait, son," said Sulliman amiably. "Alosh must be harnessed at the left. Otherwise he'll make trouble." He led the temperamental chestnut and started harnessing him. Now all Mustafa had to do was to copy him. Mustafa was minding the team when Sulliman left without a word. A moment later Mustafa heard someone calling his name loudly. It was Sulliman's voice; he turned toward it. He was on the balcony.

"Mustafa," repeated the tough voice, making this name stick for all who could hear, "come up here, you've forgotten something."

Mustafa ran up the stairs excitedly and followed Sulliman into the room. Sulliman closed the door behind them, leaning against it. For a few seconds he looked at his apprentice, and then said, "There are a few things I want you to know. I have nothing in this world but my teams. They are supporting Ghalil and me comfortably and they'll support you, too. You need me and I need you. I'll treat you like a son. By the time you are back from this trip, I will arrange another.

"Ghalil is not a Turk; he also is an Armenian. This might explain things more clearly, but you must keep it to yourself. He has been with me for the last six years. Stick along with him and you'll be all right. The life we live is not always safe. I've paid the price." He lowered his eyes to the arm missing from the elbow. "Be good-natured, but hard. Don't look for trouble, but also don't run away when it comes. Accept friendship only when you are sure."

"Thank you, sir," Mustafa said solemnly.

"Call me by my name. And by the way, I want you to know that we are not getting paid for this trip. Try to pick up a fare on the return."

Mustafa was about to leave the room when Sulliman asked, "Do you smoke?"

"No."

"You better learn. You're a wagonman now. Here, take these packages."

When Mustafa returned to his wagon, he found Ghalil waiting alone. He climbed up and sat on the driver's seat, trying hard to conceal his nervousness. It was the first time he held a pair of reins. The two chestnuts seemed to have doubled in size. Ghalil's wagon had almost reached the gate.

Suddenly he shook the reins and shouted "Yaha!" with all the energy he could muster in his voice. He watched the strong hind legs of his team; the wagon jerked and started rolling over the cobblestones. Seconds later, without any further effort on his part, he found himself in the street.

"All's well," shouted Ghalil, turning around in his seat.

"Right," Mustafa yelled. "Let's go!"

"Good luck!" shouted Sulliman, standing at the gate.

On the straight, sandy road Zaven watched and imitated Ghalil in voice and manner, and became an acceptable wagon driver in less than two hours. The long train of moving wagons thrilled him. The drivers sang ballads and teased the clownish Hasan, a diminutive, stocky Kizilbash, with an ugly face and a nasty temper. Two soldiers rode next to the wagons and joked with the drivers. One of them wanted to be friendly with Mustafa, but before he got to the point of asking pertinent questions, Ghalil found an excuse to call him. The drivers stopped every two hours or so to rest the horses. Mustafa kept close to Ghalil and talked sparingly. That night they stopped at a small inn. Ghalil preferred spending the night in their wagons instead of sharing the room, which the soldiers had provided for all.

This was their first chance to be alone, and there was a lot Mustafa wanted to know.

"I already know a little about you," he began. "I was lucky to meet you."

"I suspected that Sulliman would tell you when he called you up," Ghalil replied.

"Yes, he told me. I was a bit puzzled."

"If it hadn't been for Sulliman, I wouldn't be here talking to you."

"And now because of him, I, too, am safe."

"Right," said Ghalil in an emphatic tone. "Sulliman is respected in every way and by everyone."

"Is he really a Charkas?"

"Maybe, but that shouldn't concern you. He has been good to me, and he'll be good to you, I can assure you. Now go to sleep, we've a hard day ahead of us."

The following day about noon, the wagon train of ammunition for the southern front reached the bank of the renowned river Euphrates. Mustafa was thrilled as he gazed at its muddy, foaming water and listened to its thunderous roar.

The only way to get across the torrent was by rafts resembling oversized bathtubs and kept afloat by inflated buffalo hide. There were three of these contraptions, each large enough to carry two wagons. It took almost three hours for one of them to make the trip over and back. A crowd of travelers and merchants with their goods and pack animals was waiting at the landing, but the soldiers in charge of the ammunition convoy made the operators of the rafts see that government business came first.

There was a sudden commotion while Mustafa stood in front of his team with a tight grasp close to their bits. A team left unattended had rolled downhill toward the river. Scarcely had the horses taken a few steps in the water when a swift current dragged them down. Moments later horses and wagon were sucked into a whirlpool and disappeared from sight. No one dared to save them. The driver, a hired man, was beaten by the gendarmes. What else may be in store for him was too terrible to speculate. Mustafa was thankful that the team wasn't his.

Crossing the treacherous torrent excited him. First, the wagons were pushed onto the raft; then the horses were led on, blindfolded.

"Now, boy, hold tight on those reins," warned the man at the rudder. "I've seen them jump overboard."

Mustafa smiled confidently. Besides Ghalil and himself on the raft, there was a talkative peddler with his mule who had bribed the soldiers for the ride with a pair of cheap earrings.

"Rivers are a blessing for the land and the people living around it," said the peddler philosophically, "but not this one. It is a curse." He gestured at a massive concrete tower. "See that tower? There's one like that on the opposite bank, too. They had a heavy steel cable across the river connecting the two. It was supposed to speed the crossing with the rafts fastened to the cable and pulled by machines from the shores. But the cable broke on the second day, and all the rafts and those in them perished. It happened ten years ago. They haven't tried it again."

The raft pushed off. The man at the rudder warned again, "Don't look at the stream. You'll get dizzy."

Mustafa could not keep his eyes away. The whirling, roaring torrent fascinated him. Scarcely ten feet away from the shore, he realized that the rowing of the four men wasn't any use. Swift currents swept the raft along like a leaf. The skill of the man at the rudder was their only hope of getting safely across. The raft rushed on, almost helplessly, but gradually edged its way to the opposite bank. More than a mile downstream the raft finally touched the bank. Half a dozen Kurds were waiting there with a rope to tow it upstream.

By the time the wagons were ferried across, it was nightfall. There was a full moon. The horses were fresh and the teams received orders to start climbing. This was the most difficult part of the journey. The wagon train climbed up along the narrow winding road, with the Euphrates foaming beneath. Every driver led his team. Any misstep would send them plunging down into the watery abyss below. Mustafa was finally relieved when he brought his wagon into the courtyard of the isolated inn at the summit. He was animated by the experience in crossing the Euphrates. It symbolized something—maybe his people, as it was their river. They had their birth, growth, and glories along its banks.

After their meal of bread, cheese, spiced beef, and tea, he made a place for himself on the ammunition boxes and went to sleep. They reached the government warehouse the following day. When the last ammunition boxes were stowed away, Ghalil remarked in a joyous manner, "Well, it's all over. Now we can be by ourselves."

"That suits me," Mustafa said, thinking of Hasan, the nasty-tempered clown who had been insulting him as an inexperienced driver and trying to get a reaction.

For their stay in the big city, Ghalil chose one of the best inns and rented a room. That evening they went to see the town, and Ghalil led the wide-eyed youth down a narrow street where women without veils stood in the doorways or looked from the windows, smiling bewitchingly at all the men passing by.

Soft, enticing music came from both sides of the street. Soon Ghalil was coaxed to enter a house. Mustafa followed him, shy but curious. The roomy salon was flashily furnished, with soft cushions, fluffy rugs, and inlaid wood tables, and looked like a scene from *The Arabian Nights*. A slim, exotic gypsy girl danced seductively to the hypnotic thumping of a tambourine. A smiling, middle-aged woman with unnaturally rosy cheeks directed them to a cozy corner.

Ghalil ordered drinks. They had hardly sat down when two scantily-dressed women, smelling of heavy perfume, walked over. One was very young, even younger than Mustafa. She stood in front of him, her feminine charms on full display, with her eyes downcast. Mustafa gazed at her, embarrassed, fancying that she, like himself, was somewhat unsure of herself. She was small, very pretty, and very delicate. Suddenly she looked up, and her eyes locked with Mustafa's. His face turned red, and he lowered his eyes. Ghalil, noticing the expression on his face and aware of Mustafa's discomfort, sent the women away.

CHAPTER 5

Three days in the big city were happy ones for Ghalil, for he was drunk most of the time and made all the rounds by himself after his first evening's experience with his innocent young companion. As for Mustafa, he had to take care of two teams, but he preferred that to Ghalil's escapades.

On the morning of the fourth day, while Mustafa brushed the horses in the sun out in the courtyard, a well-dressed, elderly gentleman approached him. Mustafa threw a sideways glance at him, and kept on with his work.

"The innkeeper told me that you have two wagons for hire to Malatia," said the gentleman. "I really need a carriage and a wagon, but I was told that carriages are scarce." The gentleman circled around. "He's a healthy-looking animal," he commented.

"Speedy and strong, sir," asserted the young wagon driver.

"I'd like to see your wagon."

"That's the one, sir," said Mustafa, pointing to a well-kept and sturdy-looking blue vehicle close by.

"It's covered and it's roomy," commented the gentleman. "It can be made comfortable. Where is the other one?"

Mustafa showed the gentleman Ghalil's wagon. It was open with one small, wooden bench.

"That'll do for our luggage. There are three of us, my wife, my daughter, and myself. When will you be ready to start?"

"Anytime you wish, sir."

"It's too late to start today. Tomorrow we start early."

"Very well, sir."

"Now, what is your price?"

"You'd best talk to Ghalil about that, sir."

"Who is Ghalil?"

"My boss, sir."

"Does he own the wagons?"

"No, the wagons belong to Sulliman."

"That rogue! You mean Sulliman the one-armed?"

Mustafa nodded.

"I know him well. I have done business with him many times, but I haven't seen you before. How long have you been with him?"

"Not very long, sir," replied Mustafa curtly.

The gentleman looked at him and smiled. Mustafa felt uneasy. Neither his speech nor his wagonman's attire had fooled the gentleman, but Mustafa was not worried. The gentleman had a kind face and his attitude was friendly; besides, he needed his service.

"I've no time to wait, boy," said the gentleman firmly. "By the way, what's your name?"

"Mustafa, sir."

"Well, then, Mustafa, name your price."

Ghalil had mentioned that if they could book passengers for four liras, Sulliman would be tickled. "I want five liras per wagon, sir."

"The usual fee is three liras, my boy."

"But there are hard times, sir. We were not paid for the trip up here. Everything is expensive. You will have good service and be completely satisfied, I can assure you."

"You're a shrewd bargainer—more so than your one-armed master, boy," said the gentleman. "He would never have been paid that much from me. Now, here's where I want you to bring the wagons about dawn." He slipped a sheet of paper in Mustafa's palm and turned toward the gate.

Ghalil returned to the inn after a melodious voice from the top of the minaret had summoned every Mussulman to the midday prayer. He was in a joyous mood.

"Have you eaten?" he asked.

"No," replied Mustafa. "I was hoping that you would come with me."

"Let's go. I'm so hungry I could eat a jackal!"

They went into the small grill attached to the inn.

"Well, my boy, I've finally had my fill of the big city," said Ghalil. "I'm going to stick around the inn the rest of the afternoon and try to get fare for our return trip."

"You already have one," Mustafa smiled.

"Good!" shouted Ghalil, leaning across the table to slap Mustafa's shoulder. "Who is our benefactor, then?"

Mustafa responded by showing him the paper that the gentleman had given him.

"You know I can't read," Ghalil chided him.

Mustafa glanced at the paper. "It says here Mahmude Bey, from Malatia, and he's provided an address. We have to meet him there before dawn tomorrow."

"Mahmude Bey! That tyrant!" cried Ghalil. "What is he doing here?"

"You know him?"

"I certainly do. He is a big dried-fruit producer, and he has enough business to keep fifty wagons busy all year round. Oh, what a bargain shark! Sulliman will have another round with him. How much is he going to pay?"

"Five liras per wagon."

"What!"

"Just what I said, five liras per wagon."

"What did you do to him?"

"Nothing, just told him that it is a fair price."

"Mustafa, you're a genius! To get that much out of that skinflint," spurted Ghalil, his mouth half full of bread.

It was not for lack of room in the wagon that Mahmude Bey decided to sit next to Mustafa on the driver's bench. He watched the young wagonman's handling of his team. Mustafa acted like a veteran driver, and enjoyed himself by shouting at his team and tickling them with the whip. The Bey was talkative, but Mustafa answered him only in monosyllables. He was puzzled. Through the questions and insinuations he became aware that the Bey knew exactly who he was.

The women sat on soft cushions at the back of the wagon. Mustafa hadn't seen their faces, for they were heavily veiled. But, they looked nice and spoke very softly. The daughter, called Nouria by her parents, must have been about his age, possibly a little older. But girls of her age looked more mature, especially in veil. She must be pretty, though, Mustafa thought, gazing at the white velvety skin of her hand while she offered him a plate of cheese and fruit.

"Father told me that you're a Charkas," said the young lady. "I've heard of them but never met one, and I could hardly believe a Charkas would be a wagonman. I thought they were all warriors or highwaymen."

"Mustafa is a Charkas, daughter," said the Bey. "I even suspect him of being of noble birth. Driving a wagon may be his idea of adventure. But, ah, Mustafa...very common name; he could have chosen something more refined."

The remark dispelled whatever doubts Mustafa had about a challenge to his identity. But he laughed, since for the time being, at least, he was needed. When they reached Malatia, he was certain that Sulliman would deal with the Bey.

It was close to sunset and they had less than two hours before reaching their destination. The evening was cool, the road smooth, and the horses comparatively fresh. Ghalil, who was on Mustafa's heels, had taken the lead and sang a wild ballad. The group laughed and commented on his harsh and tuneless voice.

"Surely Mustafa could sing better than that," chuckled Nouria.

Mustafa turned sideways and looked back. Taking advantage of the dusk, the ladies had thrown their veils over their heads. To him, the Bey's wife looked older than he had imagined, but had a very pleasant face. As for the daughter, she was pretty. He thought she did not look Turkish as her skin was very fair. Everyone looked happy, and why not? It was a pleasant journey and nearing its end.

"How's everything, Mustafa?" shouted Ghalil, leaning out of his wagon.

"Couldn't be better, my friend," Mustafa shouted back.

"You're doing better than Sulliman ever did," said Ghalil. "He treated those chestnuts like babies; that's why they got so fat."

Mustafa was pleased with the compliment but tried not to show it. "It won't be long now before we're there," he said with the authority of a seasoned wagonman.

Suddenly, just ahead and close to the edge of the road, Mustafa saw a naked human form. What a strange sight! It seemed to be walking toward him. He turned to his passenger.

The Bey didn't answer, but only stared.

"Mahmude Bey, did you see that thing ahead?"

"But, why, in that state..." muttered Mustafa to himself.

He slowed down the horses.

"What's the matter?" shouted Ghalil from behind.

"There's something strange ahead. Haven't you seen it?"

"No, what is it?" called Ghalil, stopping his team and standing up on his seat. "Oh, yes, I see something, but it's not moving!"

Mustafa climbed down, held his team close to their bits, and advanced slowly. When the animals caught the grotesque sight, they made a sudden dash toward the shoulder of the road. Had Mustafa been less adept at handling them, they would have run off with the wagon and its passengers.

After observing the figure more closely, he stopped ahead of it at a safe distance and calmed the horses. Ghalil, who had followed his move, stood close behind him. No one spoke a word. The women pretended they hadn't seen a thing. Imprints in the dirt indicated that a deportation caravan had been on this road. The naked figure of a dead Armenian woman lay there, a testament to the Turks' violations of Armenian women.

Mustafa lifted the lid of his bench and took out a shovel and an old blanket.

"Would you please mind the horses, Mahmude Bey?" he asked. "They won't be any trouble now."

"Gladly, son," said the Bey.

Mustafa advanced slowly toward the corpse; Ghalil followed him. As they looked at the naked figure, their feelings of sadness turned to horror and then to rage. She had died of a dagger wound inflicted under her mutilated breast. She was young, and even in that horrible state they could tell she had once been pretty. They closed their eyes, as if that could wipe out the hideous reality. This act was more than a vicious crime: It was a deliberate attempt to degrade another race. They lowered her body to the ground, covered it with the blanket, and dug a grave deep enough to cover her.

Mustafa was stunned. It had shocked him even more than separating from his mother. Rather than feeling helpless, a strong desire for revenge came over him. He took off his fez, knelt on the fresh grave with the earth giving softly under him, and stretched his hands toward Heaven with complete disregard of those who were around him.

"Damn me forever," he cried, "but I will never wash away this shame, even if it means shedding blood!"

He rose, feeling that suddenly he had become a different person. He ran down into the field, found a heavy rock, and placed it on the grave.

"It's over," Ghalil said.

"Yes," answered Mustafa. "There is no more we can do."

They returned to their wagons. Mustafa found his passengers whispering among themselves.

"It must have been the body of one of those unfortunate Armenians," commented Mahmude Bey.

Mustafa nodded without looking at him.

"Son," continued the Bey, "I thank God for giving me a conscience to judge between good and evil. The thing you and Ghalil did was kind and humane. The monster who committed the crime was a Mussulman, but his is not the deed of a Mussulman. Evil is everywhere, in all people. The Armenians should never have been deported. Now we know that this is one of the blackest episodes in our history. As a true Mussulman, I declare that Allah will not let this crime go unpunished."

CHAPTER 6

It was dark, but the kerosene lanterns lit the way and the two wagons rolled slowly along. Faces were long. Mahmude Bey spoke very little. The patrols at the entrance of the city stopped them. The Bey, who still sat next to Mustafa, graciously accepted the policemen's humble apology for detaining them. It was close to midnight when they reached the gate of Mahmude Bey's big house.

The Bey stepped down and went to Ghalil. "The boxes in your wagon go to my warehouse. Take them there," he commanded.

He instructed the burly servant who had opened the gate to accompany Ghalil to the warehouse. Mustafa carried the luggage into the house. He was impressed by the spacious and richly decorated hall.

"Here, my boy," said the Bey, putting eleven gold pieces into Mustafa's palm. "In all my travels, I've found you to be the best driver I've had. Ten is the amount we bargained for; the extra is your tip."

Mustafa thanked him and started for the door.

"Wait!" the Bey beckoned to him. "Ghalil won't be back for some time yet; I want you to have some coffee with me."

Mustafa hesitated, but had no excuse to refuse. He followed the Bey into an elegantly furnished parlor and sat in a velvet-covered chair. The Bey took his place on the divan opposite him.

Presently an aged servant brought in the coffee and served them. Then the old man withdrew and stood, head bowed, by the door, his hand poised over his abdomen.

"You can go," said the Bey in a casual way.

The man's hand touched his chest, and then went to his forehead. For a split second, Mustafa caught the servant's puzzled eyes as he looked at Zaven. Then he closed the door behind him. The Bey went to the cupboard and took out a small gilded box.

"These are good cigarettes," he smiled. "Though I do not approve of a boy smoking, I noticed on the wagon that you already have started."

Mustafa thanked him, but did not accept the cigarette. The Bey lighted his own and went back to the divan.

"Now, tell me who are you and where are you from," he demanded, not unkindly. "You're not a Charkas, nor a wagon driver."

Mustafa was speechless. His eyes strayed nervously to the floor.

"No matter how you act and talk, son, it's written all over you. I want to help you and perhaps lessen your sadness. I've done that for other Armenians. Half a dozen families are safe and working in my farms. That's the least I could do."

"God bless you, sir," said Mustafa.

The Bey looked satisfied. "Now that we have set aside the pretense," he said, "I want to know all about you. Your real name, your family, what your father did, and the place you come from."

"There isn't much I can tell that you don't already know, sir. I'm the son of an ordinary family."

"I want to make certain that you won't be harmed, and will have a new start. I want you to trust me."

"I do, sir. I'm grateful for your kindness. Reliving my sad past won't help."

To Mustafa's relief, the servant entered to inform them that Ghalil was outside. The young wagon driver rose with an apology and was about to leave the room, when the Bey called after him in a commanding voice.

"Tell your master to see me tomorrow. I'll engage him for a trip to Sivas."

Mustafa was overjoyed at the prospect of seeing his home again, even though he risked being recognized. "Yes, sir!" he cried, and quickly left the house.

He walked straight to Ghalil, who sat in his wagon.

"Thanks for the timely call," said Mustafa. "The Bey insisted on my company longer than I cared for."

"I suspected that he liked you," said Ghalil.

"Maybe, but I'm not flattered by it. He's too inquisitive. Anyway, he has another job for us. He wants Sulliman to see him tomorrow."

They drove to the inn, put the horses in the stable, and went up to their room. Sulliman was in his bed, snoring like an out-of-tune pipe organ. They tried to slip into bed without awakening him, but he sat up drowsily and rubbed his eyes.

"Damn," he growled. "Couldn't you two stay at an inn and come back during the day?" Then he changed his tone. "How did you like this job, Mustafa?"

"I liked it," said the young wagonman and handed him the eleven gold pieces.

Sulliman counted the gold, jingling them in his palm. "Eleven liras!" he cried. "How did you do it, boy?"

"Five liras per wagon was what we bargained for, and the odd one as a tip for me."

"Why don't you keep yours?"

"I may lose it. You keep it for me."

Sulliman unloosened the belt that he wore next to his skin. At one end was a red string; he gave it a pull and out came a heavy linen pouch. One by one he placed the gold pieces in the pouch. Then he pulled the string from the other end, replaced it in the belt and fastened it around his waist. He rose, half-dressed, and walked to the door. Mustafa followed him into the stable. He walked around the horses, patted them, and examined their hoofs and legs.

"I couldn't have cared for them better myself, my boy," said Sulliman. "They are hungry. Give them an extra portion of barley and come up. You need a rest, too."

Early the next morning Sulliman went to see Mahmude Bey. Mustafa had to spend most of the morning in the stable. When he went up to their room, Sulliman was back, but he looked pensive. Mustafa wondered what was wrong.

"Day after tomorrow you and Ghalil will start for Sivas," Sulliman said. "It is a longer trip, but the roads are better—also, no river to be ferried and no passengers. Don't hurry to get back. There's plenty work in and around Sivas, but keep me informed."

He looked directly at Mustafa and added, "By the way, that's your home town. Is there a chance that you'll be recognized? Not that it matters, but I will need to get some papers for you."

"Don't worry about that, Sulliman," answered Mustafa. "No chance that I'll be recognized, the way I look."

"I know that, but I need to make sure."

Sulliman's manner and his mention of getting papers had made Mustafa less enthusiastic about going home. Mahmude Bey's interest in him had made him suspicious, but he felt that the Bey was a good Turk and wouldn't harm him.

The following day, when Mustafa met the Bey in his busy warehouse, he looked somewhat different. Clad in Western clothes, he looked even more distinguished than usual with his reddish, well-groomed goatee and sharp, greenish eyes. He did not talk to Mustafa. After the wagons were loaded with sealed boxes of dried figs and raisins, the Bey asked Sulliman to let Mustafa remain in the warehouse the rest of the day and help weigh the goods coming in. Though this sounded like a favor, Sulliman could not refuse.

"If I had someone like you to help me, I would have no worries," said the Bey, as he locked the door of the warehouse.

"I'm glad that I could help, sir," answered Mustafa. "I'd better get back to the inn."

"I want you to eat with me," said the Bey curtly, in a tone that was more a command than an invitation.

"You've been kind. I'm very grateful, but Sulliman may not approve."

The Bey waved his hand dismissively. "Stop worrying about Sulliman! I've talked to him and we understand each other."

This comment was significant. Mustafa was left to wonder what they had talked about.

Outside the warehouse, two expensively saddled thoroughbreds were tied to the post in the shade and pounded the loose dust under their hoofs. One was pure black with a white star on his forehead.

"You ride the black one," said the Bey as he gazed fondly at the animal. "He's a yearling, just broken into saddle. A bit devilish, but I'm sure you can handle him."

Mustafa felt like he was in a dream, but it was real, happening to him—riding with a nobleman, who was a Turk. Even though he hated Turks in general, this one seemed to be different. Half an hour later they were at Bey's home. On his previous visit, Mustafa hadn't seen much. Now he was amazed by the surroundings. There were three separate apartments: two built side by side, separated by a low fence overrun with morning glories, a wall of flowers serving as a curtain between the harem and a third building, which was the main living quarters. They walked through the marble-paved courtyard surrounded by flowerbeds and rose bushes with a fountain in the center. At one side was a narrow sand path leading to the stable.

They were going to dine alone, as custom did not allow a Turkish woman to share the table with men, and certainly not in the company of strangers. The supper was sumptuous, consisting of roast lamb, dried fruit, and bread. Wine was served, indicating that the Bey was liberal. After their coffee, black, unsweetened, and thick as pea soup, they retreated to the adjoining room, a cozy alcove decorated with ancient swords and firearms on the walls. They sat down, facing each other. The hookah, with the bright chunk of charcoal skillfully placed on the highly aromatic tobacco, was ready. This was the only time the Bey smoked the narghile. He again offered Mustafa a cigarette, but he refused.

"Well, I won't press you," said the Bey, "but you are welcome to smoke here."

Mustafa finally took the cigarette and pondered over the inevitable conversation that we knew was coming.

"You probably dislike me for not leaving you alone," began the Bey after inhaling deeply on the narghile's long pipe. "I sympathize with you for those you have lost. We all are puppets in the hands of destiny. Let me put it this way: If I had known your Armenian name, I would have called you by it. I was in Karput, for my father-in-law and uncle passed away, and his last wish was to have his only daughter and grandchild at his bedside. God has willed that I find you, for he has denied me a son." He looked straight into Mustafa's eyes. "This is my feeling toward you, my boy. Can you understand?"

"Thank you, sir," Mustafa gasped in amazement. "You are very kind, but I am too old to forget who I am."

"I don't want you to forget who you are, but I want you to know that there are people like me who want to do the right things."

"I know that, sir. Sulliman is good. I'm grateful to him."

"Fortunately for you, Sulliman also knows what's good for you. This will be your home from now on."

Mustafa was totally taken aback by the offer of a home he never dreamed of and could not think of what to say. The idea of becoming an adopted son of a wealthy Turkish nobleman, and all that was required of that exalted status, ran through his mind while Mustafa thought of an answer. He glanced at the tall grandfather clock facing him. It was late.

"Thank you for everything, sir. I will remember this evening as long as I live. But it's getting late. Sulliman will worry about me," he said, standing up.

"You stay here. I'll send a messenger to Sulliman," said the Bey.

"Please, no, he wouldn't like that. He has been good to me. I cannot let him down." Mustafa moved toward the door.

"Wait!" commanded the Bey. "It isn't safe for you to go alone."

He left the room and returned within a moment with the old servant hobbling behind him. "Take this boy to the inn," he ordered.

As Mustafa went up the iron-fenced stairway to his room, the timid old servant's words still rang in his ears: "The Bey is a kind man, but stubbornness aggravates him. For your own good, my boy, I hope you did not displease him."

He found the door unlocked, pushed it open, slipped in, and quietly closed it behind him. Ghalil was snoring in his bed. Sulliman sat up and lit the candle.

"I thought you were going to stay overnight at the Bey's," he said sleepily.

"You know I wouldn't," answered Mustafa curtly.

"I was pretty sure of that. But the Bey generally gets his own way."

"Not in this case, Sulliman," said Mustafa in a determined voice. "I want to stay with you."

"I don't blame him for wanting you. Anyone would be proud to have a son like you."

"So, you know all about it."

"Of course I do! He's an important man, but he is honest. I only wish that I could offer you all that he can."

"But I really do want to stay with you."

Sulliman remained silent.

"You don't want me," Mustafa mumbled.

"It isn't that, son, but I don't want anything to happen to you, and the Bey can protect you. But, if you don't want to stay with him, I hope he will understand. We will see. Now, go to sleep, and don't worry."

It was the morning they were to leave for Sivas. Sulliman and Mahmude Bey were making the last minute arrangements. Ghalil had gone to the coffee house for his farewell drinks. Mustafa minded the horses. When he turned back he saw a police officer, accompanied by a soldier, walking toward him. He instinctively sensed trouble. He pretended to be busy by adjusting the feedbags. Soon, the policeman was standing directly behind him. He felt a tap on his shoulder.

"Come along," growled the officer.

"But—I—can't c-come," he stammered. "I-I look after the horses. My master will be angry. They may r-run away. Wait until—"

"To hell with your master and his horses, too!" shouted the policeman.

He roughly pulled the young wagonman's arm as if to yank it off, and turned to the soldier. "You wait here. When his master comes, tell him where we have taken this Kavour."

Glancing over his shoulder as he walked, Mustafa hoped that Sulliman or the Bey would notice, but there was no sign of rescue. His feeling that help was once again beyond reach put him in a state of mental paralysis. He was taken to the police station and flung into an underground cell, without being questioned. Here he found several other Armenian boys, also runaways. They exchanged stories of their experiences and spoke of their families. All day he waited in agony, hoping that he would be released. In the evening they were given some soup, but Zaven couldn't touch it. Later the other boys were taken away. The next day at about noon, a policeman entered and commanded Mustafa to follow him.

They went up a stone stairway, walked down the hall, and passed through a door marked "Police Commissary." Behind a large oak desk sat a middle-aged officer in uniform. Mahmude Bey sat in an armchair to his right. Mustafa looked at him. The Bey smiled but didn't speak.

It was the Commissar who said in a gentle but authoritative voice, "Listen, my boy, the only one who can save you is here. We were going to send you back to the caravans with the others. But Mahmude Bey wouldn't let us. He wants to adopt you. He is here to take you to his home. Thank Allah for your good fortune."

Mustafa stood by the closed door, dumbfounded, looking alternately at the Commissar and his benefactor.

"What are you waiting for?" said the Commissar. "Kiss his hand and prove to me that you're worthy of his compassion."

Head down and trembling, Mustafa approached his benefactor. He kneeled before him, held the extended hand, and took it to his lips.

"Come, son, we're going home," said the Bey, patting his head.

As they were about to leave the room, the Commissar rose, shook hands with the Bey and whispered, "We didn't tell him his new name. He may not like it, in which case it will necessitate a change in the registration."

"That's right," the Bey replied. Then, turning to his foster son, he said, "I've named you Ibrahim; it is the name of my father. A much nicer name than Mustafa, in my estimation. Do you like it?"

Names didn't concern him—Mustafa, Ibrahim, it mattered not. But there were other things he wished to know. What became of Ghalil and Sulliman? Did they leave for Sivas? Did Sulliman try to save him? Was his being groomed as a wagonman a prearranged ploy, designed to ultimately deliver him to the Bey? True, there could be no comparison between the life of a hired wagon driver and a nobleman's foster son. But, Ibrahim, as he was called now, preferred Sulliman and driving his wagon.

The Commissar accompanied them to the door and paused before opening it. "I hope I'll be extended the honor of being his Godfather at the solemn ceremonial, Bey," he said amiably.

"The honor will be yours, Rashid," the Bey smiled.

That afternoon they went to the best stores on the main street. The Bey introduced his foster son, Ibrahim, with pride to all his friends. He bought him new Western clothes, including an expensive fur hat and fine underclothes.

They got home in late afternoon, earlier in the day than was customary. Normally they would not arrive until it was time for dinner in the evening. The Bey introduced Ibrahim to the family; his adoptive mother looked very happy. Nouria, a stepsister now, looked at him suspiciously under her veil.

"My child," explained her mother, "Ibrahim is your brother."

Nouria threw her veil back, but Ibrahim did not dare to look at her. She curtsied and disappeared quickly without a word. There were other veiled women, servants and two more foster sisters, one about ten years of age, the youngest about six years old. Ibrahim wondered why the Bey had not taken a second wife in hopes of having a son. They left the harem so that he could meet other attendants and servants. After this initiation, the Bey and his foster son retired to their own quarters.

"All these years I have eaten alone, except when I had guests," said the Bey while they dined on stuffed dolma and rice. "How I wished that I had someone close to eat with me. Now I do. I've accepted you as a son: Ibrahim. I hope in time you'll accept me as a father."

Then the Bey went on to describe his foster son's duties and his position in the household. He was to take his father to work and assist him in the office, as well as to help to manage the household. He was to be available whenever the Bey needed him. In the morning, Ibrahim was to go to the tutor who would teach him his new religion and duties appropriate for an adopted son of a bey. Then he was to take his foster father's lunch to the office, work there in the afternoon, and return home with him.

Weeks rolled by. The house of the Turkish nobleman became a real home for the Armenian outcast. He learned the likes and dislikes of every member in the family, and tried to please them all. His foster father's interest and care for him increased daily. Accompanied by a bodyguard, he could visit the Bey's properties and farms. This was the work he really enjoyed as he could talk to the Armenians who worked there. He attended the mosque every Friday at noon with his foster father. This was one way for the Bey to show those interested that he had succeeded in converting an Armenian.

The idea did not annoy Ibrahim, but the rituals did. He had to be absolutely clean before entering the mosque, then kneel down on the prayer rug for a long half hour and follow each move of the priest, repeating the phrase "God is great. God is merciful" over and over in Arabic. Then he would follow his foster father out of the mosque with a guilty conscience, for during the prayer he had been thinking things that were far from being a Mussulman in spirit.

Ibrahim began to accept his life. He wasn't concerned with consequences and took life as it came, enjoying the benefits of his good fortune and never being swayed by circumstances.

He had learned from his foster mother that the Bey had refused to take a second wife even when she had suggested it after their third daughter. She had kissed him and said with great affection, "Since you have come to us, my husband believes that fate had planned it so. We both love you as if you were our own, and in every way, my son, you've proven yourself worthy."

Time passed quickly for Ibrahim, and he lived in Mahmude Bey's household as a member of the family for two years. He grew up physically strong and tall. Mentally he was far more mature than his age. People respected him, as they would a legitimate son of the Bey.

He had all the material things he wanted, and this should have made him happy. Yet deep in his heart he was restless and very unhappy. He wasn't sure what he really wanted. Was it love of adventure? Or was it the reverberating echo of revenge that sometimes died away and then came back stronger? As the months rolled by, and he gained confidence in himself, this relentless fantasy began to dominate his thoughts.

His discontent changed to misery. At times it seemed he could not bear to remain another instant in a household that had been so kind to him. His foster father's concern and devotion only seemed to increase his distress. Of course, he liked him—he supposed he even loved him, in a sense—and he wouldn't have hurt his feelings if humanly possible. But in truth, could the Bey, though kind, be naïve enough to think that he could make a grown-up Armenian forget his murdered parents?

How well he recalled his parents' soothing words, which had no effect on his feelings. Nor had they succeeded in extinguishing the burning flame of revenge that consumed his heart. "Ibrahim, my boy, forget the past, and don't blame those who had no hand in it," his father had said. "I won't and I can't make you a Mohammedan. Both Christ and Mohammed gave us the words of God: Do well, be good. What does it matter which one we follow as long as we obey God's commandments? I'm proud of you, son. And when the time comes, I know that you'll carry on, not as a Mohammedan or a Christian but as a good man."

It was harvest time. For weeks Ibrahim had been away from home at one of the farms attended by a rescued Armenian family. A fall sunset and a vineyard combined in delightful harmony. He had worked hard all day and lounged on a soft mattress with no thought in mind and smoked. A gentle evening breeze swayed the column of smoke away. The teenage daughter of the family brought his coffee, and waited by the steps with the coffee tray in her hand. Ibrahim felt guilty having her waiting on him, but such had been the quirk of his destiny.

His foster mother and Nouria arrived unexpectedly and momentarily disturbed him. Lately he sensed that his foster mother's attitude toward him had become exceedingly possessive. As for Nouria, he felt that she had never accepted him as a brother. She was nice enough to him, but he saw her rarely, and on these occasions their conversation had been very short. Her reticence was accepted, but the real meaning behind it was yet to be disclosed. Ibrahim left the portico to meet them.

"I didn't expect to see you, Mother," said Ibrahim. "What brought you?"

Nouria watched them enviously. "Father is so boastful of the work you do here, that we wanted to see it for ourselves," she said breezily.

"I'm glad to hear that, but the credit goes to those who are doing the actual work."

"The Bey knows that and is very much pleased with them, too, Ibrahim," said his mother. "I am sure you expressed his feeling to them."

"Yes, Mother, they are grateful. But you must be tired and hungry. Let me make sure that you are looked after properly."

"The workers are taking care of that, son. I want you to have coffee with us after we've washed the dust off our feet."

It was a glorious night. Ibrahim spent more than two hours with his foster mother and sister. They gossiped, laughed, and talked about serious matters. As the evening progressed, Ibrahim began to feel uneasy, although he tried to conceal his feelings. Several times he fancied Nouria glanced at him almost flirtatiously, conveying unspoken thoughts that unnerved him. He imagined these were the normal thoughts of an attractive young woman in a man's company. She made the remark that she preferred living at one of the properties away from the big town house, having people around whom she could feel free, and not having to wear the black veil. She could have said more, but her mother's stern look stopped her.

Although he was tired, he could not sleep. He got up and dressed, went to the vineyard, and wandered around, looking up at the stars. There were so many thoughts swirling in his head that he could not concentrate on any one. He sensed that he was not alone and turned around. Nouria was standing a few paces away.

"I've been watching you for a while, Ibrahim," she said gently. "You're unhappy; I know that. You might never guess it, but I know what is in your heart. It's that horrid scene on the road. I saw you kneel and pray on that poor woman's grave. I also know what your prayer was. You're proud and revengeful, Ibrahim. You'll never become a Mussulman, and the truth is that I don't want you to. Right at this moment you're fighting a battle in your heart—between hate and loyalty. Can't you forget it—for my sake ..."

She flung herself into his arms. He kissed her, knowing that this is what had haunted him from the very moment he caught her eye. Like a child experiencing her first touch to a fire, she raced away.

Dazed, he watched her disappear in the vine bushes. He looked up. The moon seemed to be laughing at him. He heard a voice coming from within: "You love her, fool; but your life with her would be in bondage."

CHAPTER 7

The incident with Nouria had made things clear to Ibrahim: How could he stay and lead a life as Nouria's husband? He made up his mind. The winter was not far off. If he delayed, it meant spending another six months, possibly the rest of his life, as a confirmed Mussulman and devoted husband.

He arranged everything he needed—a small sack containing the shabby outfit of a refugee, food, and a little money that he had saved. Only one thing remained: He needed a gun. Obtaining one would be easy, as his foster father was away that night.

He tiptoed into his Mahmude Bey's room, although he had no reason to, and went to the wall where the automatic pistol hung. He kissed it and replaced it with a note that read:

Please forgive me for what I am about to do tonight. I cannot help myself. I know that I am throwing my life away; but let it be so. You have done all you can. Thank you, farewell, and may God bless you all.

He returned to his room and fastened the pistol under his waistcoat. The cold steel strengthened his resolve. Then he walked into the garden, picked up his sack, and climbed over the wall, where he found himself in the narrow street leading to the mountains. He never looked back to the house where he had experienced both joy and disillusionment.

His plan was to travel through Asia Minor until he reached the eastern frontier where the Armenian army fought the Turks. He would go across the border to join his people and fight to the finish. It sounded like an easy plan, but he soon discovered that it was hard to follow.

He decided that the best course was to travel by night on the regular roads and at daylight climb into the mountains for rest. He followed this plan for several days. Finally he entered a small village. To his satisfaction he realized that everyone whom he met took him for a Turkish refugee from the frontier, as he claimed to be. Not a glance of suspicion was cast his way. His Turkish was perfect, and his disguise convincing.

He stayed at an inn that night. In the morning he thought that it would be safe to travel with Turkish companions. It was not difficult to manufacture a story about his assumed identity: A refugee named Mustafa from Kars, captured by the Armenians, he had lost his family and was trying to find them.

He found many sympathizers willing to help; many suggested places where he might find his relatives. He listened appreciatively, and asked questions now and then to appear genuinely interested. He was beginning to feel safe, and stayed at the inn for another day.

That evening several wagons arrived on their way to Sivas. His desire to see his birthplace once more tore at his heart. Besides, Sivas was on his route and a stop there would not hinder his plan. He had succeeded in establishing a friendship with the innkeeper. It was he who introduced Mustafa, the refugee from Kars, to the wagonmen. One of them, an elderly fellow whose long, gnarled limbs reminded Mustafa of an ancient willow, would take him if he would look after the horses, adding that the only place for a refugee to find lost relatives was in Sivas.

Although this arrangement fit nicely into his plan, he would have to sacrifice his gun. He was certain that, as a refugee, he would be questioned and searched, and a gun would cast instant suspicion. Reluctantly, he sold Mahmude Bey's automatic pistol, without ever being used, to the innkeeper with the story that he had found it on the road.

Another and perhaps more important reason to go to Sivas, was that he had learned Miss Blake, the kindly American missioner, was still in the city. He wanted to see her; even if she could not help in any material way, her advice would be valuable.

Everything went along smoothly, except for one incident where he almost exposed his real identity. One of the drivers, an overbearing, vile-mouthed wagonman, swore at him. Incensed, Mustafa the refugee slapped him; the driver came back with a painful lash from his whip, but it was the first and the last. The refugee from Kars pushed him down and began beating him revengefully. Those who witnessed the beating reproached him. Fortunately, the driver he rode with took his side, and the incident was forgotten.

They reached a small town less than two days' journey from Sivas. The refugee from Kars was at the fountain on the square, filling his water canteen. A veiled woman stood beside him with a jug. The young refugee had become aware that she was staring at him through her veil. He sensed that he was recognized. Suddenly she grasped his arm, threw back her veil, and cried, "Zaven!"

He looked around anxiously and saw the wretch he had beaten standing by the stable door. Surely he had seen her grabbing his arm and shouting his name.

"Zaven, don't you recognize me?" the woman asked in a lower voice, pulling her veil to her face, but too late. "I'm Armenuhi, your neighbor."

Yes, Zaven had recognized her and remembered her only too well. But how she had changed! She had been pretty then; now her face, haggard and careworn, had grown old before its time.

"Of course I recognize you," he whispered. "What are you doing here?"

"The Turk who owns this inn is my husband. He took me away from the caravan, and since then I have been living with him."

Zaven struggled to find something to say. Should he congratulate her for being alive?

"It's so good to see you," she continued. "You can never know how miserable I've been. I wish I were dead. Where are you going? What became of your mother?"

"Don't talk now," he cautioned. "One of my companions is watching.

They think I'm a Turk."

"I should have known better," muttered the woman. "But I couldn't help it. Please forgive me. Oh, God, don't let him get hurt," she mumbled as she walked away.

He walked straight to the gate, having already decided what to do. The troublemaker, who had been watching him, shouted, "Where are you going, Mustafa?"

"I'll be back in a moment," shouted back the refugee. "I want to buy some cigarettes."

Again Zaven, alias Mustafa, the refugee from Kars, headed for the mountains to hide from real and imaginary enemies. However, Sivas was not far away. The air was cold and damp, the kind of frigid dampness that penetrated into your bones. The sky had turned sulky and menacing. His spirits were down; could he continue his journey toward the border? Winter came early here. Zaven spent the whole day in the woods. The chill of the evening was too harsh, and he knew it would be even worse at night.

He left the mountains under the cover of darkness and entered a small village, where he sneaked into a warm stable. He was up early the next morning. After buying two loaves of bread and some cheese, he began his journey along a well-traveled road. He looked like a typical refugee with the white head towel (the indisputable symbol of a Mussulman) wrapped around his fez.

That evening, tired and sore from walking, he reached the foot of a high mountain. It would not be safe to attempt the climb at night, so he looked around for a place to keep reasonably warm. He saw an isolated hut not far away and walked cautiously over to it. Peering through the opening, he found it blessedly unoccupied. He thought it must be a shelter, old and dilapidated, that had been used by shepherds. He gathered some wood and built a fire in a little pit surrounded by soot-stained rocks. He heated his loaf. Cheese in the fold of the hot loaf tasted good, and the fire comforted him. He stretched down before it and soon went to sleep.

The morning was cold and windy. He waited for a while, hoping that it would grow warmer, but there was no change in the weather. He left the shelter and began climbing. The wind became stronger and snow began to fall. At first he had no trouble following the road up the mountain. But when he was up high on the ridges leaning into the storm, he was not certain. He soon realized that he was not on the road. The snow under his feet was getting deeper and deeper. Pushing through the heavy drifts required energy, and he had not much left. Gradually it dawned on him that he was in a hopeless situation. He collapsed in the snow from exhaustion. A familiar warning echoed in his mind: Staying still in a blizzard invited certain death. He felt a surge of vitality. He got up and floundered on, hoping that he was close to the peak. Now the snow was above his knees and every step buried him deeper.

He was completely exhausted, sunk deep in the snow, unable to move. In submission, he covered his head with his coat, ready for oblivion.

Suddenly he heard, or thought he heard, a faint sound. He listened intently, unsure of himself. But the sound was real: the familiar "choo-choo" command one uses to lead a donkey. It seemed unbelievable that a man with a donkey could be about in this storm. He gathered what strength he had and shouted, "Hello! Is there anyone out there who can save a Mussulman?

There was no answer. He yelled again, louder, and heard a deep voice answer, "Who are you?"

"I am Mustafa, a Mussulman who lost his way en route to Sivas and was caught in the snow."

"I'm coming, I'm coming! Keep on shouting so that I can find you!"

In a few moments a burly peasant, wrapped in a heavy woolen cloak, stood over the helpless young traveler, who was now almost covered by the snowdrift. He kneeled down and raised his arms skyward. "Thank you, Allah!" he cried.

With his hands and feet the peasant dug and kicked away the snow and released the refugee from his death trap. He wrapped his cloak around him and helped him to get on the road where the donkey stood.

"It wouldn't have been so bad if you hadn't lost the road," said the peasant. "The snow on the road hardly covers your ankles, but that's the danger of this mountain. Strangers lose their way and get trapped in the drifts."

Mustafa tried to speak his thanks, but his chattering teeth would not let him.

The peasant gathered up the freezing refugee in his arms and placed him gently atop the donkey's back. The peasant spurred the beast to move and walked alongside as the little creature slowly snuffled through the blinding blizzard.

The descent was easier, for the storm gradually subsided. They reached the peasant's village. The refugee, feeling much warmer and in better spirits now, looked at the man who had saved his life.

"You must know how I feel," he said. "No words can express it." While he said these words, he resented the thought that abruptly entered his mind. Would he have been saved had the word "Mussulman" been left out of his cry?

"I will be all right from here on," he added. "Good-bye. I'm forever grateful."

"You will be my guest for the night," the peasant said. "A bowl of hot soup will do you good. You can start for Sivas in the morning. Maybe there will be others from the village going to the big city. It's better to travel among a company."

That evening Mustafa supped with his rescuer and shared with him a few details concerning his supposed journey, just to keep up his charade. He was a refuge from Kars who was en route to Sivas to meet up with relatives who were going to help him find work. He was willing to do anything to make some money.

The following morning the refugee was still in bed when his host bent over him. "Mustafa," he said, "I've good news for you. There are a few Kurd refugees in the village who are from the same parts that you come from.

I spoke to them about you. I think they can help you. They are peddlers and are leaving for the city. You can go with them."

"Thank you. You have been so kind," replied the refugee.

The supposed refugee did not like to associate with other refugees, especially those from the same parts he supposedly hailed from. But, he could not afford to arouse any suspicion. He needed to start out with them and, if he could help it, avoid talking about imaginary places and relatives. Maybe he could find a reason to leave them along the road. He would wait and see. At any rate, he would be introduced as a Turk. With any luck, the Kurds from Kars may not know much about the Turks.

His host left and within ten minutes re-entered with a large copper tray. There were freshly-made bread cakes that smelled good, and also cheese with a preserve made of mulberry fruit. They sat facing one another and ate their meal together. Then the host asked for his guest's handkerchief. It was a bit soiled but it did not matter. He put several pieces of bread cakes and chunks of cheese in it.

"Now let's join your countrymen," he said.

At the gate of the mosque where curious villagers had gathered to take a peek at the refugee saved from certain death, Mustafa met the Kurds. The young refugee was accepted enthusiastically and they began the journey.

The Kurds turned out to be more inquisitive than Mustafa cared for. They showered him with questions. They wanted to know everything—all the details about his family, the street he lived on, people he knew, and so on. On several occasions he was embarrassed by a sharp reminder that his stories did not quite coincide with the facts they knew.

Toward evening they were in the vicinity of a once large Armenian village now taken over by Mohammedans. Mustafa felt that the Kurds suspected him and had an idea who he was. They stopped and whispered. Mustafa's heart beat quickly, for he knew that he was the subject of their discussion. He heard the word "infidel" and his heart skipped a beat. A particularly ugly Kurd, the leader of the group, clumsily drew out his revolver. Would this be the end?

"You're an infidel!" shouted the man with the gun, and delivered a painful blow to his chest. The others joined him. Mustafa was knocked down. Five against one; this wasn't a contest of skill and strength. They beat and kicked him, yelling for a confession.

"In the name of the Prophet, stop!" he cried. "You want me to confess? Then give me a chance."

They let him sit up.

"No more lies," warned the one with a satanic smile.

Mustafa's breath came raggedly. The wild Kurds circled him like hungry wolves.

"Yes, I was an Armenian, but no longer," he said. "Thanks to Allah I'm a Mussulman." No Mohammedan could repudiate the sanctity of this claim. "And I can prove it."

"A converted one—ha!" laughed the Kurd with the gun. "I might have believed you if I didn't know your kind."

"Yes, a converted one," declared Mustafa in a bolder tone. "A converted Mussulman is a blessed one; even more so than a born Mussulman." He spoke these last words in Arabic.

"He recited the word of the Koran," uttered the eldest Kurd.

"Yes, these are the words of the Prophet; if you plan to kill me, let me pray."

They all looked at each other in amazement, muttering in Kurdish.

"Before granting you anything," said the old one firmly, "we want more convincing proof."

"Yes, I'm circumcised," he declared. But they wouldn't take his word for it. Shamefacedly, he showed them the physical proof.

"Why do you pass as a refugee from Kars then?" asked the ugly Kurd, replacing his revolver in the holster. "And why are you traveling alone?"

"Here is why," Mustafa replied calmly. "I became a Mussulman of my own free will. The last two years I've been working for an innkeeper. I'm from Sivas. My father was a rich man and I know where he hid his money. I don't want to be recognized when I get there to dig it up."

The Kurds glanced at each other. The hastily concocted yarn had produced the desired effect. The Kurds seem convinced. Was it the lure of gold? The ugly one spoke up.

"We are not going to harm you but we want our share of that gold," he said, his eyes snapping with greed. "This is our village. Tomorrow we'll take you to Sivas. And if your story is true, you will be treated as a brother."

"That's very kind of you," said Mustafa.

"And another thing," added the Kurd, "from now on you are not from Kars, but from Olti. It's a town on the Russian side of the border. You won't meet anyone from there."

Were these the same Kurds who were ready to tear him to pieces less than five minutes ago? Secretly he was flattered that they believed his story and thought how disappointed they would be the next day.

They reached the village. He was to stay with the ugly one who had suddenly taken an interest in him. After the usual meal of meat and pilaf, they led him to a room with two of his companions. He couldn't sleep. He was in a bad situation, and could not wait until the morning.

He lay quietly and listened to the snores of the two Kurds. He had taken off only his fez and shoes. He sat up and crept to the window. All was quiet. He got back to his bed, picked up his fez and shoes, and the white towel. A rooster crowed. There was no time to waste.

Quietly he approached the door, opened it inch by inch, and slipped out into a narrow alleyway. If someone should see him, he had a plausible excuse. Leaning against the wall he put on his shoes and fez, but the white towel shouldn't be wrapped around his head until he was outside the village and safe. He headed for the gate and was almost out in the street when a large and mean-looking shaggy mongrel confronted him. He had noticed the animal in the evening, and in anticipation of having to deal with him, had learned his name. The dog growled. That warned him, but he was not discouraged.

"Hush, Saru, I've got bread," whispered the desperate fugitive, throwing him a crust of bread. The animal wagged his tail and gobbled down the morsel.

"Good boy," muttered Mustafa, breathing freely as he tossed another crust.

He began walking along the mountainside for a long time, but did not know how close he was to the city. The lengthening shadows indicated that it was mid-afternoon, so he considered it safe to descend to the road.

He rejoiced on this recent triumph. He had walked by a guardhouse and had been called in. The corporal in charge wanted to know who he was and where he was going. The answers that the refugee from Olti had fabricated convinced the hard-boiled corporal of the guards that he was a poor, harmless thing and deserved sympathy. Encouraged, Mustafa had asked directions and how long it would take him to reach Sivas.

"You'll be there before dark, son," the corporal had told him.

Isn't this wonderful, he thought: only a few hours more and he would be in Sivas with Miss Blake. She would be so surprised and happy to see him. He slowed his pace to avoid suspicion.

He soon came across a vicious-looking Turk, tall and robust, mounted atop a similarly imposing horse. Cartridge belts crisscrossed his massive chest. A rifle rested diagonally over his knee, and a long saber protruded from a leather sheath attached to the saddle.

Mustafa greeted him respectfully. It was a genuine and hearty Mussulman's greeting: "Salaam-al-o-coum," pronounced cordially with hand on chest. The soldier's acknowledgement was sharp and grudging.

Then the soldier dismounted clumsily. Mustafa thought his movements betrayed poor horsemanship. Had his face shown that? Now they were walking side by side, when it occurred to the fugitive that he might ingratiate himself by a further demonstration of respect. He asked the soldier to let him lead his horse. The Turk handed him the reins willingly enough and started asking questions.

"What's your name?"

"Mustafa, sir."

"Your father's name?"

"Shukri."

"And your family name?"

"Kel-Topuz-Oglou." This was a family title of his own invention, meaning the child of a bald-headed patriarch named Topuz.

"Are you a Mussulman?"

"Thank Allah, I was born a Mussulman."

"Where are you from?"

"Olti, sir."

"Olti, Olti!" mumbled the gendarme, looking at the fugitive. "I have never heard of a place with that name."

"It's a small town on the border between Turkey and Russia, sir, under the rule of the Moscowite Kavour."

The soldier cocked an eyebrow. "So, you're a fugitive."

Mustafa nodded sadly.

"Where do you live?"

"The Kavour killed my father. I came to Sivas with my mother and two sisters but I am working for a countryman who has a tract of land and a house in the big Armenian village. He lets me visit my family occasionally."

Seemingly satisfied, the soldier didn't ask who the man he worked for was, and Mustafa, confident of himself and his behavior as a Turk, spoke quite freely. He complimented himself on his skill as a raconteur when his dangerous companion showed obvious carnal interest in his imaginary sisters. Mustafa pressed his advantage, boasting about the virtues of his sisters and invited the Turk to visit when he happened to come to the city.

Then their conversation turned to the war and the depressing problems of the refugees. The gendarme asked another series of questions concerning the enemies of Turkey and their treatment of captured Muslims. His fears faded. The fugitive from Olti spoke glibly, and let his imagination contrive the bloody tales that only an Armenian would relish hearing.

They had walked this way for some time, when suddenly the soldier stopped, yanked the reins from the fugitive's hand and roared, "Kavour! You're an Armenian!"

The fugitive from Olti stood speechless, unable to think of any words to defend himself. He knew that nothing he said would matter. His thoughts centered on his resolve to die bravely. What a strange feeling this was! He had suddenly discovered that death is not as bad as he thought. Facing this certainty, his had no fears.

He felt a heavy blow on his back. It knocked him down, but even as he fell, he knew that it wouldn't kill him, for it had come from a rifle butt. He tumbled in the dust, and like a flash, the desire to fight for his life kindled like a raging fire within him. He thought of attacking his enemy, but this would mean matching his boyish strength against the much stronger man and his deadly weapons. He looked for a rock, but could not see one within reach. He raised his head. The soldier appeared as a monster, standing over him, and preparing to hit him again if he moved. He felt there was nothing he could do but wait for the inevitable. Moments flew by, but he was not aware of time. Finally he was ordered to stand up. He got up on his feet and faced his potential killer. Everything felt like a blur, as if he was in another world.

"At first, I wanted to kill you," said the soldier. "Then it occurred to me that it might be best to take you along. Who knows? Some of you Armenians who escaped are giving us problems and you might shed some light on them."

These words terrified the Armenian fugitive more than the quick death he had expected. He imagined the tortures devised to extract information. What did he have to confess?

"Now that you know who I am," said Zaven, "and you wanted to kill me, why don't you? Save yourself the trouble of dragging me along. I've been through enough."

The soldier glared at him. "Don't rush me, cur!" he shouted. "You'll get it in time. But, I want to know a little more about who I am going to kill."

"What difference would that make?"

The soldier cursed under his breath. "All right then," he shouted. "Choose your death!"

"Shoot me."

"Have you got the price of a bullet?"

"Yes, I have." Zaven put his hand inside his shirt and took out a leather wallet. "Here, there's more than the price of a bullet."

"Keep your filthy pouch!" the Turk shouted in rage. "When I'm done with you, I'll know if you have anything more valuable."

He motioned Zaven to move on, and tramped behind him with a rifle in one hand and the horse's reins in the other.

"You acted cleverly," the soldier added. "I'd like to know where and how you learned that skill."

"I've been a converted Mussulman for the last two years."

The soldier laughed. "A snake, too, sheds off his skin, but that doesn't change him, nor does it take away its poison. But I give you credit just the same. You would have fooled me if I hadn't looked and seen your eyes while you talked of how the Armenians massacred the Turks. That's what you dream, you dog!" He backhanded Zaven across the mouth, knocking him down again.

"Come on, get up!" he shouted. "You seem too brave to tumble in the dust."

Zaven got up and continued to walk ahead. He couldn't speak or think straight. They walked this way for a while, with the soldier vigilant and very close.

"Well, that's it," Zaven heard him grumble. "I don't want to bother with you any longer."

There was a drainage ditch along the side of the road that looked fairly deep. Zaven moved to the edge and faced the soldier, who stood in the middle of the road less than twenty feet away, his rifle in hand. Zaven glanced over his shoulder at the ditch that would soon be his grave and pictured himself lying there. It was a frightening sight. He stared fearlessly into the eyes of his executioner, who avoided looking at Zaven as he raised his rifle. Zaven stood up straight with his chest out, looked again at the soldier, closed his eyes, and waited.

Nothing happened—no rifle shot! He opened his eyes and looked at the gendarme.

To his amazement, the man's expression had undergone a dramatic change. The barrel of the rifle was pointed at the ground. Something had happened to him. He stood like a statue, and stared at Zaven stony-eyed.

Zaven took a few steps forward, but the soldier did not move. He came closer. Now Zaven could almost reach his sword, and he thought of snatching it out of the scabbard and attacking the gendarme. He would have perhaps a fifty-fifty chance, but instead of trying for the sword, he picked up the reins of the horse and waited.

The soldier quivered. Then he said in an awed, faraway voice, "I've killed others, and I thought that you would be just one more. But I couldn't do it. You don't seem human. If you are really seeking death, you will find it. I have never before felt such an unearthly presence. I don't care who you are or where you are going. You are free—go!"

Zaven did not know what to say, so he handed him back the reins.

"You know," said the soldier, "I don't think you are a bad Armenian. I could even help you. Suppose I suggest that you go to my village. Will you do that?"

"I may," replied Zaven. "But I must go to Sivas first."

"It's like this," continued the Turk. "I have an old mother at home. She is alone and needs someone like you to help her around the farm. I won't be home much myself, but you will be safe. No one will doubt your being a refugee from Olti, if you do not talk about the Armenians and their massacring the Turks."

Suddenly he looked sharply at Zaven, and his eyes refocused. He gave a strange laugh.

"No," he cried, "of course you wouldn't! Maybe you're the devil. This is where we part. You follow the road on the right. It will take you to Sivas. Now go along. I granted your life thanks to the Almighty One."

The soldier mounted, turned away, and rode out of sight. Zaven watched him, still dazed and not quite certain if the events just passed had actually happened.

At sunset, he was by the river, and the city that he longed to see was on the opposite bank. All he had to do was cross the bridge, but this was not easy because the entrance was guarded. He hid behind the bushes and watched the traffic crossing. He felt discouraged when he noticed that everyone who went over the bridge was asked to show papers. He had no papers and was in no mood to answer questions. He thought he might swim across the river. This would be foolish because the river was swollen with the late rains. He would never reach the opposite bank if he plunged into the swirling, muddy waters.

While he calculated his options, a dozen ox carts loaded with grain approached the bridge. Another idea instantly came to his mind: mingle with the cart drivers and pass unnoticed over the bridge, as if he were one of them.

As the carts came closer, he looked carefully at the drivers and chose an old, simple-looking peasant who had a kind face. Zaven approached him.

"Uncle," he said, "I'm a refugee and I've been walking the whole day. I'm exhausted, and I can hardly take another step. Would you let me ride on your cart until we reach the city? I've a few piasters and can pay."

The old man looked the youth up and down. "Yes, son, jump on," he said with a kindly wink.

Zaven climbed on the sacks of grain and started a conversation, insisting on relieving the old man from the driving. His strategy worked. He passed by the guards and went across the bridge without being scrutinized. He did not leave the cart until he reached the marketplace. Then, he jumped down, thanked the old peasant, and made his way into the crowded streets.

CHAPTER 8

Undisturbed, he walked through the familiar streets. He felt safe because the city was full of dubious characters like him, supposed refugees. He wondered what had become of his house. Who occupied it now? Though he no longer had any emotional attachment to the house, he wanted to see it.

When he reached it, Zaven stood before the gate of the half-ruined, seemingly unoccupied house. No, it was occupied. A soldier in a shabby uniform walked across the courtyard to get water from the fountain. Zaven stepped aside, and looked around. The street was totally deserted. His memories of a happy childhood flooded back to him. He remembered his father, his mother, his sister, and Uncle Kaspar, who would glare at him and good-naturedly mutter his nickname, "Little Destroyer," whenever he had been up to mischief.

On those stone steps he had chatted with friends. The steps were now crumpled, and the marble-paved courtyard that his mother had kept so clean was plastered with mud. He bit his lip and walked away, his fists clenched.

Moments later he stood in front of the large brown gate of the American Missionary School. He held the knocker and, with his heart pounding, tapped gently. There was no response. He peered through the keyhole and tapped again, louder. He saw a familiar figure limping down the hall. It was Victoria, a disabled orphan girl who the government had allowed to stay.

She came to the gate and spoke in a low voice, "Who are you?"

Zaven looked around to see if anyone was nearby. A Turk standing at the gate of the Missionary School would not look normal.

"Victoria," he said, scarcely above a whisper. "This is Zaven. Please hurry and open the gate before someone sees me."

"Who?" she demanded again.

"This is Zaven, Victoria—Zaven Minassian. Don't you remember?"

Two figures had appeared in the street and were moving in his direction.

"For heaven's sake, Victoria, please be quick! I want to see Miss Blake. I'm Zaven who was deported. Hurry!"

The gate swung open a crack and Zaven slipped inside, despite Victoria's attempt to close it when she saw his white turban. He slammed the gate behind him, and turned to speak to her, but she moved away as fast as she could with her ungainly gait from a congenital birth defect. Zaven laughed. He felt good; he felt free. He was an Armenian again. He followed her into the kitchen and found her out of breath and babbling to an elderly woman.

"What's the matter, Victoria, didn't you recognize me?" he asked softly.

"Yes, yes. It's you. But I couldn't believe it. No one ever came back."

The news of Zaven's return spread swiftly around the institution. Within ten minutes the kitchen of Miss Blake's private residence was crowded by men and women eager to see a boy they thought had returned from certain death. Everyone barked questions at him. He tried to speak, but did not attempt to answer the questions. Then he heard a familiar voice shouting from the direction of the kitchen.

"Miss Blake wants to see Zaven. Let him out!"

Zaven squeezed his way through the crowd to the hallway. Brother Misak waited. The elderly man had been spared, as he was the cook of the American Hospital, which cared for wounded officers.

"It's wonderful, absolutely wonderful, that you're back, Zaven," cried Brother Misak. "Your troubles are over now."

They stood outside the half-opened door of Miss Blake's study. It was the room she always used. Zaven had been there many times, either to deliver a message or to be scolded for some minor misdeed. She walked to the door with outstretched arms as though she would have flung her arms around him, but instead she grasped his hand and led him to a chair.

"Sit down," she said while she stood there gazing at him. Suddenly Zaven felt uneasy. "I always knew that you were a clever boy, as well as a mischievous one," she said, focusing her eyes on the fez and soiled towel Zaven held in his hand. "I'm curious about the name that went with your disguise."

Zaven lowered his eyes and gazed around the room. "You mean names, Miss Blake," he muttered, as though talking to himself. "For a wagon driver and refugee Mustafa is suitable, and Ibrahim is appropriate for the adopted son of a Turkish nobleman."

Miss Blake finally smiled at him. Zaven looked up at her with relief.

"I would like to hear more about them," she said. "But you must be tired and hungry. Go along now. I'll see you in the morning. But I want you to know that you'll be safe here."

Zaven was escorted back to the kitchen. A meal of roast mutton was on the table waiting for him. Mariam, Miss Blake's personal cook, sat across the table and asked questions while he ate. Victoria stared at him suspiciously. He had hardly finished his meal when Brother Misak returned.

"We have lots of hot water and soap," he said, "and you sure need it, boy! I've smelled goats that were more aromatic than you."

Zaven followed him to the laundry room. First he had a close, clipped haircut, and then watched the large wooden tub fill with steaming water. It was inviting. He put his foot in the tub but pulled it back with an "Ouch!"

"Too hot?" smiled Misak. "We'll fix that." He added cold water to the tub.

Zaven tried again and crouched down in the warn water. Misak knew that a warm bath would make Zaven feel comfortable.

"This was the kind of bath I used to get when I was a little boy," said Zaven. "And I hated it then."

"But you like it now. By the way, what became of your mother?"

It took a long time for Zaven to answer.

"She was still at the caravan when I left," he murmured.

The change that came over Zaven's face startled the old man.

"I'm sorry that I mentioned it," he said apologetically.

"Nightmares. Will they ever go away? I came back and I am safe. Yet, I still feel that I am living on borrowed time."

"You must forget, my boy; I know it was bad. But living in the dark past will not help. Here you're among your own. The Turks respect Miss Blake. She likes you. Don't ever disappoint her."

"Thank you, Brother Misak; I'll try to be good."

Zaven emerged from the bath as a new man in clean underwear and a good suit and followed Misak to his room. The high bed with white sheets looked very inviting. He took off his clothes and sank into it. Brother Misak said goodnight as he closed the door behind him.

He was still in bed with no desire to get up when he heard a knock on his door. It was Victoria with the breakfast tray.

"Don't expect this kind of service in the future, Master Zaven," she chided him. "We all work here, and the same is expected of you. Hurry up and get dressed, you slugabed! Miss Blake wants to see you." She placed the tray on the table and hobbled quickly out of the room.

Zaven enjoyed his breakfast. It was like the ones his mother had made with warm choreg and yogurt. He dressed and went to the window. On the porch of the four-story building across the yard, Zaven saw Miss Blake talking to a Turkish officer. He watched them until the officer bowed slightly to her and walked into the building. This building, formerly the main classroom area, was now a military hospital. The Turkish government had appointed Miss Blake as its supervisor, as she had offered the building and the services without cost to the government. Her reward was a sanctuary for Armenian men and woman who worked there, and a home for a hundred or more orphan girls.

As Zaven left his room and walked across the yard, he noticed several girls watching him. One of them whispered, "With you around, life won't be so dull." Zaven glared at them. A high-pitched giggle filled the air, but he didn't look in their direction.

As he stood in front of Miss Blake's study, he felt more nervous than he had been the previous evening. He knocked gently and was immediately invited to enter.

"Had a good rest, Zaven?" asked Miss Blake. "You look nice in spite of your haircut. It's a shame, but never mind, it will grow. The girls are bound to make some fuss over you. You're the only boy. I hope they won't spoil you. Sit down."

She settled down and looked at him expectantly. Zaven was not sure where and how to begin, but made a fairly good job of summarizing his experiences. Miss Blake listened with intense interest and interrupted occasionally with questions.

"You've been through a lot," she said when he finished. "From now on, you will be where I am, and if some day I should go back to the United States, I might find a way to take you along. There are others like you who escaped. They are helping me with the work in the hospital and in the orphanage. Not once has the government asked me to explain who they are. They won't question you—that I can assure you. You can help me by buying food cheaper directly from the peasants at the marketplace. That is your job."

"Thank you, Miss Blake, I will do my part," said Zaven, and walked out with a good feeling that he would prove himself to be useful.

He had lunch with several others who worked in the hospital. One of the young men in his mid-twenties had escaped from the caravans like Zaven. He had been hit with an axe on the back of his neck and hurled into a ditch. Somehow he had lived and had crawled away from the dead bodies piled over him. He had reached Miss Blake and was treated in secret. Now he looked healthy and full of vim and vigor. Zaven had sensed the similarity of their feelings, even though they hadn't spoken a word about it.

A burly porter with two large baskets full of groceries on his back followed Zaven from the market. They were at the gate of the Missionary School when Zaven was startled by the appearance behind him of a familiar figure in a black uniform. The gate wasn't opened quickly enough for Zaven to avoid the Commissar, who had called his name.

"I heard the news of your return from Miss Blake the day after you arrived," said the Commissar. "I'm glad that you came back, and looking none the worse for wear from your ordeals."

The gate was open. The Commissar signaled the porter to move. Zaven had no choice but to listen to what he had to say.

"I have an idea of what you have been through," continued the Commissar. "What's done can't be undone. For your own sake I hope that it hasn't made your rebellious attitude worse. It might have been better if you hadn't returned, but I hope that no harm will come to you here. Miss Blake is a good woman. She and I understand each other, and both of us are concerned with your well-being. I hope you won't disappoint us, young man."

"Thank you, sir," said Zaven and hurried on.

For a while Zaven seemed satisfied with his work and the privileged position he enjoyed as Miss Blake's steward. Then, once again, the old restlessness began to eat away in him. In Seroupe, the young man who had been hit with the axe, he found a confidante. They talked and agreed to leave the hospital in the spring to join the Armenian forces across the frontier. This plan was offered to several others, and four of them agreed to join.

Having formed a band, other problems needed to be solved. First, and perhaps most important, was finding a capable leader who knew how to fight his way through the country, and finally across the border. They selected Hagop Chavoosh (Sergeant Hagop), who had visited the hospital disguised as a Turk. With his pencil moustache and fearless eyes, he looked at once dangerous and debonair. He had served in the Turkish Army and had received his rank there. Later he had made a name for himself as an outlaw. Already he had crossed the border several times. From Hagop they learned that there were others hiding in the city who would join them. Hagop agreed to lead them across the border if they could secure guns.

"For now you are safe here," he had said. "I won't take you out unarmed to hand you over to the Turks and be hanged as outlaws. Get the guns; I'll see you again within a few weeks."

Now it was up to them, Zaven and the rest, to acquire the guns. It was no easy task for any Armenian attempting to buy a gun.

Weeks passed and the best that Zaven and his companions could do was to steal three revolvers and one old-fashioned single shot rifle from drunken Truks. Hagop was not satisfied. Now, as spring had arrived, they were getting desperate.

"I've a plan that might work, Seroupe," said Zaven one night while the two were alone. Seroupe looked at him attentively. Zaven continued, "I believe we can buy guns from the Turkish refugees settled in the surrounding villages."

"Maybe," said Seroupe, "but who will do the buying?"

"I will," said Zaven.

Seroupe was about to laugh, but stopped when he saw Zaven's serious face.

The following day, Zaven, disguised as a refugee with a white turban and the habiliments that went with it, posed as a peddler collecting eggs and cheese. He went from one village to another in the vicinity of the city settled by the refugees. Yes, he bought eggs and cheese, but had no luck in meeting those who had the goods he really wanted. On his way back he came across a large Armenian village, now fully settled by Turkish refugees. There he became the guest of an old, simple-looking Kurd named Hussien, from whom he bought some eggs.

"It's getting late," cautioned the host. "If I were you I wouldn't start for the city now. Lately there have been holdups on the road."

It was bad enough to be away from the hospital all day, but to stay out at night as well would be difficult to explain. But Zaven's instinct tempted him to take the chance. After their meal, the two talked about their escape from the frontier; Zaven was quite successful at telling stories he had heard from other refugees. He had mentioned that he had picked up a rifle on the way, and sold it for a good price to supply capital for his business.

"I've found two rifles myself, but don't know what to do with them," commented the old man.

"Why don't you sell them?" asked Zaven.

"To whom? Besides, they're not the kind that can be sold easily."

"What are they?"

"A Russian Mauser and a Turkish military rifle."

"Damn!" cried Zaven. "The mention of a military rifle alone would hang you."

"I haven't mentioned it to anyone else but you," replied the old man in a conspiratorial whisper, "and that's because I know you are not the kind who would let a countryman be hanged. I lost an ox. Here it is spring, and I haven't yet tilled my patch of ground. Yes, the government has given me the land. But what good is it if I can't plant?"

"We, who live in the city, are no better off, Hussien. I wish I could help you."

Hussien's eyes flashed. "You can, if you really want to, by finding someone who wants to buy these guns."

Zaven remained silent for a few moments. Then he looked directly at his host. "Listen," he said, "tonight I have eaten your salt, and I really want to help you. I know one or two shady characters that could dispose of your goods. How and to whom I don't know, and would not care to know."

"I don't either, even if they are dealing with the devil himself, as long as I can get some money to buy oxen."

"We're playing with fire, Hussien."

"I'm aware of that, Mustafa."

The old Kurd gazed at the guest confidently, then passed his tobacco pouch. Zaven rolled a cigarette. The old man offered him a light from a red-hot chunk of coal picked up with tongs from the fireplace.

"Thank you," said Zaven, taking a long, satisfying puff. "I think—yes, I'm quite sure I can sell these guns. Can anyone hear us?"

The Kurd walked to the door and stood there for a moment, then returned and took his place.

"Go on," he said.

"I'm taking a chance and want to make a little profit myself. This peddling business hardly keeps me alive. How much do you expect to get for them, Hussien?"

Zaven watched the old man's face while he stroked his beard.

"Ten liras each," he said, rubbing his hands. "How's that, Mustafa?"

"I don't know. How many cartridges go with them?"

"The Mauser has two hundred, the military rifle one hundred, but I could get more if you wish."

"Yes, I'd like a hundred more for the rifle, but you are asking too much. How much do you think I can get from my contact?"

"Fifteen apiece."

"Impossible, Hussien. No one would pay that much, not even a Kavour."

"I'm not interested in whoever the buyer may be."

After fifteen minutes of bargaining, they agreed on the price, which was fifteen liras for the two guns, plus a hundred more cartridges for the rifle. They went to the barn. Zaven examined the guns and found them in good condition.

"Now the big question," he said, turning to his host. "How are you going to deliver them to my contact?"

"That won't be hard," said the cagey old Kurd. "I'll put them in chaff bags. You meet me in the bazaar, we bargain for the chaff, and the guns will be delivered wherever you want."

"Good," said Zaven. "I'll meet you in the bazaar in the morning the day after tomorrow."

The next day when Zaven entered the kitchen, Mariam was preparing dinner.

"A fine boy you are!" exclaimed the cook. "Out all night! Miss Blake is angry. You better go see her right now."

As he entered Miss Blake's room, she rose without a word, went to the door, looked outside, closed it, and then returned and stood facing Zaven.

"I know what some of you are up to," she said, "but I've closed my eyes and ears. You are too young for that kind of thing. Besides, you can be more helpful to your people right here, with me. Now give up your foolish plan! I'm sure you've already done your share. Where were you all night?"

"Buying guns," replied Zaven calmly.

Miss Blake rubbed her forehead and gazed at him with mingled disbelief and admiration. "Did it ever occur to you what might happen if you are caught? And I'm not just thinking of you. So, did you buy any?"

"Two good rifles," smiled Zaven.

"How much did you have to pay for them?"

"Fifteen liras."

"Too much," Miss Blake grunted.

"I could not afford to be a bargain shark."

"Did the one who sold the guns know who was really buying?"

"That's his worry. People are hanged for selling guns," he said.

She went back to her chair.

"I've had a long talk with Hagop," she said. "He's a wise and courageous man. He didn't have to work too hard to persuade me to be on his side. Now that we both have played our parts, I want you to stop. You can do much more here than going out to kill a few Turks."

"May I go now?" asked Zaven.

"Yes, but I want you to remember what I said."

Zaven was in the bazaar at the appointed time. He saw Hussien with his cartload of chaff. But he was not in any hurry to get to him. He hovered around, stopped here and there to bargain for chaff with other peasants, and finally approached him. After they had gone through the genuine bargaining processes, he instructed the old Kurd to follow him with his cartload. He went straight to the orphanage and found Seroupe waiting. Within a few minutes they had the bags in the barn. They emptied the chaff and pulled out the two rifles. Seroupe's eyes brightened when he saw the guns. He checked the barrels and firing mechanisms and pronounced the guns sound. Zaven counted fifteen gold pieces into Hussien's palm, and then added another for his service.

The successful transaction gave the old Kurd an incentive to peddle more guns. Several days later, for a higher price, Zaven bought two more rifles and three smaller firearms from him.

At the close of the deal, after packing the gold in his money belt, the old Kurd turned to Zaven.

"With all these guns, your contact could start a revolution, Mustafa," suggested the cagey Kurd. "And if you want my opinion, that wouldn't be a bad idea. Then I wonder if your contact could be a Kavour."

"I wouldn't speculate on that kind of thought, my friend," said Zaven. "Even I don't know who he might be. But one thing I do know, whoever he is, he is high and mighty. If our shady deal is ever revealed, you and I will hang. But he'll be above reproach. What matters to us who gets the guns?"

"Of course not, I was just curious. It may be a bit too late, but I have come to realize, in these treacherous times, to get by and perhaps even profit, one must be out only for himself, Mustafa."

He pressed Zaven's hand, got on his cart, and drove off.

CHAPTER 9

The obsession that had been the directing force of Zaven's life for the past two years became a reality. Fourteen men were hiding in the barn of the American orphanage. The atmosphere was tense. The women, frightened about the fate of their companions, whispered to each other. Hagop Chavoosh was in Zaven's room, waiting for nightfall to lead his band out. Everyone had a gun; Zaven's was an automatic pistol.

That morning Miss Blake had talked to Zaven again. "It is all right for the others to go," she had said. "But with you it's different. You are safe with me. I've made sure of that."

He had a ready answer but kept it to himself. But he became suspicious. To please Miss Blake, Hagop might play a trick on him and leave him behind. The only way to be sure was to know the getaway plan. He stole into Hagop's room and questioned him.

"There seems to be strong opposition to my coming with you," said Zaven. "I want to make sure now that I will not be left behind. If you won't take me, I'll start on my own if I have to."

The leader looked at him and smiled. "Sit down, Zaven. Of course you're coming with us! Just try to act normal until we leave. Tell Miss Blake that you've changed your mind. A small white lie won't hurt. Frankly, I want you in the band more than the others. I know I can depend on you. You can do things that the rest of us can't."

Those words excited Zaven. Hagop was a man worthy of admiration; a compliment from him was the ultimate gesture of respect. It was the first time in his life Zaven felt he could idolize a man.

"How are we going to get away?" asked Zaven.

"After dusk, we will leave by twos. You and Seroupe will be the last ones, but I don't want you to leave from the barn. This morning I promised Miss Blake that I would leave you here." He smiled. "Stay in the yard so that you can be seen. Then join Seroupe when he comes out. Should anything go wrong, we'll meet in the valley behind the Red Hill."

The night was murky and black. The men in the barn waited impatiently for Hagop to give the word. As for Zaven, he walked outside, trying to appear that nothing unusual was going on.

He saw the barn door open. A man walked out, stood there for a moment, and looked around. All was quiet. The frightened group of women had locked themselves in their rooms. The man approached the gate, opened it, waved his arm, and disappeared. After a few seconds, two men followed him. This procedure was repeated several times. Finally, a lone man came out of the barn. He stopped momentarily and looked around. Zaven slid out from behind the bush.

"Got your gun?" asked the man.

"Yes," answered Zaven in a whisper.

Seroupe was wearing a long coat to hide his rifle. They walked out into the street, following the pair barely visible ahead. The few people they encountered on the street may have wondered at seeing a number of shadowy characters passing along two by two at definite intervals, but they were not looking for trouble.

Luck was with them and they reached the edge of the city without incident. The pair whom Seroupe and Zaven followed were at the top of the Red Hill. The houses loomed behind them in the inky darkness. Zaven looked back and saw three dark forms not far behind. He brought this to Seroupe's attention, and pressed his arm, whispering, "Let's move fast."

They hustled up the hill. The dark forms behind them seemed to be moving faster after them. Glancing back again they noticed the faint gleam of rifle barrels in the dark.

"Must be the night patrol," whispered Seroupe.

They were about halfway up the hill when they heard a shout: "Stop, now!"

Seroupe whirled, dropped down on his knees, and Zaven followed his maneuver. The pursuers in the dark were running up the hill. Seroupe took out his Mauser and pointed it toward them.

"Stay where you are," he cried, "or I'll shoot!" Turning to Zaven, he barked, "Quick, crawl up the hill while I keep on eye on the patrol. When you reach the top, throw a pebble, and watch them while I move up. If you see any of them move, fire and try not to miss."

Excited, Zaven worked his way up the hill. At the top he crouched down and signaled. As far as he could see, the enemy lay flat at the bottom of the hill. It seemed to him that one was slowly edging toward the left. Bullets poured out of the automatic as if from a machine gun. He was satisfied to see the Turk throw himself to the ground. Had one of his bullets found him? Grimly, he hoped so.

The Turks started shooting back. It had never occurred to him that the bullets whistling by his ears would thrill him. Seroupe was beside him.

"Hurry!" he said. "Things may get worse."

They ran downhill into the valley and saw a lone figure standing in the dark.

"What happened?" asked their leader, Hagop Havoosh, moving closer.

"Patrols," answered Seroupe.

"Many?"

"Only three. Zaven had to empty his pistol."

Hagop grabbed Zaven's arm and shook him briskly and with affection. The youthful outlaw was trembling.

"You're shaking," Hagop said softly.

"I'm not afraid," protested Zaven. "It's just the excitement, that's all!"

Within seconds their anxious companions surrounded them. After counting to make sure they were all there, the leader said, "Let's go—we'll have to get into the mountains. Before long this place will be swarming with soldiers."

They made their way quickly across uneven fields. Zaven followed his leader closely, trying to imitate his movements, but he lacked the finesse and found it hard to keep up with him. He looked back to see how the others were doing and was comforted to see Seroupe and their confederates close behind him. Hagop stopped at the foothills of the towering mountain, which formed a natural barrier for the city.

Hagop saw Zaven standing near, breathing heavily. "With a little training," he smiled, "I believe you'll beat me yet!"

Zaven was too short of breath to answer.

"Let's rest," Hagop said, sitting on a rock. "We've a long, hard climb ahead of us."

"Can we clear the mountain before daybreak?" asked Zaven.

"I doubt it. Even if we could, I wouldn't take the risk of taking you down to the fields in daylight."

The last in the line, an elderly man who perhaps had no business being there, crouched down. There was no sign that they were pursued. The trail up the mountain was hazardous, but they were in no hurry. Sudden movement in the brush ahead startled the men, but the leader laughed. A stray jackal dashed across the trail, then stopped to watch them from a safe distance. At daybreak, they stood on a high peak. The outline of the sleeping city lay below them. Zaven watched the glowing horizon. He had never seen such a beautiful sunrise.

"We'll stay up here during the daytime," said Hagop, "then move on."

For several days they took things easy, heading slowly toward the east. Their only contact had been a shepherd, who sold them a sheep for a good price. Then the leader decided to test his men. He took them down the road, and had them hide behind bushes and rocks to wait nervously for their first prey. Peasants passed by with their ox cars and pack animals. The outlaws peered at them but Hagop told them to let them alone.

Some time later, several mounted men appeared on the road. They looked more promising. With three of his men, Hagop stepped out into the road and told the group to halt. The rest of the band remained in hiding. No shot was fired. The travelers surrendered without so much as a whimper. They were relieved of their money and food, but best of all, two guns. Then they were allowed to go with a warning to tell no one of the robbery. That was a ridiculous demand!

A bigger prize came toward the evening when they were ready to leave the road. There were three civilians and two soldiers.

"They may give us some trouble," Hagop commented. "We must not give them a chance to use their guns."

They set a trap at a narrow part of the road. Hagop, who was next to Zaven, raised his head and commanded, "Drop your guns! You don't have a chance."

The astounded men gazed around wildly, seeking a way to escape. Muzzles pointed at them from all directions. One hasty move would be fatal.

"We give up!" cried one of the civilians.

"Drop your guns and dismount!" Hagop yelled.

The next command was to stand in line. While the band was searching them, one of the civilians, a haughty one with a large pouch of gold, said insolently, "That's government money. You won't get away with it."

The leader's face turned grim. "Tax collectors!" he growled. "I detest your kind worse than the cur standing beside you," referring to the soldier.

The sentinel watching the road ran up to the leader and whispered in his ear. Hagop listened attentively, nodding grimly at the news.

"Bind them," Hagop ordered. "We'll take them along."

The outlaws hurriedly left the road with their prisoners and started toward the mountains. According to the sentinel, troops had appeared on the road in the distance. The horses were stripped and abandoned at the start of the trail up the mountain. In silent satisfaction Zaven followed the leader up the trail.

At their hideout the outlaws thoroughly searched the prisoners, burned their papers, and tucked away whatever was useful. The big question was what to do with them. There was a strong argument to let them go so as not to attract too much attention, but the decision was up to the leader.

"They have learned too much about us," said Hagop. "Not that it matters, but these are the Turks we are after."

He walked toward them. His face was cold and menacing; his finger on the trigger of his rifle was itchy. "I'm an Armenian. This should explain everything!" Hagop snarled.

The haughty Turk who had warned the outlaw of robbing the government fell on his knees.

"Have mercy, please!" he whined. "We're decent men and had no hand in the killing of your countrymen. We have wives and children. Spare us for their sake."

"You villain," cried the leader of the outlaws. "You're begging me to spare you because of your wives and children. Did you spare the lives of our women with children? You'll pay as long as I live." He turned to his men and commanded harshly, "Take them away and get rid of them for good!"

Hagop looked ferociously at Zaven. "I want you to take care of that soldier," he said in a voice that made the young man wince.

As Zaven followed the prisoners, he shuddered and felt sick at his stomach. Now that he faced the reality of killing another human being, he felt that dreaming of revenge and killing in cold blood were not the same. The tax collector didn't look any different from the one who had adopted him, and the soldier he was assigned to kill looked like the one who did not kill him earlier.

Again, he moved in a daze as he had when he had walked to the edge of the ditch along the road, leading the bound soldier. Though the roles were reversed, the feeling was the same. He felt like a puppet in the hands of fate. He wished he were back with the Turk who had adopted him. He wished he had stayed in the hospital. He would accept any kind of life, do anything, if only he could be spared from this bloody initiation that would brand him, once and for all, as a callous outlaw. But by refusing he would lose Hagop's respect and surely be exiled from the murderous band for his cowardice.

He had only one option: In a surreal fog, he carried out his leader's orders.

Upon his return from the ravine, Hagop gazed sharply at him. He did not know how he looked, but from the depths of his despair he heard Hagop comment, "I want to see you look like that from now on. Grim. Determined. Merciless."

Speechless, Zaven sat down beside him and tried to quell his nerves by gazing at the distant slopes of the mountain. He had begun the grim, bloody course of an outlaw. There was no turning back now.

The following day Hagop and his no longer timid pack descended to the valley again. Hidden behind a rock and peering through field glasses, Hagop reconnoitered the field.

"There!" he cried suddenly. "They are not in uniform, but they have rifles and we want them!"

He replaced the field glasses in their case and surveyed the surroundings. Kneeling on one knee close beside him, Zaven observed every change in the leader's face. With a stern look, he turned to Zaven.

"Tell me, Zaven," he said, "what course do you suppose those wretches are likely to follow?"

"I think they'll pass by the foot of this hill we are on," answered Zaven.

"Right!" cried the leader. "Do you know why?"

Zaven shook his head.

"They want to stick close to the road, and not far from the mountains. That makes their identity fairly certain—deserters. We'll set a trap behind the hill. They won't see us until they're right upon us."

The outlaws gathered in a circular formation covering an area of about a hundred yards behind the hill. Unaware of the approaching danger, the deserters walked right into the trap. A hard voice cried, "Surrender, turncoats! You don't have a chance."

Bullets went flying in all directions in response to the ominous demand before Hagop's first shot was fired. One of the deserters made a flying leap behind the bushes where Zaven hid. With the rifle of the soldier he had killed, he fired a shot and the man tumbled down, dead, at his feet.

There was no hope for the others, but they fought to the bloody end. One of them muttered, breathing his last, "You're bandits. We thought … you … were Turkish soldiers …"

"Bandits, but not Turks," Hagop mumbled.

The affair had its consequences. As the outlaws picked up the rifles and were ready to depart, a troop of soldiers emerged at the farther side of the field. They advanced in battle formation, spread wide. Hagop ordered a hasty retreat to the foothills flanked by a forest-covered ravine, leading to the depths of the mountains. This was an important position, for it commanded the way into the mountains. Four men were dispatched toward it while the rest positioned themselves to hold back the soldiers.

"Don't waste cartridges," instructed the leader. "Shoot when you know where your bullets are going."

He crawled toward Zaven. "Their plan is to hold us until they get reinforcements," Hagop said. "We must act quickly. Follow me!"

Zaven and a few others followed him. They made a wide circle and positioned themselves on the enemy's flank. The sudden burst of well-timed firing gave the illusion of multiple guns in action at their rear. The enemy maneuvered a hasty retreat, leaving three behind.

CHAPTER 10

The encounter with the soldiers was a real test. Hagop was thoroughly satisfied. Two men were wounded. He dressed their wounds. "Not serious," he commented. "The bullets went straight through. You'll be all right."

Turning to the others, he added, "We must move fast. If they had held us for an hour longer, we would have been surrounded by an army."

They went deeper and deeper into the mountains. At dusk they reached the spot that the leader apparently had in his mind. It was a natural fortress, circled by a wall of rocky precipices, except for the narrow steps that had brought them there. Hagop looked around and sent two men in different directions as sentinels.

"Don't smoke," he commanded. "Climb a tree. You can see and hear better. We must be careful. The Turks know that we're somewhere in these mountains and they'll be watching for signs."

This was their first real hideout. Zaven crouched beside his leader and watched the grim, unshaved renegades around him. He was one of them, maybe the worst. Whatever shock and tribulation he felt at the start had gone away. He had become a coldy efficient killer, who would kill without remorse. The obsession for revenge, too, had faded. Once he had prayed (to whom, he wasn't sure he remembered) but he could no longer pray. From now on his life boiled down to a simple edict: He must kill or be killed.

They had stale bread and cold meat for their meal since the leader would not allow them to build a fire. Faces were stern and no one talked. Only one thing could have cheered them up, but that, too, was forbidden. Hagop, lying flat on his back gazing at the stars, suddenly sat up.

"Damn it!" he mumbled, and took out his cigarette case. "All right, boys, light your cigarettes in your hats and keep them there."

He showed the way it was done. Zaven lit his cigarette from the leader's, who had held the burning cigarette tucked in his hat in front of the young outlaw.

"We will lie low for a while," Hagop said. "We have done enough for now. My plan is to stay here for a few days, then go south. There is a group of Armenian outlaws operating there. We may join them."

The night passed quickly. Hagop was up early. Several men still lay dozing when he returned from his reconnaissance down the side of the mountain.

"Get up, you lazy bunch!" he shouted. "I don't mind you sleeping, but I don't want to see you lying around half-awake like lizards." He turned to the man in charge of the food. "How much is left to eat?" he asked.

"Not much," he answered.

"I want six of you to come along. You, too, Zaven."

Zaven and the others followed their leader in single file down to the valley. They approached a lone farmhouse. Hagop posted the men around the house. Zaven alone stayed with him. They stood in front of the heavy closed gate. Hagop knocked fiercely with the butt of his rifle. There was no answer.

"Open it," roared Hagop, "or I'll blast it and whoever is in there along with it!"

"Who are you?" asked a feeble voice. "There are no men in the house."

"Don't flirt with my temper, woman!" Hagop thundered.

The gate swung back. An old woman stood trembling before them. Zaven would have felt better had challenging bullets answered the arrogant demand, instead of this decrepit creature in rags.

"Don't be alarmed, mother," said Hagop in a softer voice. "We're not going to harm you or anyone else. If there's a man in the house, send him out."

"No, Kurban, I'm alone."

"Well, then, we've come to buy food."

"But I haven't anything to spare," whimpered the old woman.

"We will take what you have. Then, you can buy yourself twice as much with the money I will give you. We want flour, cereals, cheese, and butter. Now be quick about it!"

"The house is open to you," said the woman. "Take what you want, and live with your conscience, for I am but a poor old woman. The war took my two sons. I have five grandchildren and two daughters-in-law to feed."

While searching for food, Zaven felt like he was snatching away a crust of bread from a starving child. The poor woman had told the truth; there was not much food to take. But, whatever there was, they dumped it in sacks. Then they went to the barn, where they picked up a few chickens and loaded up the donkey with the provisions. The pitiful old woman watched them in silence with tears in her eyes.

"Kurban," she whimpered. "That donkey means a lot to us."

"We'll send him back," answered Hagop curtly.

The old mother said hopefully, "If you let him loose and no one catches him, he'll return."

When they were about to leave, Hagop took out his moneybag and put a handful of gold pieces in the woman's palm. She made a faint cry of joy. The pathetic figure knelt down before the leader of the outlaws, hands clasped on her chest.

"Allah preserve you and your brave men," she said. "You've been good to an old woman."

"Don't worry about your donkey, mother," said Hagop. "We'll send him back."

Zaven was delighted to see that the old woman had received in return ten times as much as they had taken away. But this generosity shown by Hagop for a Turkish woman puzzled the young outlaw. For her part, the gold had driven away the woman's fear.

"You are welcome in this house anytime, son," she said.

"I'll remember that, mother," smiled Hagop. "As long as we're around, we'll see that you and your grandchildren are fed well. In the meantime, for your own good, forget that you ever saw us."

Walking away from the house, Zaven commented, "I see you have a soft heart toward the helpless—even for a Turk."

The leader seemed annoyed. He shot his protégé a flinty look and retorted, "My generosity wasn't prompted by tender feeling. Never abuse the peasant in whose territory you work. Nine out of ten outlaws have come to their end by the betrayal of a boor they had ill-used. A peasant's creed is his own welfare. Disregard her feeling for us. That old witch will not talk because she knows that she is better off with us than against us."

This was Zaven's first lesson in bandit/peasant psychology. Before entering the trail that took them to their hideout, they unloaded the donkey and let him loose. All was well. The sentinel reported they had sighted some soldiers in the valley, but they had not attempted to climb up the mountains. There was much activity in the camp during the rest of the day. At night they made bread and roasted meat in a cave that concealed the smoke. Hagop, lounging on his blanket, summoned Zaven.

"We are leaving soon," he said, bringing his lips close to Zaven's ear. "To tell the truth, I'm in no hurry to reach the border, and when we join those I have in mind, there is no telling how troublesome we can be to the Turks—right in their own nest."

"You must be quite sure that you'll beat these others," commented Zaven.

"Yes." After a moment's hesitation, he confided, "In that, I'm greatly depending on you, Zaven."

The journey towards the south began shortly after midnight. They were no longer individuals but a well-oiled and formidable whole. They reached a high peak overlooking a sprawling town whose lights winked to them from below.

Zaven had slept all night undisturbed. The sun was high when he half opened his eyes and saw Hagop leaning against a rock and writing on papers on his knees. In a few moments he carefully folded two sheets, rose, and walked toward Zaven.

"I'm going to send you to that town," he said, "and I expect you to be back by noon. It shouldn't take you long to get there. So, get in your refugee outfit, and wrap that good old white towel around your head once more."

Without comment, Zaven opened his sack and took out the things needed for his disguise.

"Don't hurry," said the leader. "Eat first."

"I don't feel like eating," answered Zaven. "Besides, when I get into the town, I can have a bowl of hot onion soup. That's worth waiting for."

"It certainly is," laughed Hagop. "We don't happen to have that on our menu this morning."

"What am I going to do when I get there?" Zaven asked.

"You know why we came here. I'm sending a message to the men we want to meet. It won't do to meet them accidentally. So, here's where you come in. In that town there is a Kizilbash innkeeper. His name is Omar; they call him Omar Agah. He is the contact. You'll find him easily enough; just ask for his inn. He knows me well."

Hagop handed Zaven the two folded sheets and said, "You had better read them. One is your introduction; hand that one to him first. The other, written in Armenian, goes to the men I have in mind. Omar will take care of that."

Zaven ran through the notes hastily. Hagop had designated the rendezvous point. He folded the papers, wondering where to put them. Hagop read his thoughts.

"You mustn't be caught with them," he warned.

"Have no fear; no one will get a hold of them, even if I'm cut to pieces."

"You might put them in your shoe."

"They would look there first," smiled Zaven.

He rose, went to the provision bags, and took out a flat loaf of bread. He sliced it with his dagger and slipped the folded sheets inside. Hagop watched him with admiration.

"To a Turk, a loaf of bread is sacred. They would never tamper with it."

"I'm not too old yet to learn," smiled Hagop. "Going unarmed?"

"Of course," Zaven answered. "Any weapon, even a knife, would be difficult to explain, and even I could not talk my way out of its possession."

"Good luck, but don't take chances."

Half an hour later Zaven was down on the road, feeling safe in his disguise. He caught up with several peasants on their way to the town with donkeys carrying firewood to be sold in the bazaar.

"Salaam-al-okum!" he shouted in a friendly manner.

"Al-okum-salaam!" shouted back the peasants all at once.

"Going to the town?" asked Zaven.

"Yes," answered one, adding, "You look as if you have been on a long journey."

"That's right. All the way from Sivas," said Zaven.

The peasant examined him curiously. "You are not from these parts?"

"No, I'm a refugee; I'm going to see my cousin. He is working for Omar Agha."

"The innkeeper?" hinted the peasant.

"He is the man," Zaven declared.

"You know," said the friendly and talkative peasant, taking a second look at the refugee, "Omar is from my village. Once, he and I were next-door neighbors. I knew him when he begged for a piece of mutton or barley. Then suddenly he got rich. They say he found hidden gold while plowing. Some are born lucky! He came to the town, bought the inn, and is now a rich man who won't even recognize me."

"Luck indeed," commented Zaven. "As for Omar not recognizing you, you and I would be just like him if we happened to strike a pot of gold. Wealth changes a man, and not always for the better. I suppose you know his inn?"

"Everyone does. It is the best one in town. We'll pass it right by the gate."

Eventually they came to the marketplace. Zaven had enjoyed the companionship of the peasants and liked listening to their ribald jokes.

"That's Omar's inn," said the talkative peasant, pointing to a wide-open gate. Zaven found the coffeehouse in the courtyard. Every inn has one where men drink, gamble, and discuss war and politics. Entering with a careless manner, he walked among the marble tables, and made his way to a corner. A teenaged Turkish boy with a colorful apron served the customers. He stopped now and then to shout in a musical voice, "Coffee for two! Make it without sugar! Tea for one!" Another man stood in front of the charcoal fire repeating the orders. As soon as Zaven sat at a table, the boy approached.

"Tea, boy," ordered Zaven, "and lots of sugar."

The boy repeated the order as given to him. A moment later, as he placed the tea glass and a small plate of sugar on the table, Zaven said, "I want to see Omar Agha. Will you take me to him?"

"Sorry," replied the boy. "The master left town yesterday."

"When do you expect him back?"

"Don't know; he may come at any moment, or maybe in a day or two."

"Do you know where he went?"

"I believe he went to his village. I heard him mention buying some land there."

"How far is his village?" Zaven asked in a voice that did not hide his disappointment.

"Four hours if you're a fast walker," said the lad, glancing at Zaven curiously. "Is your business urgent?"

"I can wait," Zaven answered hastily.

As he sat there, sipping his tea, he thought about his next move. He wasn't sure that he would find Omar in his village, even if he went there. On the other hand, he did not like the idea of loitering around. People would ask questions. Finally, he thought it best to remain in the coffeehouse for a while. So, when the boy came to take away the empty glass, he told him that he intended to await Omar's return.

From the minaret, the call the prayer invited the faithful for the mid-afternoon worship at the mosque. Customers began to leave the coffeehouse. Zaven noticed some of them glanced at him suspiciously. He was a stranger, and strangers are always looked upon as questionable. He contemplated joining the faithful on their way to the mosque. That would provide some cover. He felt a sudden premonition of danger, urging him to leave the inn. He left his table and was on his way to the door when a police officer blocked his way.

"Who are you?" he demanded.

"A refugee," Zaven answered.

"One finds you wretches everywhere. You've become a public nuisance. Where are you going?"

"To the mosque."

"That doesn't sound right. I've never yet seen one of you ragamuffins entering the mosque."

"But I always do," Zaven declared piously.

The policeman looked at the refugee scornfully, but refrained from revealing the thoughts in his mind. He shot a generous wad of spit in the direction of Zaven's feet and asked, "What are you doing in this town?"

"I want to see the innkeeper."

"Do you know him?"

"No."

"Then why do you seek him?"

"I'm very handy in the stable and thought he might give me a job."

"You had better come with me," said the policeman decisively. "I don't like your looks."

It was out of the question to resist. He contemplated escape, but before he had the chance to look around and find a place to run, he was in the police station. Without being questioned or searched, he was thrust into a cell. It had a low ceiling and concrete walls turned a somber and depressing gray by dirt and smoke. The inmates sat in groups. One of the old men invited Zaven to share his mattress. Zaven felt resentful but soon realized that in his position he couldn't be choosey.

"What are you in for?" asked the one who offered him a place.

"I don't know," answered Zaven curtly.

"You know—you mean you won't tell," sneered the convict.

"Neither. I am a stranger in town, a refugee."

"Bah, they won't bring you in for that!"

Zaven fell silent. A few paces away, two prisoners were playing an animated game of backgammon, emphasizing every move with their profane remarks. Presently, the man who had started the conversation with Zaven found it more interesting to watch the players than waste his time with the newcomer who wouldn't talk.

Now that he was left alone, he needed to quickly get rid of the notes. He took out the small loaf of bread that he had kept in the folds of his handkerchief and began eating. A paper sandwich—it wasn't particularly palatable, but he mouthed it with a great show of appetite. He was chewing the last bite when the police officer who had brought him there appeared in the doorway.

"What are you doing?" he shouted.

"Only eating a piece of bread," answered Zaven nonchalantly, as he folded his handkerchief and put it in his pocket.

"Come along," the policeman commanded. "The Commissar wants to see you—now."

He was led into a room where a haughty officer sat behind the desk. A policeman stood by the door.

"Search him," commanded the Commissar.

The order was carried out thoroughly. The young refugee was stripped naked. Zaven saw a faint ray of hope. When the Commissar's face showed signs of satisfaction, Zaven realized the unquestionable evidence of his circumcised penis proved he could be nothing but a Mussulman.

After Zaven was dressed, the Commissar said, "What are you doing in this part of the country? We don't see many like you around here."

"I have come from Sivas, sir," answered Zaven. "It's hard to make a living there. I thought I might have better luck around here."

"What is your name?"

"Mustafa, sir. Kal Tahir Oghlu Mustafa."

"Where is your birthplace?"

"Olti, sir."

"When did you leave Olti?"

"It's been almost two years now, sir."

"Have you been in Sivas all that time?"

"Not all the time. I have been in different places around the city."

"Do you know anyone in this town?"

"No, sir, I have arrived only today, and wanted to see an innkeeper for a job when I was brought here."

"Can you give me an address in Sivas? Someone whom I can contact and get information about you?"

"No, sir, I don't know anyone in Sivas." The Commissar's expression showed rising suspicion. "I mean..." Zaven caught himself. "I don't know anyone who would recognize me by my name."

The Commissar eyed him in silence. It was very evident that he was not satisfied with Zaven's answers.

"Take him away," he said. "He seems a tough nut to crack, and I'm not in the mood now."

CHAPTER 11

For Zaven, the Commissar's last remark shattered all hope of his being set free. He was led back to the jail. What was worse was the thought that he would not see Hagop and his outlaw confederates again. His situation was hopeless. A chance for escape might come later, but even the next day would probably be too late.

His cellmates, who had accepted him as a harmless, unlucky refugee, seemed surprised to see him back. Some of them were perhaps glad that he would share in their misery. He chose a place on the bare floor near the door. The bully who had earlier invited Zaven to share his mattress tried to make room for the refugee beside him. Zaven was content that there was no room to be made. One should know these jailbirds better before accepting favors.

"So, you are back," said the convict. "You don't have to bow your head to anyone. Come on, you rogues!" he bellowed. "Pull your rotted beds closer to make room for him next to me." From his tone and the way the convicts responded, it was clear that he was the leader in this cell.

Days passed. Zaven learned all he wanted to know about the prisoners around him. He discovered that misfortune is the great leveler of all things, and that friendship grows the same within prison walls as it does in the sunshine and freedom. Here he learned how to play backgammon. Hour after hour he would sit shaking the dice to take his mind away from his troubles.

At first he thought that the boy in the coffeehouse might have told the innkeeper about the incident and the man might carry enough influence to get him out. But the days passed uneventfully, except for the endless backgammon.

He was shaking the dice vigorously, trying for a six and one, when a guard opened the door. "Kal Tahir Oghlu Mustafa!" he shouted.

"Yes, sir, here I am," Zaven answered.

"Come along."

Zaven walked out, with the guard following close behind. He stood before the Commissar who had questioned him earlier.

"Now, young man, tell the truth," said the Commissar sternly.

"Sir," answered Zaven, "I've told you the truth."

The Commissar rose and angrily pushed back his chair. "You're lying!" he shouted. With two swift steps he reached the prisoner and slapped him. Zaven clenched his teeth.

"You won't leave this room alive if you don't tell me who you really are," he warned. "I can see things in your eyes. I want to hear them from your damnable lips."

"There's nothing to tell, sir. I've told you everything."

"Don't toy with my patience!" roared the officer and slapped him again.

Zaven was dazed, but struggled to remain on his feet and to keep his mouth shut.

"Talk—talk!" the Commissar seethed. His words were like an echo that resounded forever. "I have a feeling that you're worse than the devil."

"What do you want me to tell you, sir?"

"Tell me who you really are and why you came here."

"I've told you that already, sir. I'm a poor refugee. I came here hoping to find work."

"For the last time, you son of a bitch, tell me your right name!"

"Mustafa, Kal Tahir Oghlu Mustafa. And my father's name was Shukri; the Kavour killed him."

"I want your right name, the name by which you were known in the army, and I want you to confess that you're a deserter and a traitor."

"No, sir, no," Zaven protested with relief, for he had not been accused of being what he really was.

"I'll make you confess if I have to break every bone in your body. Lay him down," he yelled.

One of the attendants forced Zaven to the floor. Another walked in with two sticks. Zaven had seen these implements of torture before but he had not felt them. One was short and heavy with a strong cord fastened at the ends. The other was a club for beating.

"This is your last chance," the Commissar warned. "Are you going to talk?"

The prisoner just stared at him.

"The stick will make him talk, sir," said one of the attendants with a cruel sneer.

The Commissar nodded, went to his desk, and lit a cigarette. "Go to it," he muttered, blowing out a cloud of smoke.

While the guards removed Zaven's shoes and socks, a mean-looking one entered. He cast a hateful, menacing glance at the prisoner, and waited for the command.

"Go on!" shouted the Commissar.

Zaven was on his back. The gendarme grabbed the beating club, while the other two held his feet high up in the air and twisted the corded stick. Zaven closed his eyes. The Commissar approached, grabbed away the club from the gendarme, and pressed it on the helpless one's lips.

"Kiss it," he mocked. "This will loosen your tongue."

Zaven was hurt but the mockery infuriated him beyond the limits of self-restraint. He pushed the club back savagely. It stuck the Commissar on the chin.

"Go on, do your dirty work," cried Zaven. "You can't do more than kill me!"

"He thinks he has guts," mumbled the Commissar. "I'll break him. I'll break his guts." He handed the stick back to the guard. "Give it to him!"

The blow aimed at the bottom of his bare feet was vicious. Hot stabs of pain ran through him. At the height of his agony, the Commissar bent down over him and whispered mockingly, "Now, are you going to talk?"

The challenge had a strange effect on the young outlaw. He laughed. This might have been hysterics, but he was more certain than ever that they would not get a word out of him.

The second blow, more painful, followed with the demand, "Talk, dog. Talk!"

The third, the fourth, and the fifth blows were delivered with the word "talk" punctuating each savage strike. The hated word echoed and re-echoed through Zaven's mind, but he didn't feel any more. How many more had they given him? When he opened his eyes, he found himself back in the cell. He was paralyzed and could feel nothing. Yet, he was consoled, for he hadn't talked.

"Mustafa, son," said the convict who had befriended him. Despite the man's bullying nature, Zaven had learned to like him—or at least tolerate him. "Those sons of bitches have beaten you badly. I know, for I, too, have tasted the stick. You'll be all right."

Zaven attempted to sit up but fell back and lay motionless, gazing at the ceiling half-consciously. After a while, aided by the man, he sat up, curious to know what had become of his poor feet. He couldn't look at them. They had turned black; his toes were covered with dried blood. He got dizzy and fell back, wondering whether he would ever again stand on his feet.

"They look bad now, son," said the man, "but they get that way. Don't let that worry you. You'll be all right sooner than you think."

Within a week he could hobble around, and at the expense of a little pain could put on his shoes and socks. He had been in this jail almost a month. Now he was considered one of its prominent occupants. He had learned the use of bad language, and could curse as colorfully and maliciously as any other jailbird. He played backgammon skillfully and insidiously. He had learned tricks on setting the dice. His strength and agility in wrestling was tested against the best: an uncouth, burly farmer who was there for strangling a neighbor. The farmer put up a good fight, but Zaven beat him. He always shared his good adventures from the outside, as he reflected that by now Hagop was across the border. His feet healed, and he could walk without difficulty.

One morning a guard called his name. He trembled inwardly, wondering whether he could hold out again as he was taken to the Commissar's office. From his seat, the Commissar looked up at him. Zaven fancied the torturer's eyes looked milder, seemed almost friendly.

"Mustafa," he said, glancing at a paper in front of him, "I have here instructions from Sivas to send you there. If you can prove to be who you claim you are, you'll be given identification papers that will save you from further trouble. That's all now; you'll start in the morning."

"T-thank you, sir," replied Zaven, more than a little dumbfounded by this extraordinary turn of events. "I'm sure I'll be all right there."

Would he be all right? Who would interrogate him before issuing the papers? He remembered the Commissar of Sivas; a vision of the hard look of the man in black uniform loomed in his mind's eye. And the words rang in his ears: "I hope you won't disappoint us." Suppose he was not brought before the Commissar? What storekeeper in the marketplace would not recognize that bargain shark Armenian lad who vanished suddenly? A few days later a tax collector and soldiers had been killed. Then the government had lost track of these rogues. Later on the one calling himself Mustafa was caught in a coffeehouse, in a town not far south of Sivas. To make certain, wouldn't they call Miss Blake to identify him? What then? What would happen to the orphan girls and hundreds of other unfortunates? No, he resolved that he could never reach Sivas alive.

Early the next morning he was taken out to the courtyard where three other prisoners and two mounted soldiers were waiting. He was handcuffed to a convict charged with murder who was being sent to the capitol city for his trial. The other two were deserters. As for himself, from the point of view of an average bystander his status was simply that of a dubious character—an unfortunate Turkish refugee who could not identify himself.

"Mustafa, there is no justice in this world," said the convict he was bound to soon after they began their journey. "The innocent suffer with the guilty. Take you: What wrong have you done? Just trying to make an honest living. But they won't leave you in peace. Yes, I killed a man and they'll hang me for it. But I tell you, should I be hung hundreds of times, I'd do it again. I needed money and borrowed from the moneylender. The greedy rat's rates were so high, and the time so short, that I couldn't pay him. The law gave him all I had. I thought I could get back on my feet again as long as I had my wife. She was a good woman, but women are like cats. They stray away when their tummies are empty. I knew that the usurer had his eye on her, in spite of having two wives already. He took mine as his third."

Zaven wanted to say something that might give him some kind of hope, while his subconscious mind envied the convict and his situation in comparison to his own.

"How did it happen?" he asked. "Did you plan it?"

"I killed him in a fight at the marketplace. If I hadn't, he would have killed me."

"If you have witnesses who will testify that you did it in self-defense, you shouldn't worry."

"Will you visit me?" smiled the man.

"Of course I will."

They had been on the road for three days. The next day they would reach Sivas. So far, Zaven had no opportunity to attempt escape, but he had begun to form an idea, based on his observation that the soldiers were lenient with him. Seemingly, they believed that he really was a poor refugee. For his part, Zaven had tried to convince them that he was happy returning to Sivas.

Seeing that he was having some difficulty walking handcuffed, the corporal had set his hands free and let him walk in front by himself. Once he had even let him ride on his horse for a short distance. This small incident gave him real hope. Now he was pretty certain that they wouldn't take him to Sivas, alive or otherwise, but he kept pretending and waiting for a real opportunity.

That evening, in a small village, the corporal bought a room at the inn—free of charge for all of them. Soon after arriving, they settled down.

"Mustafa," he asked, "will you brush my horse? I haven't touched the poor thing for days."

"Why certainly, corporal," Zaven answered readily.

"Do a good job and you'll get two piasters," the corporal smiled.

"Thank you, corporal, it will be a small way of repaying you. You've been very good to me."

"I wish I could do more, son. But I'm under orders to take you to Sivas. Still, I may help you a little by recommending you to people I know."

Zaven thanked him again.

"The other guard, Ihmed, is going to the stable to clean up his horse," said the corporal. "Go along with him."

While Zaven was currying the neglected animal, a Turkish gentleman entered the stable to attend to his own horse tied in the next stall. He stopped to watch Zaven work.

"You're doing a good job on that animal, son," he said. "Are you the stable boy?"

"No, sir, I'm a prisoner."

"I would hardly take you for a criminal. What have you done?"

"Nothing, sir, but I'm suspected because I'm a refugee and have no papers to vouch for my identity."

The Turk shook his head.

"No one seems to be watching you. Why don't you just walk away?"

"There's a guard watching me," said Zaven, looking in the direction of Ihmed brushing his horse. "Even if there wasn't, I wouldn't. They are taking me where I want to go."

"Whose horse is this?"

"The corporal's."

"I was thinking of giving you the chance to make a few piasters."

"I'd be glad to attend your horse, if the corporal will let me."

"Is that him?" he asked, pointing to the soldier.

"No, he's with us, but the corporal is in the inn."

The gentleman walked over to Ihmed. After a few words with him, the gentleman left the stable and soon returned, saying the corporal had given his permission. Zaven was pleased. He went to work on the gentlemen's horse, taking plenty of time, hoping that the gendarme would get tired of waiting and go away; but he was disappointed. It was unwise to arouse any suspicion at this stage.

Now that he had found another sympathizer, he finished the job and strolled back to the room. The gentleman was there, facing the corporal across a low stool, playing cards with him. Unobtrusively, Zaven took his place beside the other prisoners at the lower end of the room. The gentleman looked up.

"Come over, son, I want to talk to you," he said. "I was told that you have stayed in Sivas for some time. I, too, am from Sivas. Do you know anyone there?"

"I know many, sir. But they won't know me except by sight. You see, I was a porter in the bazaar. I know Shevket Effandi; he has the wholesale store at the bazaar. I know the butcher, Tewfik, a big fellow who talks and looks hard, but has a kind heart, and I know the innkeeper, Hassan; his place is in the square of the gilded fountain."

The gentleman smiled. "I know all of them. Tewfik is a good friend of mine. Probably I, myself, have given you jobs, but there were so many of you ragamuffins, if you'll pardon the term, about. It's hard to remember all the faces one sees casually. My store is in the covered bazaar."

"I seem to know you!" cried Zaven in triumph. "You sell dry goods."

This was a shot in the dark, but Zaven was not taking chances: Most of the stores in the covered bazaar sold dry goods.

"That's right. Now tell me, why did you leave Sivas?"

"You know, sir, it's hard for a porter to make a living there. If I got one job a day, which would be the price of a loaf of bread, I considered myself lucky. A countryman told me that things are better in the south. That's why I left Sivas."

"Corporal," said the gentleman, "I'll be responsible for this boy. He's a good worker. When we get to Sivas, I intend to take him on as a servant."

"I'm glad to hear that," said the corporal. "The poor thing deserves a break."

"I'll be in your party tomorrow. We'll straighten that out when we get to the city."

Three more men joined the card game. They were playing for fairly large stakes and the game was getting interesting. At midnight the three convicts leaned against each other, snoring. Zaven was waiting on the gamblers, who made gruff demands—"Mustafa, glass of water; Mustafa, empty the ashtrays; Mustafa, order coffee"—all through the evening.

The corporal was losing heavily. He opened his cigarette case and found it empty. He fished in every case on the table, but in vain. But he must have a cigarette. It would change his luck. Ha! A fresh pack would do it. He seemed to have forgotten that the wily young refugee who had made himself so useful was his prisoner. It also helped that the corporal had drunk perhaps too freely of the gentleman's liquor.

"Mustafa!" he shouted. "The damned cases are empty, every one of them. Go get us some cigarettes from the coffeehouse."

He placed a large silver coin in Zaven's palm.

"Get two packages for me, too," shouted another gambler.

"Wait!" commanded the gentleman, handing Zaven a gold piece. "Get us a dozen packages. I'm the winner and can afford it."

Zaven walked out with the money. This was the chance he had been waiting for. His escape with the money in his pocket would not in the least change his status as a refugee, or worse, as a deserter, which was what his conviction papers labeled him.

He went down to the courtyard, but instead of entering the coffeehouse, he passed out into the street and took a path that would take him to the mountains.

CHAPTER 12

That invisible hand of destiny once again had snatched the young outlaw from danger, but he felt shaky in the dark, tense solitude of the mountains, even though this was not a new experience. Every tree, every rock, every shadowy object had taken on some fearful imaginary form, and his mind made them real as he approached. Once, he timidly approached a sinister object, which turned out to be the trunk of a gnarled old tree with branches outstretched like open arms, and he laughed at himself. But his fevered brain would again invent the dreaded forms. He told himself he was a fool, a coward, and moved on carefully, keeping a weather eye on inanimate things that might not be what they seemed.

As he planned his new course, he had learned—through the short week's experience as an outlaw—the futility of attempting to reach the frontier alone. If he were caught again, he would never get out of it. Certainly he could not return to Miss Blake; that was out of the question. He must find a place where he could pass with a new identity.

He was a fugitive with no place of refuge, a criminal in the eyes of the Turks, who would not give him a chance if they recognized him. And yet, there might be a safe place. The thought kept reoccurring to him as a possibility until finally he decided to pursue it. He had learned that the Armenians in Constantinople were not deported. If he could reach this famous capitol, he might find sanctuary. Going there meant a long journey through Asia Minor. The only thing in his favor was that, along the way, a refugee would not appear to be a suspicious character.

After days of being hungry and afraid, he was halfway to the city of Kaiserieh. At dusk he entered a small village and asked a boy who was driving a few goats home if there was an inn or coffeehouse in the village.

"There isn't any inn here," answered the boy. "The refugees go to the Muhtar."

For a small coin the boy took him to the Muhtar's house. The Muhtar was the name for the head of the village. An old hunchbacked peasant with a gray beard and shaky knees hobbled out, supporting himself with a clumsy cane.

"Ah, another one," he cried as soon as he caught sight of the young refugee, "but what can I do? Can't let you starve to death. It's the devil's curse, which has already taken two of my sons. Allah, will I ever see the end of it ..."

"I understand, father," replied Zaven. "The curse has stricken all of us. For me, not one member of my family—four brothers and a sister, grandparents and parents—is living this day. I will pay for food and lodging."

"They all say that," grumbled the Muhtar, "but in the morning we find that they have nothing to pay with."

"That won't be the case with me."

"Well, follow me then, but I advise you to pay the man I am taking you to."

They walked down the narrow, litter-strewn street and stopped in front of the gate of a dilapidated shanty. The Muhtar pounded the gate with his club. No one stirred. It seemed like the whole village could hear the thumping, but there wasn't the slightest sign from within that people lived there. Zaven looked at the old man, who was getting impatient.

"Tefuk, you confounded idiot!" he shouted at the top of his lungs. "I know you're in. Open the door, else I'll run you out of this village!"

That threat fetched a fat man whose face was a picture of stupidity to the door. Zaven followed the two Turks into the house.

"I've brought you another one," said the Muhtar. "He says he'll pay."

"He had better or I'll work it out of him," said the peasant, appraising Zaven's physical condition.

The Muhtar disappeared without any further comment. The peasant looked suspiciously at his self-imposed guest, but, seeing no alternative, led the refugee through the main living quarters into a small room, where another refugee sat cross-legged on a mat.

"His name is Abdullah; he, too, is a refugee," said the host. "Make yourself at home while I have your meal prepared."

Zaven took his place on a small carpet in the opposite corner and glanced at this Abdullah. He had yellowish skin and looked wicked. The small eyes shined greedily under long eyebrows that gave him the appearance of a human hyena.

"Refugee?" asked Abdullah.

"Yes," Zaven answered.

"What part?"

"I hail from Olti."

"I'm from Sari-Kamish. Been in these parts long?"

Zaven nodded. "Stayed in Sivas almost two years."

"Where are you going?"

"Kaisarieh."

"That's where I'm going. We can start together tomorrow then."

Abdullah picked at his rotten teeth in an uncouth manner Zaven didn't like, but he hid his distaste. "Why not?" he said. "There is safety in numbers, as I've learned."

"Yes, and two refugees traveling together would look more natural," mumbled the man.

"I'd guess you're of military age," Zaven conjectured. "Have you papers? I have had lots of trouble for not having any."

"Why didn't you get any in Sivas?"

Zaven shrugged. "Too much red tape."

"I see," said Abdullah. "Well, I'm not of military age."

Zaven looked at him suspiciously. He was tempted to press the point, as this hyena man looked plenty old enough for the army, despite his close shave. Abdullah was clearly masquerading as a youth, and a smooth face was key to putting over the artifice. He doubted if Abdullah was even his real name.

"Well," Abdullah sneered, seeing Zaven's disbelief, "you can see for yourself."

He unbuttoned his coat and pulled out a greasy wallet and held out the document. "Can you read?"

Zaven shot Abdullah a dirty look and studied the paper. "Why, this is original and gives your age as seventeen. It must be a forgery—"

"That's right. Had the soldiers I've shown it to been as suspicious as you, I would not have come so far." He snatched the paper away and placed it in his wallet.

They had their meal of sour milk and pilaf. Zaven paid the host; his unwelcome companion followed his example reluctantly. After some more desultory conversation, they prepared themselves for sleep. The refugee with the fake identification paper stretched himself down on one of the filthy mattresses that the host had dragged in, but Zaven could not quite bring himself to lie on the other one and preferred the uncovered boards. He listened to the snoring of his companion and disliked him even more.

Though their mutual hostility was obvious, the next morning they started out together. As the day advanced, and they learned more about each other, their hatred reached the breaking point. Every suggestion Zaven made, Abdullah pronounced as stupid. Every ancecdote Abdullah shared, Zaven branded a lie. They could not agree on anything.

Before dark they arrived in a small village. Zaven announced his intentions to stop there for the night. His companion looked at him sharply.

"There's a better place ahead," he said. "It'll take only an hour to get there. Besides, there is a guardhouse in this village. You won't like that."

"True enough," agreed Zaven, "and I have no papers."

"I thought so," snorted the man. "As long as you have papers to show, you get along."

Zaven didn't like the snakelike smile that accompanied his words. During the day he had observed this disgusting hyena man with mounting contempt and felt that an explosion between the two was inevitable. It got to the point where Zaven, supremely confident in his fighting ability, wished that the man would start something. To the winner would belong the spoils: ID papers that suited Zaven much better than the long-in-the-tooth hyena man.

As they walked, Abdullah turned off on a trail that appeared to lead toward the hills.

"Why don't we follow the road?" Zaven asked.

"This is a short cut," came Abdullah's sharp explanation.

Zaven walked beside him pretending to be unconcerned, but he watched every move. Soon they were out of sight and hearing in a desolate spot in the midst of overgrown foliage. A crow shrieked ominously and flew over their heads. They looked up momentarily. Zaven was sure that something was about to happen.

"You don't seem like a refugee to me," said the hyena man in a belligerent voice.

"Bite your tongue, you slimy hyena," Zaven retorted. "And that fake paper of yours, who knows how you got it!"

"I will tell you now," growled the Turk. "That's why I brought you here, so that we can understand each other. If it'll do you any good to know, I'm a deserter. I don't mind telling you that I got the papers by killing a refugee."

In silence, the two took each other's measure. Zaven stepped back, without taking his eyes away from him. The hyena man carried a dagger tucked in his belt. He also had a money belt, which Zaven had coveted since first laying eyes on it. Zaven had picked up a heavy stick, which would serve nicely as a club. Abdullah observed Zaven's cold eyes and tried to make light of the fearlessness he saw in them.

"Don't be an ass!" he said, half laughing, half sneering. "I could have killed you a dozen times. But I won't because you'll be useful to me. The story of my being a refugee from Sari-Kamish will sound better if I should say that the papers belong to you and I'm your father. Then I can let my beard grow. I'm getting tired of those close shaves every day."

"Let's move on, then," said Zaven, "and tell me more about yourself and of your foul deeds."

"Ha! There isn't much life in the army—hard work, hunger, lice, and the ever-present chance of getting killed. But I had my days. Those were the days when I volunteered to be a soldier when the Armenians were deported. That was the life!"

Abdullah kept on talking, but his words had become an incoherent jumble in Zaven's ears. He trembled; his face became as twisted as his feelings.

"Why so excited?" shouted the hyena man, his eyes fierce. "Why tremble when I speak of Armenians?"

"I tremble not of fear, that much I want you to know," cried Zaven, "but out of hope that you'll try to kill me when you learn that I am an Armenian outlaw."

"You cursed Armenian!" roared the Turk, pulling out his dagger. "Had I known that, you would never have had the chance to boast."

"I know that, and this is the difference between us. While you didn't know me, I knew you. But I wouldn't strike you in the back. Now let's see how good a killer you really are."

The Turk rushed, whirling the dagger in front of him. Zaven sidestepped him, with the agility of a cat. The dagger missed his chest by inches, and the club crashed squarely on the charging killer's head, opening an ugly gash. The outlaw leaped in front of his enemy, readying himself for the next charge. Abdullah was hurt; he staggered momentarily but soon regained his balance. Then he charged. Again the club found its mark. The hyena man went down. Blood gushed from the wound.

The outlaw had turned into a beast. He hit the fallen enemy again and again; ugly words poured from his lips and rang back in his ears as an echo. He had already killed him, but he wanted to make doubly, triply sure. He picked up the dagger and administered a final blow. Then he took the dead man's papers and the money belt, which held a small fortune. It would serve him well. He threw the dagger in the brush, covered the body, and took the trail back to the road.

The next morning at a small town on the road to Kaiserieh, Zaven assumed his latest guise: a Turkish refugee with authentic papers bearing the name of Kadir Oghlu, Abdullah, age seventeen, from Sari-Kamish, who was looking for a carriage going to Kaiserieh. He had seen the innkeeper in the town, told him what he wanted, and produced money to convince the man of his ability to pay. While he sat with his teacup in the coffeehouse, he played backgammon for money with an old man who would learn too late that the young refugee was a more skilled gamesman than he had bargained for. The innkeeper approached and tapped the refugee on the shoulder.

"I've spoken to the driver of a carriage going to Kaiserieh," he said. "It's hired by a military doctor. The driver will take you on if the doctor consents. I spoke to the doctor, too; he wishes to see you."

Zaven put the dice on the board. "I concede this game," he smiled. "And we'll call it even. How's that, uncle?"

"But you've practically won it!" remarked the old man with smiling eyes.

"That's all right; next time, don't be so sure of yourself."

The old man grinned. "Not after the skill you showed me."

Zaven rose and followed the innkeeper. He was introduced to an agreeable-looking officer, lounging on a cot.

"Are you the young refugee who wants to go to Kaiserieh?" asked the doctor.

"Yes, sir."

"Have you identification papers?"

"Yes, sir." Zaven took out the precious document and handed it to the doctor.

"Good," said the doctor. "Without it, I wouldn't have taken you."

"When will we leave?"

"In half an hour. Do you have any baggage?"

"Not even a sack, sir."

"Then you can help me get my things into the carriage."

Now, with authentic papers and in the company of a respected officer, Zaven felt safe. He was beyond suspicion, and experience had taught him what to say and how to say it. He carried on a steady conversation with the doctor. It seemed they were enjoying each other's company while their carriage jerked and shook them along the bumpy road.

"I'll have to admit, I've been prejudiced against the refugees," remarked the doctor. "Maybe I haven't met the right ones. You seem a decent and intelligent boy."

"Thank you, sir," said the refugee. "I have had some schooling, and I owe a good deal to a gentleman whom I served while I was in Sivas."

"Why did you leave him?"

"I want to go to Stambul," declared the refugee boldly.

The doctor's face registered sudden surprise. He looked at the bold refugee with a smile in his eyes. Zaven liked it.

"Have you any relatives?" the doctor asked.

"Not one living," answered the refugee from Sari-Kamish in a sad voice. "A shell hit our house during the siege. My father was killed on the spot. Mother died on the road. I've no idea where my two brothers are. They were in the service, and my sister disappeared just before we fled." The story sounded so good, Zaven half-believed it himself.

"The battle of Sari-Kamish, a disastrous one," said the doctor thoughtfully. "I remember it well."

Just before entering the village, where they intended to stay overnight, the carriage stopped at a checkpoint. A tough-looking guard with a loud, braying voice stuck his head through the side opening of the carriage. His tone and manner became fawning when he saw the uniformed occupant.

"Sorry to stop you, sir."

"Don't be apologetic of your duty, man," said the doctor as he produced his identification.

After a hasty look, the guard passed the paper back. "I assume the boy is your servant, sir."

"No, he's traveling with me. He has his own paper."

Zaven showed his to the guard , who just glanced at it and said, "Pleasant journey, sir."

The carriage rolled on. Zaven hadn't felt this good for a long, long time—self-confident, unruffled, money in his pocket, and an influential friend with him. Yet beneath this superficial cloak of security laid the irony of the truth. He didn't dare to flatter himself. Just one slip, a weak link in the chain of events, and he would be cast to his doom once again.

They drove into the courtyard of a ramshackle inn that looked more like a cattle shed. The man who owned the place had appeared and assured them that he had a good room in the back. Whether the place would meet the doctor's approval or not was immaterial, as the next overnight station was too far. Zaven helped the peasant carry the luggage into the room. It was a small room, spartanly appointed, with tiny windows—a tidy, cozy little place.

"Will the young man stay with you, sir?" asked the innkeeper.

"Yes," said the doctor.

"I will make it comfortable for you both, sir."

"I don't want a mattress; just set up my cot and bring us something good to eat."

"Yes, sir. I've a pullet. It won't take long to prepare it."

The doctor turned to the refugee. "What about it, Abdullah," he said, "do you like broiled pullet?"

"Very much, sir," smiled Zaven.

"The pullet then," said the doctor.

The peasant saluted and left the room. Zaven was wondering if it might be better to stay with the carriage driver rather than sharing the room with the doctor. He would feel more at home with the driver, who was a friendly fellow. Zaven had asked the driver to let him drive and surprised him with his technique.

"So, you want to go to Stambul," the doctor said unexpectedly.

Zaven was caught unprepared.

"Sit down, my boy," continued the doctor. "Has it ever occurred to you how hard it would be? No one can enter Stambul without passport and traveling orders. It isn't easy to get these papers, and as for a refugee, it's almost impossible."

"I know that, but I still need to try," said Zaven thoughtfully. "If I get close enough, some day I may get there."

"Have you a particular reason to go there?"

"Yes, I have an uncle there who has done well. I lost his address, but it won't be hard to find him through some countrymen once I get there."

The doctor did not speak for some time. Zaven noticed how his face changed expressions as he sat, lost in deep thought. Finally, the esteemed doctor of the army looked at the refugee and smiled.

"There's a way to get you there, but it's risky and uncertain."

"I don't mind the risk, sir," answered Zaven enthusiastically. "I'm willing to take a chance, any kind of chance, to get into Stambul. If you help me, I'll be grateful forever."

The doctor leaned forward and whispered his plan. "There's one sure way. It would be defrauding the government, but larceny, they say, is good for the soul. First, you must be bitten by a mad dog. Then, when you reach the capitol, they will take you directly to a hospital to receive the needle treatment. I warn you, boy, you won't like it! And after all you have been through, they may not let you stay."

"Please, sir, I'll suffer anything to go to my uncle. It won't be hard to find an ill-tempered mongrel along the road."

"Suppose the beast turned out to be a really mad one?" smiled the doctor.

"What of it? I'll be treated."

"You may really turn out to be a mad one yourself before I get you to a hospital," chuckled the doctor. "No, there's a safer way," he added. "And if you're smart enough, which I believe you are, you can spare yourself from those painful hospital treatments."

"Please, sir, go on.

"I could make a report that you had been bitten by a mad dog, and then they'd have to give you a passport. Not only that, but the government has to send you there as quickly as possible. To be convincing, you would have to cut wounds on your ankle resembling a dog's bite."

"I'll do it, sir!" cried Zaven.

The doctor smiled again. "You've been pretty friendly with the carriage driver. Do you think he'll sign the paper as a witness?"

"I'm sure he will," said Zaven confidently. "He told me that he'll try to get a fare in Kaiserieh that would take me closer."

"Go ahead, talk to him and invite him to eat with us."

Zaven found the carriage driver in the stable and talked to him while they were brushing the horses. The man was very understanding. When they came to the room the meal was already set and the innkeeper made his graceful exit.

"Doctor, Effendi," said the carriage driver, who always addressed the army doctor with that compound title. "Abdullah was telling me about a scheme that would take him to Stambul. I think that's very decent of you to save him from his miseries. I don't know how to write my name, but I'll put my seal under the paper as a witness if you make the paper."

"Good," said the doctor.

"I will always remember you both, and your kindness," said the supposed refugee softly.

CHAPTER 13

Under the dim candlelight, Zaven sat cross-legged, holding the scalpel in his right hand and digging holes in the flesh of his left leg. The doctor had marked the places for him and suggested using his scalpel instead of Zaven's jackknife. The pain was excruciating, but Zaven performed the task almost with pleasure, scarcely wincing as the incredibly sharp utensil made deep punctures in his flesh. Meanwhile, the doctor sat on his cot and wrote the report describing the incident of a rabid dog attacking his patient. Finally, he put the paper aside and went to see how the patient progressed.

"Abdullah, that's enough!" he cried. "This is supposed to be a dog's bite, not a lion's."

Zaven put the scalpel aside and took out his handkerchief to wipe away the blood.

"Don't touch it," commanded the doctor. "I will do the rest." He cleaned the wounds with a professional's touch, opened his satchel, took out bandages and antiseptic, and dressed Zaven's leg. He was satisfied that the boy had created authentic-looking bite marks.

"Now get up and walk," he said. "Does it hurt? It should."

"Not much." Zaven smiled. He hurt, but it was a good hurt.

"Nevertheless, limp." Zaven complied. "Ah, that's better. Now read the paper I've written aloud so that Hasan can hear it."

The carriage driver, who had witnessed this operation from a distance, straightened up. Zaven picked up the paper and began reading:

"As a witness, I, Captain Jemal Kazim of the Medical Corps of the Army, certify that Kadir Oghlu Abdullah, a refugee, was bitten by a rabid dog.

Said refugee was walking within about one hundred feet of my carriage when a dog attacked him. I fired at the animal but failed to kill him. After examining the boy's wound and taking into consideration the behavior of the beast, I came to the conclusion the animal was rabid. Therefore, I urge immediate action in sending this unfortunate boy to the hospital in Stambul where he can receive proper treatment.

Captain Jemal Kasim,

Army Medical Corps"

The doctor took the paper from Zaven and went to the carriage driver. "Now, Hasan, put your seal right here," he said, pointing to the space under the word "witness."

The following afternoon, in the city of Kaiserieh, the refugee bitten by a mad dog was taken to the government building. Over a glass-paneled door was the sign Commissar of Passports in gilded letters. Dr. Jemal instructed his ward to wait outside while he explained their situation to the authorities. After five minutes of waiting, the patient was called. He stood before a well-groomed officer in civilian clothes. The doctor, with a smile on his face, occupied the chair beside the desk.

"You're a refugee, your name is Kadir Oghlu Abdullah, and you were bitten by a dog. Is that right?" the officer asked gently.

"Yes, sir," replied the refugee.

"My boy, you're lucky Dr. Jemal happened to be around when the dog attacked you," said the commissar with a nod to the good doctor. "Now, Abdullah, I want you to be brave because I have some bad news for you. The doctor thinks that the dog that attacked you was a rabid one and urges that you receive proper treatment immediately. Therefore, we're going to send you to Stambul."

The officer walked to the door, opened it, and commanded to the attendant waiting outside, "Take this boy to the hospital at once!"

The doctor rose, stopped momentarily to tap the refugee on the shoulder, and walked out. The Commissar of Passports went back to his desk and picked up three documents: his own recommendation, Dr. Jemal's falsified report, and the refugee's forged identity papers—all of which looked completely authentic. He placed them in a folder and gave it to the attendant. Now, the wanton outlaw was beyond reproach. Behind the mask of a sad face, he was excited at the thought of getting on his way.

He enjoyed the sights of the city on the walk to the hospital, but kept up his act, hobbling along and making occasional moans of pain. His escort, walking beside him, whispered comforting words. The hospital was not far, although it had taken a half hour for them to arrive.

After a short wait in the lobby, he was summoned before the head surgeon, a colonel in military rank. Sad-faced and seemingly in pain, Zaven stood by the door while the colonel glanced over the papers handed to him.

"Did the dog bite you?" he asked without raising his eyes.

"Yes, sir."

Zaven walked to the chair next to the desk. He sat down, pulled up his trouser leg, and began to undo the bandage.

"Don't touch it!" commanded the surgeon severely. "We'll see to that."

A young woman in a crisp white uniform entered with a tray of surgical instruments. One look at her and Zaven knew that she was an Armenian. She kneeled in front of him, raised his feet, and gently rested them on a stool. Then she started cutting the bandages. Zaven's thoughts wandered. What would she think if she learned that she was caring for an Armenian outlaw in a Turkish military hospital?

The wounds looked bad; the leg had swollen and the skin was a purplish red. The surgeon began to probe around the injuries.

"Ow!" cried Zaven loudly, but it was more pretense than real pain.

The colonel shook his head. "It's bad," he mumbled. "We must send him to Stambul right away."

He went to his desk, scribbled something in his doctorly hand on an official sheet, signed and sealed it, and then attached it to the other documents lying on his desk. He asked for the attendant who had brought the refugee to the hospital.

"We will keep him here until we are ready to release him," he said to the attendant. "Take these papers to the Commissar and tell him to have the passport ready."

The patient was brought to a ward occupied by several wounded soldiers. For two days he ate rice soup and enjoyed the company of sympathetic roommates. On the third day, he was ordered to get dressed to see the colonel.

"Abdullah, you're leaving for Stambul by truck," he said. "That's the fastest way to get you there. It wasn't easy to arrange. We had to hold back an officer to make a place for you. He can wait, but you can't. Don't worry, my boy, you will be all right. I hope to see that you are well when you return."

Zaven thanked him and followed his guide into the street to a busy square where two German trucks, enormous vehicles with heavy iron wheels, were waiting. He was thrilled. He so much wanted to ride in one of those trucks, and here he was, a guest of the government!

A group of uniformed officers was gathered around the trucks. Zaven was beginning to wonder if a place had really been reserved for him when Dr. Jemal approached.

"Didn't I tell you that you'll get there before me?" he said, smiling.

Zaven looked disappointed. "Can't you come, too?"

"No, there are too many ahead of me. I have to wait my turn if I want to travel in one of those trucks. I'll see you in Stambul. Here is my address."

A young, good-looking lieutenant with the Engineers' insignia on his lapel elbowed his way through the men. He stood before the doctor.

"Dr. Jemal!" he cried, extending his hand. "I'm very much indebted to you. I wonder if you remember me."

"Of course!" answered the doctor. "Lieutenant Shavket. How's that battered leg of yours?"

"Thanks to you, doctor, good as new." Shavket looked toward the trucks. "It won't be a comfortable ride, but we will get there faster."

"I'm afraid I won't be going with you," Dr. Jemal replied. "I have to wait my turn, but this boy is going and I'm responsible for him. You see, a mad dog bit him, and I recommended that he be sent to Stambul for treatment. He's a refugee—a good boy. I'd appreciate it if you would look after him."

"Of course," said the young lieutenant, eyeing Zaven with a friendly look.

The doctor pulled the refugee aside. "Don't worry," he said sotto voce. "Even if you can't find your uncle, I'll be there soon. I advise you not to go to the hospital at all. You're a smart boy and can make friends."

They shook hands. The good doctor turned and left. About this time, a sergeant holding a piece of paper began calling names and the men responded by getting into the trucks. These were anxious seconds for the refugee. Kadir Oghlu Abdullah was the last name on the list. He saw the young lieutenant waving his hand from the back opening of one of the trucks. Zaven went toward him and climbed in with the lieutenant's help. He was the only civilian. That was very unusual. The refugee bitten by the rabid dog smoothly told his story, generating sympathy, as they bumped along the road. The engineering lieutenant, who was on his first leave home since the beginning of the war, seemed to have taken a special interest in the unfortunate boy.

"I always dreamed of seeing Stambul," said the refugee, "but not this way. Dr. Jemal told me the treatment would be painful."

"Oh, I shouldn't worry, you look like a stout lad," said the lieutenant cheerily. "Are you sure that the dog that bit you was really mad?"

"I don't know. Dr. Jemal, who saw the attack, too, thinks so. The colonel at the hospital agreed that the aggressive dog's behavior suggested it might have rabies. But to me, the dog didn't look sick."

"How long ago did the accident happen?"

"It's been four days now."

"Does it hurt?"

"The pain comes and goes. It mainly hurts when I walk. I don't look as if I'm going mad, do I?"

The lieutenant laughed. "No, my friend, you're not foaming at the mouth—yet! Today we will reach Aski-Shihar where we take the train, and in two more days we'll be in Stambul. That will make a week, won't it?"

Zaven nodded.

"If, during this time, you feel well," continued Zaven's newfound friend, "you can be pretty sure that the dog wasn't mad. Then, if I were you, I'd try to slip away when we reach the station in Stambul without showing papers. If you do, they will surely take you right to the hospital."

"That's probably true," groaned the refugee, "and what troubles me more is that after going through the treatment, they will send me back to Kaiserieh."

Of all the places Zaven had seen so far, Aski-Shihar was the most impressive. The streets were paved and the houses were over two stories tall. The stores had plate glass windows. He dined with his friend in a good restaurant and wanted to pay his share but Shavket wouldn't let him.

It was here that he saw a train for the first time and was fascinated when the long chain of cars drew into the station. How lucky he felt to be alive to see it! The passenger cars were divided into small, two-benched compartments. He and Shavket took one. They had a bottle of cognac and delicacies to go with it. They drank, laughed, and told stories. After two days of companionship they were close friends. In his heart Zaven cursed the shadow between them.

"Abdullah," said the lieutenant, "two more hours and we'll be in Stambul. The dog that bit you wasn't mad—otherwise you'd be trying to bite me by now! I won't let you show your papers."

"I know I'm all right, Shavket," answered Zaven, "and I don't intend to go through the treatment for a rabid dog bite." He looked at his friend and, after a moment, said, "Shavket, would you condemn two friends, who—of no evil intent—had schemed against the law? Should I tell you why I don't have to go to the hospital?"

"Go on, you scoundrel," smiled the lieutenant. "Dr. Jemal is too human to be an army doctor."

"I'm grateful to him, and to you, especially." Even as Zaven said these words he wondered how Shavket would feel if he knew the truth. Well, if the lieutenant were a true friend, he would take Zaven as he was: the good and the bad. There was only one way to find out.

Zaven sighed heavily and said, "The story and the papers saying that I was bitten were a ruse to get me to Stambul."

The lieutenant threw back his head and roared with laughter. "This is the best scheme I've heard yet! Rules and regulations, most of them senseless. Listen, my friend, do you think I am without fault? Do you think I could get this leave of absence with some chicanery of my own? Go on, tell me what happened."

"The whole thing's a pack of lies. Even the wound on my leg isn't from a dog's teeth."

"Now I admire Dr. Jemal even more. Of course, you have to escape, but we'll find a way. Stambul is big and unfriendly to strangers. You'll have to come home with me."

"That's too much to ask, Shavket."

"If I hadn't offered, or if you refused to accept, it wouldn't be the kind of friendship that we both thought, Abdullah."

"What about your family?"

"They'll welcome you. I have a mother and a sister. My father, also an officer, was killed in the Italian war. They live with my uncle, who has a high-ranking position in the government. He can help you. In the meantime, you'll be useful around the house as a sort of adopted brother."

"I only hope that I don't disappoint you, Shavket."

"You won't, I'm sure of that. Now, we have to think of a way to get you out of the station. I have an idea," he offered. "Just before the train stops, you jump out onto the platform and pretend to be a porter. I'll give you my trunk to carry." He examined his friend's appearance as though he were seeing him for the first time. "You'll pass for a porter all right, but don't answer any questions. I'll do the talking."

"Very clever, Shavket," Zaven said as he seized the lieutenant's arm.

"Don't flatter me too soon; we're not through yet. First, you need a rope. Have you ever seen a porter without a rope? It's practically part of their uniform."

Zaven untied the heavy rope that held Shavket's trunk and bedding together and threw it over his shoulder.

"That's it!" cried Shavket. "Now, when the train slows down, get on the stepping board and jump, but make sure that no one sees you."

The train entered the station at a slow crawl. The place was crowded, but no guards were in sight. Zaven stood on the step for a moment, and then jumped down onto the platform, holding the rope over his shoulder. Shavket was fumbling around in the compartment, killing time, so that others who were in the car would move on. Then he appeared on the stepping board and shouted, "Porter, porter!" Zaven was quick to answer his call before half a dozen others rushed toward the lieutenant.

"All right, boy, you'll do," said Shavket as he pointed to Zaven. "Come up and get my luggage."

Zaven stepped into the car, threw the rope around the trunk and bedding, hoisted the bulky load on his back, and stepped back down to the platform. Bent under the load, he followed the lieutenant through the station to the fenced iron gate. Here, two policemen were examining passports. As Shavket handed his papers to one, Zaven kept going and was almost out of the gate when he was stopped.

"He's a porter carrying my luggage, officer," Shavket explained.

"Go on," mumbled the policeman without taking another look.

Zaven straightened up enough to catch the lieutenant's smiling eyes and followed him to the wharf, where they took the ferry for the European side of Stambul. Then they hired a carriage that brought them to Shavket's home.

The sights on the streets of the great capital excited Zaven. Here, for the first time, on the wide cement walkways he saw women without veils wearing hats and stylish clothes, but no one seemed to pay attention to them. He was content and felt secure. He liked the lieutenant and saw him as a friend. There seemed to be two ways of life open to him, an outlaw or a settled-down, respectable Everyman, but he couldn't yet decide on one or the other.

Shavket's mother and sister, who were pleasant but very shy and retiring, seemed excited about having a guest. They bent over backwards making Zaven feel at home. Then he went out with Shavket to buy clothes and shed his refugee rags. When they returned Zaven felt comfortable in his new look; now he could walk in the street without attracting attention.

That evening he met his friend's uncle, an arrogant bachelor who obviously loved to listen to himself talk. He wanted to know all about the Turkish refugee, but Zaven's sad stories did not impress him.

"You're lucky to be here," he said coldly. "And now that Shavket has brought you into this house, we have to look after you; I hope you'll prove worthy."

"My only wish is to measure up to your expectations," the refugee said, but his thoughts were quite different.

The following day the lieutenant went to headquarters. Zaven walked out with him, but they separated at the stop for the electric trolley. From the window the lieutenant shouted to his friend to be back for lunch, as he would return then, too. But at that point Zaven had already made up his mind never to see him again.

As Zaven was wandering in the streets admiring the buildings and displays in the store windows, and speculating what to do next, he overheard two women ahead of him speaking in Armenian. He approached them and asked for directions to the office of the Armenian Patriarch. The place was not far, and he had no difficulty finding it. After a short wait in the hallway, he was led before the venerable clergyman. He told him part of his story and asked for help locating a family friend who had come to Constantinople several years ago and who worked for the American Mission Board.

"If the man you are looking for works for the Board," said the Patriarch, "the best way to find him is send you there."

He gave Zaven directions to the American Board. Here, to his great satisfaction, he learned that Brother Levon, the man he was looking for, worked in that very building. Within a few minutes Zaven was talking to his old family friend and was invited to his house that evening.

Later, a small, select group of friends gathered in Levon's house to see and hear from the young boy who had escaped. They knew little of what had happened to their countrymen outside the city. The disturbing memory of the sudden disappearance of a dozen Armenian leaders had faded, and life in Constantinople went on as usual.

Sunk in a chair, Zaven told his grim story while the group stared at him as though he was from another planet. A well-groomed young man with an insolent twinkle in his eyes asked bluntly, "Have you killed anyone?"

The cold, stony expression that suddenly clouded Zaven's countenance made the vain young man wish he had held his tongue. The rest of the group who had witnessed this transformation learned all they cared to know about this hardship-haunted refugee.

"Zaven," said Brother Levon when they were alone, "here you can forget the past. You'll be safe like the rest of us. I believe we can even get you an Armenian identification card. It won't be hard to find you a job. In the meantime, you can stay here until everything is straightened out."

"Thank you, but I really don't want to be a problem for you."

"You aren't any problem, boy. And let me tell you, whatever I do, it won't be one tenth of what your father did for me."

Levon had a large family: four young children ranging in age from three to twelve. Soon Zaven learned that food was rationed. Even if he helped financially, which he could, the good man would not accept any money from him. Besides, ration tickets were more valuable than money and he could not get any. Zaven decided to leave Brother Levon the evening of the third day when he learned that there was a job for him. The American Girl's College wanted a helper in the kitchen. There he would be fed, sheltered, and—most blessedly—above suspicion.

CHAPTER 14

The American Girl's College was a congenial place to work, and to an outlaw it was a haven of safety. Weeks passed, and Zaven seemed content. Then people began to talk. Pampered, romance-hungry young ladies, despite Zaven's tight lips, had learned about him. There he was, in the kitchen serving tables, a handsome outlaw. It was not obvious from a casual glance that he could be a killer. A dark-haired girl, not pretty but attractive, was the only one who challenged the young outlaw's cold, hard look with her coquettish smile. She wasn't one of the students; she was the daughter of the cook and she worked there as a secretary. The cook invited him to her home one Sunday evening. She was good to him, so he felt he couldn't refuse. After the tea dishes were put away, the mother asked to be excused and walked out.

He was alone with the young woman. Mariza, in her short-length gown, looked stunningly feminine. Zaven felt uncomfortable as she curled up on the sofa, displaying her legs above the knee. Never before had Zaven been so conscious of a woman's sexual appeal. With sparks in her eyes, she patted the unused portion of the sofa in invitation. The young outlaw sat timidly beside her.

"Now, tell me all about it," said Mariza, in a coaxing voice.

"There isn't anything I can tell that you don't already know," Zaven answered indifferently.

"Oh, yes, there is." She cuddled closer and held the young man's hand. "I want to kiss the hand that has avenged our people," she whispered.

A black kitten with shiny fur and a blue ribbon around its neck imitated her mistress and cuddled down on the other side of the outlaw. With a sudden explosion of fury, the outlaw grabbed the innocent creature by the neck and hurled her through the air. The poor thing lay there motionless on the hard floor in the middle of the room. In a flash Zaven was on his feet. He cast a glance at the innocent victim, lying there apparently dead. His eyes softened. He took a few paces toward the door, then turned and looked back. The dark-haired enchantress's hands covered her face, but she laughed.

"I'm sorry," mumbled Zaven.

"Don't worry, she won't die," Mariza said softly. "Cats have nine lives. I should be thankful that it was she..." She went over and picked her up. The poor innocent thing was dazed but otherwise all right. She caressed the puss and put her out of the room. Zaven was ashamed.

"I thought men like you existed only in books," she said, walking back to her place. "Your kind can be adored, but not touched. Please sit down." Her voice was sincere; she now looked calm and dignified. "I want to talk to you. Not of what you've done, but what you intend to do, and how I can be of help."

Zaven looked at her apologetically and sat down in a chair, puzzled more than ever.

"Let me tell you about myself," she continued. "I'm a member of the underground organization. You are the first person we know of who has returned from the deportations. By itself, that is proof of what you are. Zaven, we have men hiding in the garret. They have the spirit, but few have the experience. Until now, no one has been able to move their spirit into action. There's one now ... you. Take them out and lead them, Zaven."

Mariza walked over to him, sitting in the chair. "Will you give me your hand now?" she said, smiling. Zaven fought against his impulse to embrace the enchantress and ravish her, an action that could only lead to trouble.

She had ignited the fuse. Zaven was restless again. His comfortable life annoyed him and his feverish brain worked day and night.

It was Sunday; there wasn't much work to do in the kitchen. By chance he came across an illustrated English textbook. He had studied one of them a very long time ago, and he was curious to know how much he still remembered. He picked it up and walked outside. It was a pleasant afternoon in mid-June. Zaven settled down in the shade of a tree, with the book in his lap. The campus with its white buildings and garden of flowers, and the blue, curving strait of Bosporus with palaces of sultans along its shores, were in his view. Although he had seen no one approach, he felt that he was not alone. He turned and saw a girl whose table he routinely served standing a short distance away.

"I'm sorry, Zaven," she said gently, taking a few tentative steps forward. "I hope I'm not disturbing you; this is my favorite spot, too."

"It is beautiful."

"What's that you are reading?"

"Not reading, just looking at pictures."

"Ah, an English book. Interesting language. Do you wish to learn it? I will help you. By the way, my name is Sonia."

"Thank you, Sonia. I don't believe I can be sincere about books and learning."

Zaven detected a look of disappointment on her face, but she sat down. He thought it was time for him to leave.

"Hope I'm not chasing you away," Sonia said, as he stood up. "There's no harm in both of us enjoying the scenery, and I promise not to talk about books."

"No harm at all. But I'm afraid it's about time for me to go to work."

"Zaven, would you think I'm silly if I tell you that when I learned a little from Professor Calomian about you, I wanted to know more."

"It isn't a happy story."

"Is there anyone of your family living?"

"No."

"I wouldn't believe it, if you were not standing there. That one could escape all those horrors and reach here safely. It's remarkable."

"I've been lucky."

"It couldn't have been all luck."

"I'm sorry," said Zaven awkwardly. "I really must go."

Between the three—Zaven, Mariza, and the leader of the underground, a pleasant-looking, smooth-talking man in his thirties who owned and operated one of the best restaurants in the European sector of the capitol—plans were developing. Securing guns seemed to be the biggest problem, but Zaven did not demand an armory.

The school was about to close for the long summer vacation. Some of the girls had left already. These were his last days of a peaceful life, and he was trying to make the most of it, now that he was at peace with his own conscience. The girl who had tried to talk to him while he was examining the English book told him that she was going to leave for Bulgaria within a few days. She had hinted of her need for a guardian during the journey and that Sofia was a fine place to spend the summer. Whatever her intention, Zaven did not take any notice.

It was rather late at night. Zaven was in his room, absorbed in his dreams, when he heard a tap on his door. He went to the door and discovered to his surprise that the unexpected visitor was that old respected professor of history that Sonia had mentioned.

"I'm certain it will surprise you to learn why I've come," he said, as he accepted Zaven's invitation to sit down. "Sonia sent me. She is the daughter of an important Bulgarian officer. The Bulgars are the allies of this government, and I know that she can do almost the impossible, which is taking you out of this country where you will no longer be hunted. Don't ask me why. I'm an old man and have seen most of the vagaries of life. But this one, I can't figure it out. The truth of the matter is that the silly girl thinks she's in love with you."

"That's ridiculous!" laughed Zaven. "She only feels pity."

"Let me speak," said the old man in a domineering voice. "Nothing would have made me come to you if I hadn't seen and heard her. I admired her courage. Yes, Zaven, her courage. It couldn't have been easy. Can you understand that? I know you've been talking to Mariza. I know what she is. I'm telling you, Zaven, no good will come of it. As an Armenian, I would be proud if I had a son like you, but as a father, I wish that you would leave this hellhole and go with Sonia."

"Why didn't she ask me herself?"

"From her words, I know that she had given you a hint. You're a hard man to talk to, Zaven, especially hard for a young girl."

"I appreciate her kind thought," said Zaven, after some hesitation. "Had she known me better, I am sure she wouldn't have been that silly."

"Zaven, you're a fool, a fanatic! This girl can make a happy life for you. I hate to think what may become of you; you cannot always escape."

"I understand that, but my work here isn't finished yet."

"Now listen to me, son. I, too, am proud of my heritage. In my youth I worked toward what I believed to be a cause. But there's no longer a cause. If the whole Turkish population were killed by a supernatural force, there are not enough Armenians to be liberated. Men have killed one another ever since creation. Revenge is not a cause but an obsession."

The young outlaw rose and circled around the room, then stood in front of the old professor. His breathed deeply; his eyes were cold and his face austere.

"I thank you both," he said coldly. "I'm not worthy of that sort of consideration. I've already chosen my path. Tell Sonia I'm grateful for her kind thoughts."

The old professor shook his head and left, muttering to himself.

With the aid of Mariza, Zaven visited his prospective companions at their hiding place. They looked to him like the kind of men he could rely on. Among those who impressed him most was a man in his early forties. His name was Avak; Zaven nicknamed him "Dio," for uncle. And Dio he remained for the rest of his life. He was tall, awkward, bony-cheeked, and a messy mustache hung low on either side of his lips. His expression was one of simplicity, but courage and loyalty were also writ large on his face. Zaven liked him. Dio was a native of a town not far from Stambul and knew the European side of Turkey well.

Zaven had just finished the breakfast dishes when Mariza walked nervously into the kitchen.

"Zaven," she said, "there's a policeman downstairs in the office. He says you're wanted at headquarters for matters concerning a passport. Have you applied for one?"

"No," said Zaven, imperturbably. Had that Bulgarian girl anything to do with it? That was immaterial. He was through dealing with the government. The links with his current situation were weak; it did not require much strain to break them.

"It doesn't look good, Zaven," whispered Mariza, drawing him to the corner of the kitchen. "You're not going there."

"I'll go," Zaven said calmly. He didn't wish to involve those who had been kind to him. "Will the garret be a safe place until ..." he asked.

"Yes," answered Mariza. "You'll be safe, but do you know how to get there?"

"Yes, I know the way. Wait, I'll be back in a minute."

He went to his room, stood in front of the dresser, and caught his face in the mirror. It was the face Hagop had seen when he had said, "I want to see you look like that ..." He pulled out the drawer and from under his clothes he fished out something that looked like an ice pick. He tucked it in his sleeve, and walked out to meet Mariza in the kitchen. He followed her down the stairs to the office of the Dean, a nice, elderly American woman. A fortyish policeman, robust and self-assured, sat on a chair near the door. After a quick glance at him, Zaven turned his eyes away.

"It's about your passport, Zaven," said the Dean of Women. "The officer wants you to go to headquarters with him for some routine questioning."

"Yes," reassured the officer with a smile. "Routine questions, such as name, place of birth, and so on."

This subtle acting didn't fool Zaven, but he, too, could act. "Of course, officer," he said with a submissive smile.

As they were about to leave the room, the policemen turned to the Dean and said, "We won't keep him long, ma'am."

"That's all right, officer. We can spare him for a while. He is a good boy," said the Dean, as she closed the door behind them.

The Girl's College was on an isolated hilltop in the suburbs. A narrow, winding trail that started from the gate ran down the slope for a good mile between the gate and the trolley line. Zaven had the exact spot in mind: a desolate bend in the trail overlooking a deep ravine, hidden from everywhere and everything. How many times had he stopped there and reflected subconsciously about it—a ten-foot-high wall on one side, the deep, jungle-like ravine on the other.

The policeman seemed very sure of himself. Their conversation up to this point had been more or less friendly when the policeman asked bluntly, "Are you from Anatoli, and have you come recently?"

"Yes," replied Zaven.

"Been deported, of course. That doesn't matter if that's the only thing against you. All is forgiven and forgotten."

The words infuriated Zaven. Forgiven and forgotten—but who had to do the forgiving and forgetting? Zaven's panther-like leap brought the policeman down flat on his back. Before the man could scream Zaven's steely palm covered his mouth and the deadly weapon had pierced the victim's heart. Zaven stabbed the officer again to make sure he was dead. The incident had taken mere seconds. He picked up the officer's automatic pistol, and then kicked the body down into the ravine. He looked up and down the trail. He saw no one. He brushed away the telltale marks with his feet and hastened down the trail to the trolley line. Very conveniently, one was coming. Zaven got in and took a back seat, looking as innocent as a child, as calm as a nun.

CHAPTER 15

Late in the afternoon, during the quiet hour of business, Zaven entered the restaurant operated by the underground leader. He was a popular man with friends in official circles. He was startled when he saw Zaven walk in. A prosperous-looking Turk and a lady in a wide-brimmed hat sat close together in the corner, but they did not notice Zaven. He followed the leader to his office.

"What's up?" he asked, after closing the door behind the young outlaw.

"Nothing much," answered Zaven, calmly. "Had to kill a policeman."

The man stared at him, unable to think of an appropriate answer. Recovering from the shock, he demanded, "Did you leave any trace behind?"

"No."

"Are you sure? If not, tell me, so that I'll be prepared. Avak—your Dio—he, too, killed a man, a stool pigeon who stuck his nose where it didn't belong. A messy job."

"Don't get fidgety. I would not have come if I had the slightest concern over covering my tracks. I took the trolley to the Turkish sector, and then traveled all over the city before coming here."

"Let's go downstairs, then."

They went to the back of the kitchen and stood by innocent-looking chests of canned foods. The leader pushed on a portion of an adjacent wall, and the chests moved as though by magic. After a moment's pause, a small round hole opened in the wall. The leader squeezed through. Zaven followed him. They descended a dozen steps and found themselves in a good-sized basement with beds along the wall. Nine men, pale-faced and unshaven, huddled like moles in a burrow. They sat up erect, blinking in the dim light.

"Here he is," said the leader of the underground in a casual way. "We must get you boys ready soon."

"That suits me," cried Dio, jumping to his feet.

"The sooner, the better," commented a young man from Zaven's hometown, who had come to Constantinople before the war—a deserter from the labor battalion.

"Ah, to breathe fresh air again," sighed another.

"You'll breathe plenty of fresh air," said Zaven. "That I assure you, if nothing else. Now, if someone would tell me, where do I bed down?"

"That cot in the corner is reserved for you," said Dio.

Zaven walked to it, took out the pistol, and shoved it under his pillow.

"I see," smiled the leader. "You've brought your own."

"One less headache for you," Zaven commented curtly.

"I must go," said the proprietor, taking Zaven's arm and walking toward the steps. "I wouldn't tell them anything about the incident," he whispered. Without comment, Zaven walked back to his cot.

In the garret, time moved slowly. Morning papers brought in with the food did not carry any account of a policeman being murdered.

"Had it been in print, I would be disappointed," whispered the proprietor in Zaven's ear.

"Might take days to find the body," Zaven mumbled.

In the early hours of the morning, when most good people were sleeping and every place, respectable or otherwise, in the city had locked their doors, the round hole above the stairway opened.

"Come up, Zaven," came the proprietor's voice.

The outlaw walked up. Mariza was in the kitchen.

"You're a worse demon than I thought you were," she said. "Did you have to kill him?"

"Did you convey your sympathy?" Zaven grinned.

"Don't be funny. I may have a limited education, but I know what things need to be done to calm a mourning wife. The institution took care of her."

She rose and got closer to him. "You really put us in a spot!"

"Isn't it over yet?"

"Somewhat," she said airily, adding, "but it wouldn't have been if the trolley conductor had been able to identify you taking his trolley and getting off at the Turkish section. The investigator said that he has an idea who you are, but it would be difficult to prove until he gets his hands on you. He seemed quite confident that he will. He mentioned a name you used as a Turkish refugee allegedly bitten by a mad dog. It was a great relief when he said, 'You are not the only ones beguiled by this insidious hornet, ma'am.'"

"What about Brother Levon?" asked Zaven.

"He is not in the picture at all," said Mariza nonchalantly. "We told them that you came to us directly with your story and asked for help."

Zaven smiled. "I believe we can see you off tomorrow," he said. "You have the guns?"

"Not the kind you want, but enough to start you off—three revolvers and two automatics."

Zaven paced around the kitchen.

"Does that include mine?"

"No," replied the leader.

"That's not bad for a start but we need more," said Zaven. He thanked Mariza as she poured him a cup of coffee.

The following day, with the help of the women, the men disguised in yashmaks—the veils traditionally worn by Muslim women to cover their faces in public—went to a house on the outskirts of the city. At night they got out. Zaven's plan was to first arm his band. To do that he needed to stage a few quick holdups, then decide on their course of action. But at the very start he became suspicious that some of the men would not stand the test. If so, he had to weed them out. Those he doubted were the ones who had not suffered. To them, life was sweet. They were only with him because they hoped to go to a Christian country across the border to enjoy life and live in peace. That was not Zaven's idea. The men he wanted were those ready to give up everything to fight for justice.

Zaven proposed descending to the road to see if they would have any luck in getting rifles. Most of them were shocked and one spoke out.

"We didn't come with you to kill and rob," said the man. "We want to slip out without making trouble."

"And how do you propose to do that?" retorted Zaven.

Nothing more was said. Those few who shared Zaven's opinion looked at him warily. Zaven made up his mind then and there about who would stay and who would go.

Several days later, after wandering half-starved through the forests, the opportunity that Zaven was waiting for came. He had purposefully brought them back to the vicinity of Constantinople. Their last meal had been eaten twenty-four hours before, a sheep that Dio had stolen. The argument as to who should provide the next meal had reached its height among the men. Zaven, who was sitting alone with Dio within hearing distance, rose and walked over to the group.

"Listen," he commanded, "I've stood this long enough. It's time for us to understand each other. There is going to be discipline from now on. And that discipline will be my words. Anyone who hasn't got the stomach to take it can leave now. I've brought you close enough to your rat hole to go back safely. Those who choose to stay with me will rob and kill. Those who don't have the nerve to stand under the gallows with the noose around your neck had better take off right now, because I assure you that's where I will be leading you."

Trembling with rage, he glanced from one to another. Dio alone looked him squarely in the eyes. Three of them slipped away immediately; others dropped out later. Five stayed with him. Among those who remained was Eremia, a boy from Zaven's own hometown. The other four also were from Asia Minor and had lost all they possessed.

Restless, Zaven paced. The men watched in silence with mingled awe and admiration. Suddenly he stood in front of them.

"There are only seven of us, but I feel safer," he said solemnly. "Now that we understand each other, we will live and die together."

"Your word will be law," avowed Dio.

"I have nothing to live for," declared Eremia.

"Eremia spoke for all of us," added another. "We will revenge the blood of our loved ones as long as we live."

"There is one more thing I want to say," the leader declared humbly. "No longer am I an individual but a part of all of you."

Late that afternoon, hidden behind the bushes that covered the low hill, they lay looking over the road. Traffic was quite regular. Someone passed by every fifteen or twenty minutes: carriages, wagons, and peasants with their pack animals. Finally, in the distance, a mounted figure and two others walking behind him, all in uniform and armed with rifles, appeared on the road.

"Soldiers," muttered Dio.

"They are the ones I have been waiting for," remarked the leader.

"We may have some trouble handling them," reflected Dio.

"We would if we're fool enough to give them the chance to reach for their guns," Zaven said as he crept downhill through the brushwood.

At the place where the road turned into a narrow pass, Zaven planned the ambush. He left one of the men on a hill as a lookout. He placed Dio and Eremia under the bushes, close to each side of the road less than twenty feet away from the edge. The two others were positioned in the rear. Zaven alone crouched behind a large rock in the front. He made it clear to his men that their lives depended on getting the Turks with their first shots. Dio and Eremia were to take care of the soldiers. He would handle the mounted soldier himself.

They had just placed themselves in position when the three soldiers entered the trap. The mounted figure, who proved to be an officer in the Army, led the way with the two soldiers close behind.

Instantly, Zaven leapt out from behind the rock and shouted a fierce command to surrender. The soldiers' hands jerked toward their rifles, but two distinct shots dropped both of them flat on their faces. The officer glanced back for a second and realized that he, too, had no chance. The muzzle of the outlaw's automatic was squarely against his chest. He looked at Zaven and dismounted submissively.

In the meantime, Dio and Eremia came out from hiding and picked up the rifles. The lookout on the hill signaled that all was well. Nevertheless, the outlaws hurried away, and headed toward the mountain with their prisoner, leaving behind them no visible trace that death had struck just moments before.

Just beyond the forest ridge, they paused. In addition to the three rifles, including a brand new Luger belonging to their still-alive prisoner, they had acquired some much-needed food. Zaven was experiencing mixed emotions. This was his first strike. He should have finished off the officer and his horse. He could not explain why he hadn't, but he knew it must be done. Zaven looked at the officer as if to say something, but then changed his mind. He walked away and in his mind saw himself kneeling beside a grave close to a wagon road. Words echoed in his ears; they were his own words but sounded as though they came from the hollow grave. He turned back; his expression was more of pity than violence.

"If I had my way, I would not let you live," he said. "You will expect no other explanation when I tell you that I am an Armenian."

"I know that," declared the officer in an unemotional voice. Zaven's face registered surprise. The officer continued. "I understand why you have to kill. If you let me go, I will think of you as a fool. You won't mind if I speak my last words, will you?"

"That is your privilege," Zaven snapped back.

"I will reserve expressing my opinion of you and your kind because you may misinterpret my motive. Ignore race and religion—one's loyalty to his country comes above everything else. Though I'm in uniform, I hate this government as much as you do, although my hatred is for a different reason. Should the Germans win, this country will become just a colony. Those at the head of the government are puppets. They are not responsible for what you have become. Do you think that they could plan and carry out an atrocity of that magnitude without approval? And do you know why? So that you could become hungry for revenge. The Germans do not want to inherit the headache of a Christian minority when they take over."

"You're not a Turk," declared Zaven.

"That is immaterial. I was born Mohammedan, but my religion is my conscience."

Zaven was skeptical. "Your religion and your philosophy do not interest me. I want to know what you are," he demanded harshly.

"I'm Charkas," the officer answered smartly.

"I thought so. You're tall and handsome—traits the Charkas are known for."

"Thanks for the compliment," the officer retorted, eying him. "It looks like we have that much in common."

"What's your name?"

"Badjad."

"Where are you from?"

"A small town not far from here."

"How long have you been in the service?"

"Since the start of the war."

"Married?"

"Just for a few weeks. I have not seen my wife since. I'm curious to know what happened to her."

"Doesn't she write?"

"She cannot write. Others write for her. I have not received many letters from her."

"Are you on a leave of absence?"

"I wrote my own papers and forged the colonel's signature."

"That is desertion," laughed Zaven.

"Must you remind me of it?"

"Show me your papers. I want to see how good a forger you are."

As he handed the papers to Zaven, he smiled sardonically and said, "Are you thinking of using them? If so, I warn you, you won't get away with it."

"Looks authentic," Zaven mocked. "But I have no use for them. What about the other two, were they deserters, too?"

"Yes, and potential followers to me. I had no intention of going back to the Army," answered the officer, looking straight into Zaven's eyes.

"What is your plan?"

The officer hesitated. "The same thing as yours."

"Then we have another thing in common besides our looks. We hate the same people. You are clever." Zaven laughed.

For the first time, Badjad's face became angry.

"I have told you all you wanted to know." He flushed. "And I want to remind you again, I will think of you as a fool if you let me live."

Zaven looked at him. The prisoner's eyes were defiant.

"Don't rush me," Zaven muttered and walked away.

His companions were watching him. Zaven had a difficult decision to make. Whether all that he heard was true or not, the soldier was not the kind he wanted to kill. Yet, could he take the chance of letting him go? He thought hard for several moments. Then he turned to his prisoner.

"I have decided not to kill you," he said in a cold, calculating voice, "and let you think that I am a fool. I want to remind you, however, I did not come to this decision because of what you have said. I have no reasons to kill you. You remind me of another lieutenant. I don't know how he would have felt had he known who I really was. Now, the point is, how to get rid of you."

Zaven looked at his companions. They looked uneasy, but his calm, confident eyes reassured them. What sort of multiple personalities did this ruthless killer and leader of theirs possess? Any revengeful Armenian would not have given a second thought to killing the soldier.

"Now that you have ignored my warning," said the prisoner, "may I make a suggestion?"

"Go on," Zaven said curtly.

"I promise that if you leave me here, I won't show my face to anyone for twenty-four hours, and after that, no one will know what happened today."

"I might be a fool, but not that big a fool," Zaven smiled.

Badjad looked directly at him. Their eyes met and shared experiences they both had felt. Badjad meant what he said; Zaven was sure of that.

"Have you any cigarettes?" he asked.

Badjad produced a silver cigarette case and passed it around. "There are several packs in my saddlebag. You're welcome to them."

"We can certainly use them," said the outlaw.

"Do you want my money?" Badjad asked.

"No, I've taken from you what I want," Zaven retorted sharply, drumming the Luger at his side with his fingertips.

"It belonged to a German officer," Badjad reflected. "He was a nasty wretch."

"Did you kill him?" Zaven grinned.

Badjad looked at him. "He died in combat right in front of me."

Zaven nodded understandably.

"I suppose you're heading for the border," Badjad continued. "I wish I could go along with you, but since that's unthinkable, do you want some tips?"

"Thank you," Zaven snapped back, " but I don't need your damned advice. We will depart at dusk, but before I leave you, I will tie you up in a nice tight bundle. It will take you some time to break loose. I thought about killing your horse, but I won't. He, too, will be tied securely to a tree near you."

"You're very generous," snapped Badjad.

"I want you to know that what I do is not a gesture of kindness, as I have none."

The night was moonless. The outlaws descended the mountain in a single file with Dio leading the way. They left Badjad and his horse behind as Zaven said he would. They stopped momentarily at the summit of a foothill overlooking the plain in front of them. The men gathered around their leader.

"From now on," he said, "we will forget that we are Armenians, and speaking in that language is forbidden. The Charkas we left behind will serve my purpose well. We will operate as Turkish bandits. My name will be Daly Mustafa, the Mad One. Each of you should also pick out a Turkish name. Dio, you don't need to since your name is Turkish anyway. Eremia, call yourself Ibrahim. It's close enough. I was called Ibrahim once." After a pause, he added, "How far are we from the Sea of Marmora, Dio?"

"We can get to the shore before daybreak," Dio answered.

Zaven reflected for a long moment, taking in the panoramic view. "I don't like this part of the country," he said at length, as to himself. "It's too crowded. These puny mountains are not to my liking. I want big mountains and wide, open spaces. We will travel all night, and get across the sea before any rumors reach the government."

Shortly after daybreak, the band of the Daly Mustafa took shelter on a hill where the great stretch of shore was in view. They spent the whole day in hiding. At twilight, they saw a sailboat approach and anchor below.

"Fisherman," said Dio, "coming ashore for the night."

"They'll serve us well," remarked Mustafa, the Mad One.

As darkness closed in, they approached the fishermen. There were two of them, an old man and his young apprentice, sitting by a campfire. The unsuspecting fishermen were paralyzed when a harsh, commanding voice behind the muzzle of a Luger warned that nothing would happen to them if they did exactly what they were told.

"They're Greeks, Mustafa," whispered Dio.

"What do you demand of us, master?" said the feeble voice of the old man in broken Turkish. "We haven't anything that will be useful to you."

"Just a service," said the outlaw, advancing. "I want you to take us to the opposite shore."

"That won't be difficult, but it will take the whole night. Do you want to start right away?"

"If you think it's dark enough not to be spotted by the coast patrol," observed the outlaw, then added, "I take it you're Christians."

The two fishermen gazed at him in alarm.

"Don't be scared. I have nothing against Christians, but there is one thing I want you to bear firmly in mind. After you have done your job and leave us, I want you to forget that you have ever seen us."

"Yes, yes, sir," cried the old fisherman.

Within half an hour they were on their way in a tiny fishing boat under full sail. The young outlaw knelt at the bow, as handsome and proud as the figurehead on an ancient man-o'-war, his silhouetted profile projecting the symbol of a future legend. As the boat plowed through the waves, the fog appeared to wrap around him, like an apparition. What were his thoughts? It didn't matter. He knelt there insensitive to joy or sorrow, the emblem of a ruthless obsession.

Near dawn, and without mishap, the tiny boat arrived at the shore of Asiatic Turkey. The outlaws stepped out. The young leader rewarded the Greek fishermen with several pieces of gold. Dio's lips moved close to the leader's ears.

"Do you trust these fishermen?" were the words. "If ..."

The leader's stern look silenced him.

"A thousand apologies, I did not mean to doubt you," Dio mumbled with downcast eyes.

CHAPTER 16

As they climbed the shale slope that rose from the shore, Daly Mustafa watched his companions bent under their satchels. He congratulated himself for reaching the heights of his aspiration so soon. How distressing it was to contemplate that life alone could make Hagop his idol, and how much did he know about life? He was afraid of the monster he had created.

The men had discovered a narrow trail leading to the depths of the wooded mountains. At the sound of approaching footsteps, they hastily threw themselves into the brush along the trail until the intruders went by without suspecting their presence. They were peasants with donkeys. Mustafa was tempted to stop the intruders, thinking they might offer something good to eat, but butter judgment restrained him.

"We need someone who knows this territory, Mustafa," Dio commented.

"We'll find someone in time. Until then, we will watch our steps," answered the leader.

They emerged from hiding, climbed some more, and finally found a spot where they could rest. They stretched out on beds of pine needles. With his back against a towering pine, the leader gazed at the sky. The course he would follow was not clear in his mind. Although he had assumed the false name of a bandit, in his mind there was a big difference between an outlaw and a bandit, despite the obvious similarity. Bandits seek gold, and Zaven had no craving for it. An outlaw, on the other hand, was a nobler breed—lawless, yes, but possessed of a lust for loftier goals than mere riches, and endowed with a righteous man's spirit and code of conduct. Gazing at the skies and treetops, he felt certain that ambitious Turks with ideas of getting rich quick would want to join him. Should he take them in?

"I have a feeling that these mountains will be hospitable to us, Mustafa," said Dio.

"I have the same feeling," replied Mustafa, "but don't forget the odds are not in our favor. To survive, we must act and think as one person. Now, we must lay the foundation."

"Mustafa, will you take anyone in the band who isn't Christian?" Ibrahim, aka Eremia, asked.

Zaven had not expected to have an answer so soon, and he was still undecided.

"I don't know," he said meditatively. "The events that lay ahead will give me the answer. However, I want to make one point very clear: No one will be allowed into the band unless he is acceptable to every one of us. I say this with all my heart. If I didn't feel this way, I could throw a newborn Turkish baby into a fire. But, I can't. Neither can you. Would any one of you force yourself upon a Turkish woman, or would you rob a poor helpless peasant, and take your revenge upon a kind-hearted Turk who condemns evil men as much as you and me? I know that there are good Turks. The proof is I, standing before you and talking to you." He stood up. The men sat up erect, looking up at him admiringly.

"We'll operate on these principles," he continued. "Our grudge is against the wicked. There is another point I want to bring up. If we live long enough, we will get rich. But the gold that comes into our hands will be a means, not an end. Anyone who would join us for no other purpose than gold will have no scruples about how they get it."

He kneeled down and raised his right arm. The men followed his example. "This will be our code," he said in a solemn voice. "Spare the poor and the innocent. Never harm women or children. Money belongs to all."

They remained on their knees with eyes downcast in silent prayer.

"May I add a law to your code, Mustafa?" Dio asked meekly.

"Certainly, Dio, you and the others are free to contribute for the good of all."

"Here it is," he declared emphatically. "The leader's word and his decisions will be the law of the band."

"Yes!" confirmed the others at once.

The band was on one of their reconnaissance missions. They stood on a summit where they could see the vast wooded slope and below that the plain with scattered villages and isolated farms that resembled a painted landscape. Mustafa focused his binoculars on a spot along a swiftly running stream not far away. He was observing two figures: one with his trousers above his knees paddling in the stream while the other stood by. He was puzzled. If they were fishermen, certainly that was not a good spot. He handed the field glasses to Dio.

"They seem unarmed, whoever they are," commented Dio. "I don't like the idea of having them so close."

"I agree with you," said Mustafa, replacing the binoculars in their case. "Let's find out."

They began descending. Along the stream at a safe distance from the men, Mustafa instructed Dio and a confederate to cross to the other side to stop the fishermen from getting away. Once they went into the brush, they would be out of sight and lost to Mustafa. The bandits got close enough to see a large number of appetizing brook trout lying on the grass. The mysterious fishermen were getting ready to leave. Dio waved his hand across the stream. Mustafa crept closer. One of the fishermen looked around nervously. He started toward a shotgun that was braced against the tree. The bandits crouched behind the bushes ready for action.

"Quick, I hope we don't have to kill the poor devils," whispered Mustafa to Dio as he sprang forward. "Stay where you are and you won't get hurt!" he commanded harshly.

Heedless of the warning, the man grasped the shotgun and jumped behind a rock. Two bullets from Mustafa's Luger smashed against the rock, missing the man by inches.

"I don't want to kill you, but if you don't drop that shotgun and come out from behind that rock, the next one won't miss your fat head," cried the bandit leader.

The man with the shotgun, short and stocky, stood up with his arms above his head. The other had dashed across the stream, but Dio suddenly stood in his way.

"You brainless, jumping gazelle!" laughed Dio. "Go back and gather up your catch. I love brook trout."

The two fishermen walked back to where their catch lay. The bandits circled around them. There was enough fish to satisfy all of them.

"If this is the way you make your living, you've picked a poor spot," said the young leader.

"Is that so?" said the younger fisherman with wounded pride. "For such a poor spot, we seem to have quite a fine catch."

The stocky fellow, who was the elder, calmed him with a firm touch to his arm. "This is not the way we make a living, Affa, but we want to live," he said.

"What nationality are you?" Mustafa asked.

"Would that make any difference?" answered the man.

"Not a bit. I'm just curious."

"We're Greeks. Just harmless fugitives from the law. We won't cross your way."

"I know that."

"Will you let us go, then?"

"In time. Now let's find a safe place to cook the fish."

"We have just the place," cried the tall, well-built younger man, adding proudly, "It's a veritable citadel!"

"It wouldn't be a trap, would it?" smiled the bandit.

The elder fisherman shook his head briskly. "God forbid, you've been good to us, Affa."

"My name is Mustafa. What's yours?"

"Joseph."

"And yours?" asked the bandit, looking in the direction of the younger one.

"Yorgi."

Joseph displayed such skill leading them up ascending slopes that it appeared as if he knew every bush and rock in the mountains.

"He is the answer to our prayer, Mustafa," whispered Dio in the leader's ear.

They crept on hands and knees onto a rocky ridge.

"Here we are," said the man, and advanced to the crest of the ridge.

The perpendicular rocky wall of the ravine several hundred feet below looked treacherous. The man squeezed through a narrow opening in the rocks.

"Is this where you hide?" Mustafa asked.

"Wait until you see the inside," Joseph answered.

Squeezing through the rock, Mustafa stood in front of a window-like opening. He crawled in and found himself in a large chamber dug out of the rock. By whom, he wondered? And when? There was a fireplace and what looked like beds made of dry grass. There were some smoke-covered cooking utensils and discolored copper plates. Mustafa thought it would do for a time.

One of the bandits remained on the ridge on guard, while the others entered the cave. The younger Greek fugitive lit the fire and began broiling the fish. While they feasted on trout and freshly-made bread cakes, they talked.

"Now tell us, Joseph," asked Mustafa in a friendly way. "Why and how long have you two been in the mountains?"

"Over two years," answered the stocky Greek, then paused, looking directly at Mustafa. "You're the Albanian, aren't you?"

"The Albanian?" murmured the young outlaw.

"Yes, the Albanian," emphasized the Greek. "We know that you are around. A week or so ago you held up a carriage on the main road. The carriage driver, whom we happen to know is Armenian, is with you now."

"Go on," coaxed the leader.

"You aren't him, then," mumbled Joseph in a voice that was quickly losing its confidence.

"Go on," smiled the agreeable but relentless-looking young leader. "I like you and your story."

"Please don't think me bold," pleaded Joseph. "I would just like to know who you are."

"Oh, that. I'm a fugitive, too, but not from these parts. This is Dio," he went on, introducing the others by their Turkish names.

The man's face darkened.

"Go on. Finish your story, Joseph," smiled Mustafa, gently tapping the stocky Greek's shoulder.

The friendly gesture encouraged the fugitive.

"Very well," he said, "I've been a fugitive from the very first day I was born, as I lost my parents before I was old enough to remember them. My grandmother brought me up—a good woman, but she was poor. So, I had to work and became a shepherd before I was ten years old. When the government wanted me in the army, I didn't like it and took to the hills. Then my wife and children were deported with all the other Greeks from the coastal areas. Yorgi is from my village. They took him and put him in the Worker's Battalion. But he ran away, and joined me, so here we are—harming no one."

Mustafa savored a bite of the delicious trout. "A sound philosophy. You hurt no one, and no one hurts you. But suppose it's a reversed situation. Someone has hurt you and you set your heart to hurt that someone, Joseph. This may jolt you a bit, my friend. All of us are in the same fix. We are Armenians."

The faces of the two fugitives brightened. Yorgi was sitting next to Dio and could not resist throwing his arm around the sourpuss, who had not said a friendly word to him the whole time. Joseph turned to the young leader of the outlaws and extended his hand.

"This calls for a celebration," he said, and rose. He walked to the innermost corner of the cave, rolled away a rock, and came out with a bottle and two cups. Yorgi jumped to his feet.

"Love and life to Daly Mustafa!" he cried.

The Greeks' ouzo was a potent drink, but Mustafa drained his in one gulp and tossed the cup around. When it came back to him, he discouraged a second round. The two Greeks were then sworn in as members of the band.

"You mentioned an Albanian, Joseph. I would like to know more about him. Two cocks in a barnyard; it is not good."

"Yes, one of them must yield," commented Joseph.

"Are there others?" Mustafa asked.

"Who knows? I had no idea that you were around until you surprised us. Anyway, if there are, you don't have to worry. From now on I won't be careless."

"You didn't quite finish your story of the Albanian and Armenian carriage driver whom you thought was one of us," Mustafa reminded him.

"Well, it's like this. We found the bodies of the government officer and the guard in the forest. The next time we spied on the Albanian from a good distance, we learned that there were six of them, and they were five before the holdup."

"That's a reasonable deduction," Mustafa commented, "but an Albanian wouldn't have much use for an Armenian."

"There's only one way to find out, Mustafa," said Dio, rubbing his nose, which was his habit when confused.

"Yes," said the leader, turning to the fire to light his cigarette, "but there is no need to be impatient, is there, Joseph?"

The shepherd pouted his lips and shook his head.

"Your experiences as a shepherd, and your knowledge of the land, will come in very useful, Hasan—for that will be your name from now on," said the leader as he eased toward the opening of the cave and stepped out. He remained there for a few moments, looking around, then returned.

"By the way, someone has to relieve Ihmed. His fish is getting cold."

"I will," said Yorgi and sprang to his feet.

"Take a rifle, and you, too, pick out a Turkish name for yourself." Mustafa had suddenly fallen into a meditative mood. "Rifles," he muttered. "There are nine of us and we have only three."

The men were looking at him. He walked around the cave, banged the rocky wall here and there with his fist, and finally settled down on a solid rock bench projecting from the wall.

"There's a secret passage leading to the ravine," remarked Joseph, alias Hasan. He rose and showed Mustafa where it was.

"Does anyone besides you know of the existence of this place?" Mustafa asked.

"Maybe, but all the time we've been here, we haven't seen anyone coming near it. The place is too treacherous to reach for those who know it."

Mustafa stroked his chin thoughtfully and said, "It would serve us well as a storage place or an asylum of temporary rest, but I hate to be caught in it with an army of soldiers outside. They may not get in, but we won't get out, either." He rose again, pacing back and forth. "Rifles," he mumbled. He stood in front of Hasan and asked pointedly, "Have you any idea where to get them?"

The Greek shepherd, aware that he had already become a prominent member in the Daly Mustafa band, was thinking. "There's a place where we can get them," he smiled cunningly, "but ..."

"Go on," the leader stressed.

"The guard post, at the junction of the roads outside the village. There are several of them there."

Eyes shot around. Dio rubbed his nose. Hasan looked scared and wished that he had kept his mouth shut. Mustafa's eyes were cold, his face blank.

"How far is the post?" Mustafa's voice sounded like an eerie echo.

"N-not far," answered Hasan's frail voice.

"We'll call on them tonight, shortly after midnight, Hasan. Keep that in mind."

Nine figures, in a straight line, descended the narrow trail winding through the dark forest. Above, the moon played hide and seek in the clouds. The short and stocky figure in the forefront stopped at the edge of a barren cliff. Below him, like a patchwork quilt, lay a wide stretch of fields. The moon had just emerged from behind a dark cloud and sailed through a transparent gray cloud. The second figure moved closer. A thin light, barely visible, turned and twisted its way through the quilt-like fields—the sinuous beam of a flashlight, Mustafa thought. The stocky figure acknowledged that he, too, had seen the light in the vastness. The others had grouped around the two in the forefront.

"Good. Let's move," whispered the leader. "If things work out the way I've figured, this is going to be a one-man job. The rest of you stay close, but not too close."

Dio had moved squarely in front. Mustafa glanced at him, with a suppressed smile.

"All right, you awkward elephant, come along. But I warn you—"

"I'll be quiet as a field mouse," chucked Dio.

"Hasan, from our vantage point, will we be approaching from the rear?" asked the leader.

"No, Mustafa. We're facing the front," advised the guide.

"Better move over to that bend of the road beneath the hill and approach it from the rear," Mustafa replied. "When you're out in the open, don't stick close together—move through the fields and crouch down. The stalks are high enough to hide you. Before we close in, I'll give you the sign. Circle the place and lie low until you get my second signal."

They moved on through the brushwood over the cliffs. Then they descended to the field. Nothing stirred the peace and the tranquility of the night, not even a breeze. Crouched low like a wildcat, Mustafa moved swiftly through the grain field. A box-like shack with small square windows stood less than fifty yards ahead of him. His hand appeared above the stalks and waved. Dio was close behind him.

He was less than fifty feet away from the shack. There were no stalks to hide him, but he had not seen anyone, nor was there the slightest sign that the shack was occupied. He slowly crept closer on his hands and knees, stood up erect against the wall, cautioned with his hand to Dio to lie low, then hugged the wall and began moving. He stuck his head out from the corner to see where he was. He could almost reach the door, but there was no one standing in front of it. His mind began to speculate. Had the guards locked the door from the inside and were asleep? If so, this would make things awkward. But good sentries should keep a watch on the road.

He waited; these were long moments. He stood on tiptoe and peered though the window. He saw the outline of beds stretched flat on the floor. As his eyes became accustomed to the darkness, he observed other objects: a table, chairs, and rifles hung on the wall. A flashlight illuminated the place and died out instantly. A figure moved toward the door and opened it. Mustafa saw the uniformed figure standing outside with a flashlight and a rifle suspended from his shoulder. He walked toward the road and left the door open wide behind him. He walked around aimlessly. The flashlight had, for a brief spell, brought the surrounding scene in view.

Finally, the soldier sat on a rock at the edge of the road and lit a cigarette. He was conveniently close with his back toward Mustafa, still hugging the wall. This was the chance Mustafa had waited for. He tiptoed forward in a crouching position, with a tight grip around the barrel of his Luger. *Smack!* Then a grunt, and it was over. The soldier lay senseless at his feet.

Mustafa grabbed the flashlight and the rifle, made sure that it was loaded, and went to the open door. Dio emerged from behind the wall, while the others rushed toward the shack from all directions. He stepped inside. The flashlight threw its beam around the room. Five of them still slept.

"Wake up, you cursed hounds!" shouted Mustafa.

One of them sat up; the others still snored infernally until Dio awoke them with a rude prod from the rifle barrel. The other outlaws joined their leader.

"Anyone attending the dog outside?" cried Mustafa.

"Yes, Mustafa," came the answer.

The leader looked around. Yorgi was not there. The action had overwhelmed him and he had tucked tail and run.

Mustafa curtly ordered his men to tie up the guards.

While this was done, Dio went around the room picking up rifles, cartridge belts, swords, and a box of ammunition too heavy to handle alone. His eyes rested enviously on a shining pair of high boots standing at the foot of the corporal's bed. He quickly shed his tattered shoes, stepped into the boots, and was pleased to find them a perfect fit.

Within fifteen minutes the outlaws were on their way up the hills with their prisoners. There had been a brief stop in a ravine. Shots momentarily disturbed the quietness of the night. Then the nine men reappeared in a straight line on the same trail that had taken them to the fields.

CHAPTER 17

The outlaws felt safe in their hideout and enjoyed whatever goodness their uncertain life could offer. The membership in the Daly Mustafa's band had increased to sixteen; three of them were Mohammedans. The latest one initiated was an Armenian picked up when they raided the villa of a Turkish overlord that very morning.

The midsummer afternoon was scorching hot. The men had shed their heavy armaments and garments and relaxed in the shade. Dio and Hasan sat with the leader. The one-time shepherd in the role of guide had become a prominent and respected sage among the band.

Faint vibrations in the air made the three sit up and listen. They were repeated again and again. They glanced at one another.

"Too many shooting at the same time. This isn't a target practice," said Dio, rubbing his nose.

"Close enough to be annoying," commented the leader.

"German rifles. No other guns hiss like that," interjected Hasan as he stood up. "Could be the Albanian. We'd better find out."

"Yaw," grunted Dio, throwing his cartridge belts over his shoulders.

"You and the rest get ready, Dio," ordered Mustafa as he picked up his binoculars and rifle. "We won't be gone long."

Mustafa and Hasan made their way through the forest toward the direction of the gunfire. It became clearer as they advanced. There was no doubt now, two hostile parties where shooting at each other. Was the Albanian in one of the parties entangled with the soldiers? They climbed the rocky precipice; the mountain range lay before their eyes. Far in the distance were the foothills and the vast valley. Hasan pointed to a wooded foothill over which a cloud of dust hung.

"That's the spot," remarked Mustafa, handing his binoculars to Hasan.

"Most of the shots are being fired from the level ground around the hill," observed Hasan. "The Albanian must be on that hill."

"How do you know that it's him?"

"This morning on our way back, did you notice that I lingered behind? I didn't tell you because it was just a suspicion. I was thinking of going back again to make sure. The road was blocked. I watched it for a long time but no one went by. And that is a busy road."

"If it is the Albanian on the hill, he's in a tight spot. What do you think, Hasan?" muttered the leader. "Is his hide worth saving?"

"That I don't know, but here's your chance to kill two birds with one stone, Mustafa."

Mustafa stood there watching for a while. The shooting became spasmodic.

"Looks bad for the bandits," commented Mustafa.

"Won't take long to get there," Hasan suggested.

"Doesn't make sense. I should let dog eat dog," Mustafa replied. "Only one thing I'm curious about—the carriage driver. I want to find out who he really is."

The men arrived, ready and eager to join the fight. Mustafa looked at them with a defiant smile in his eyes.

"This isn't going to be much of a job," he said in a grim voice. "All we have to do is to sneak behind the soldiers and blast them out. They don't like surprises."

There was no talking as the tight-lipped men moved through the woods. When they got closer to the skirmish and could see figures crouching behind the rocks, they crept on hands and knees. Mustafa reached a point where some of the entrenched soldiers were easily visible. They were open targets, but he waited calmly and lay flat on his belly. Then, he fired. Instantly, answering shots joined the uproar. A screaming volley of bullets rained on the soldiers. The bandits bunched together on top of the hill suddenly came to life. They, too, were giving all they had, but it lasted only a few short moments. The soldiers who could get away had already done so. Mustafa stood up.

"All right, whoever you are. You're among friends. Leave your guns and come out."

"I won't leave my gun," cried a defiant voice, "but if you really are who I think you are, you'll accept my promise of not using it."

"All right then, you stubborn Albanian, come out with your gun."

Mustafa moved forward. Five weary figures descended the hill, rifles suspended from their shoulders. Dio followed the Mustafa. Others still crouched around with their guns ready for action. Mustafa stopped; the bandits walked toward him. The one in the lead looked agreeable.

"You're the Albanian," Mustafa said casually.

"I'm not ashamed of it," replied the Albanian boldly.

"Just the five of you?"

"We were eight; one is gone, the other two are on the hill. One was hit badly."

"We will do what we can."

"Do you want my gun?" the Albanian asked in a complacent tone.

"Should I take it, what would you do without it?"

"Try to get another one."

"And have you in my hair again?" Mustafa turned to Dio. "Bring the wounded down," he ordered. His cold eyes had appraised the others and rested on one of the men. He was shy and dark complexioned. "Were you a carriage driver?" he asked. "I've a soft spot in my heart for carriage drivers. I, too, drove a carriage."

"You know who he is, then?" interjected the Albanian somewhat uneasily. "Any objections—"

"Objection to what? Because he might have a reason to fight?" Mustafa's eyes had a faraway look. "Sixteen and seven will make twenty-three," he mumbled. "It's a respectable number."

"My name is Hazim," said the Albanian, extending his hand.

Dio showed up with the wounded. Several men were dispatched to scan the battleground. They picked up stray weapons and relieved the soldiers still breathing of their miseries.

In the dark at an isolated confine in the woods, two leaders sat facing each other. The expressions on their faces were strained.

"You didn't have to tell me everything," said the Albanian. "The way you looked at the carriage driver, I knew you were concerned, but not about his being a driver. Like him, I'm a Mohammedan. You have already taken in other Mohammedans. I have two Christians with me who I trust more. Our enemies are those who are destroying this land. Yours and mine."

Mustafa turned to him. "Those are not the words of a common bandit."

"I'm not a common bandit. Neither are you. We both have our own purposes. Yours is revenge, mine less so, but we have a common enemy."

"We understand each other then, Hazim."

"Yes, we do, Mustafa. Because I know that you won't do anything that I would not."

By the early fall the fame of Daly Mustafa had spread far and wide. He had become a menace in the land and the bane of the soldiers. A day did not pass without news of Mustafa and his band marauding some hapless village or caravan and disappearing like the wind. Rumor was that the Mad One had gathered together hundreds of desperadoes, but the actual number of his followers was less than thirty.

At his hideaway deep in the mountains, Mustafa and his lieutenant, the Albanian, sat across from an elderly peasant whose face was the portrait of servility. Only his small keen eyes signified hidden wiliness.

"If we let this situation prevail, and pick up all the stray deserters, soon we will have an army, and we would not know what to do with it," Mustafa declared caustically.

"Maybe you have to kill a few to discourage the aspirants, Mustafa," the Albanian jested.

The peasant looked from the lieutenant to the leader and mumbled, "But this one claims that he knows you, Mustafa."

"How did you meet him?" asked the leader.

"A few days ago someone held up the mail on the highway. I knew that this wasn't your job, because at the time you were nowhere near. My service to you, Mustafa, for which I'm being paid liberally, called for finding out who the bandits were. They picked me up while I was wandering in the hills where I thought they would be hiding. My excuse was that I was looking for a lost sheep. The leader, a tall, red-haired Charkas, asked me if I ever had seen you. I told him that no one can see you, but you see them."

A spark of recognition flashed in Mustafa's eyes. "Did he tell you his name?" he asked.

"He did. His name is Badjad, and he said that less than two weeks ago he was at the other side of the sea."

"How many did he have with him?"

"I saw only four. He has sharp eyes and keen wit. He told me I am the very shadow of the demon he seeks and that he knew I was not looking for sheep. He put five gold pieces in my palm and whispered, 'Tell the Mad One where he can find me.'"

"Do you know this one, Mustafa?" asked the Albanian.

"The name and description fit," Mustafa answered. "I must find out why he is here and what he is up to."

It was a moonless night. The bandits were on the move. The peasant led the way, hobbling along with the aid of a stick. At the base of a rocky, towering peak, they spread out along the slope and began climbing. Then they stopped halfway. The sun was beginning to rise. Mustafa was giving instructions to the peasant when he saw a lone figure, unarmed, descending the slope. He stopped. The chubby, dark complexioned man walked toward him.

"Will you come up, or do you want me to come down to meet you?" asked the man with an accent obviously not Turkish.

"I'll come up," Mustafa replied curtly.

The stranger nodded and led the way. Dio glanced back. The men were alert and ready. A tall figure, fully armed, with a black shawl wrapped around his head emerged from behind the rocks. Mustafa advanced. Badjad stood ramrod straight, arms folded upon his chest, watching the one who had left him tied up in the woods.

"Though you have picked up the name Mad," said Badjad, "I still think that you are a fool. But a gallant fool."

"Why did you come? How did you know?" Mustafa asked coldly.

Badjad smiled. "The daring deeds of Daly Mustafa could have been committed by no other but the one I happen to know: one who would spare the life an enemy at the risk of his own neck."

"I hope you won't make me regret it," Mustafa smiled.

Badjad grasped his arm. "I want the two of us to be alone for a little while."

They found a sheltered spot in the rocks and sat side by side.

"You know, if you had taken me with you then and there, you would have prevented a crime."

Mustafa stared at him curiously but didn't pursue the subject. "How long did you stay there after I left you?"

"Not very long, but I kept my promise and did not leave the mountains until the following evening."

"Did you talk to anyone?"

"No, I didn't have the chance. You see, the following night when I surprised my wife, I found the lord of the town in bed with her. I don't blame her. I was a poor husband to her. And he could give her all that she wanted. But I killed both of them."

"Where have you been all this time?"

"Across the sea; I crossed it only a few days ago and picked up the Greek sailor who ferried me across. He is the one I sent down to meet you."

"How many men have you?"

"Five besides myself. Three of them are Charkas, one Georgian, and one Greek."

Mustafa looked at him disapprovingly.

"I know what you are thinking," said Badjad, "but my activities were strictly directed against the government, not against bandits."

"But I am a bandit," Mustafa reminded him.

"I am very much aware of that, but you are the kind I want to join with."

"I have another one like you," Mustafa declared. "Had to rescue his hide from the soldiers. You two should get along nicely except for one thing: He hates officers. Killed one and took to the mountains."

"I understand that," smiled Badjad. "I could love you as a brother, if you could accept me as such."

Mustafa faced him squarely, grasped his arms, and shook him briskly. "Thank you, Badjad."

Thus, the pact of two brothers in arms was sealed.

As winter approached, the bandits constructed a number of dugouts in the mountains. They intended to pass the season of cold and snow comfortably in these hideouts. In order to stock up with food, they demanded tribute from the surrounding villages. The arrangement worked, as the villagers considered their contribution a cheap premium for protection and refused to accept money. However, in one instance, the Mad One met opposition.

A large and rather prosperous village had dared to send a note instead of cereal sacks, cheese, and butter. Its head, an old, well-respected patriarch, had placed his name and seal at the bottom of the message. It read:

Already we have contributed our tithe to the government, and are not inclined to pay another to a scoundrel. Your days are numbered, Mad One. If you have the guts, come and collect it. We promise a reception befitting your notoriety.

Mustafa sent back the messenger without a reply. The Mad One could not ignore the challenge and risked the possibility of widespread peasant uprisings against him.

"The stupid ass," Badjad remarked sulkily after Mustafa had read the note to his men. "Did he send that note because we have been too complacent toward them? Or could this be a trap for us?"

"Whatever the cause or the motive, it matters little," Mustafa answered grimly. "We must teach the villagers to respect us. In the process we may hurt them. I don't like to do that, but we cannot let him get away with it."

"I agree with you. If this poor village is set up as bait, we'll meet them on their own terms. I like the idea," declared Badjad.

"You've a good point there, Badjad," Mustafa agreed. "But we're not walking into it blindly. The shepherd of this village has served us well."

The village was situated on the banks of a river in the valley. That night the bandits surrounded it so quietly that even the mongrels roaming around the slimy streets were not aroused. Two men from opposite directions went to the closest barns with kerosene-soaked torches. The dismal yelps of the dogs gave warning. Soon the flames shot out from the chaff room, and bullets hissed over the rooftops. The objective was to subdue the villagers, not to kill them. Stunned men and women clad only in undergarments ran out of their homes shouting, "The Daly—the Daly!" Soon the fires were nearly roaring out of control. If not checked, it would be too late to save the village. The solitary figure of an old man shouting and waving his arms on a rooftop was a pathetic picture.

"Mustafa! Mercy, mercy, to women and children," he cried. "I sent the note, but it was not my doing. All we have is yours."

"Is that you, you old buzzard?" came the Mad One's response.

"Yes, Mustafa, it's I, the fool; I'm your slave. Think of the one who nursed you. Spare the innocent and helpless."

The wretched old man hadn't exactly struck the right note. If Mustafa thought of his mother, he might not have let a cat come out alive.

"Get the people out of their houses and come this way," he commanded. "Those who take a different route will be killed. One false move will be your end."

"Nothing will happen, Kurban. We cannot fight you. But the fire, if not checked, soon will leave nothing."

"Quench the fire!" Mustafa bellowed. In a flash, the outlaw band sprang into action, forming a bucket brigade to aid the town folk in extinguishing the blaze. Even the women and children pitched in, beating down the flames licking the barns with blankets and old feed sacks.

When it was all over and the village was safe, a quivering assemblage of soot-covered villagers stood before the bandit. The old man was in the forefront. Mustafa walked toward him. Badjad joined the leader after the signal to cease-fire was given.

"You risked your life to save the village," declared the bandit. "I want you to know that nothing else would have saved your hide. Tell me, have I given you any cause for bad feelings?"

"No, Kurban, no. Long life to you and your braves. You've been good to us," whimpered the old man, falling to the bandit's feet.

"Was it, then, the few sacks of cereal you could not spare, you miserable wretch?"

"No, Kurban, no. I myself could have sent you all you wanted, twice—nay, thrice as much."

"Why, then, did you send that note? How stupid of you, when you must have known you couldn't back up your boast."

"I had to do it, Kurban. I had to. They wrote the note, then forced me to seal it and send it to you. Had I refused, they would have accused me of sheltering you and taken me away. Then they would have confiscated my property and turned my children into paupers. They've done that to others for lesser offenses."

"Who are 'they'?" asked Badjad harshly.

The old man spat in the dirt. "In this case, the tax collector and his two bloodhounds."

"Are they still in the village?"

"They left at twilight, telling us that they would return with a large force of soldiers , in case you were foolish enough to fall into their trap."

"Why didn't they come back, then?" asked Mustafa.

"I knew they wouldn't, but it was too late to send you another message of warning. If you had only waited one night."

Mustafa looked at Badjad, who stepped forward.

"I'm thinking that those who forced you to send us the note really wanted us to destroy this village and kill half of you," declared Badjad. "We're fighting them so that you and thousands of others like you will get a fair deal. We're not after gold. Had that been our aim, we know where to get it. Someday we'll make your lives free without fear."

"May the eye of the Almighty be on you, my son," uttered the old man.

"We're sorry to do this, but the damage is small. We will fix it," Badjad replied. "Send us what you can in way of food and don't refuse the money in return. It's the best way to give away what we get from those you have made rich. Now, get back to your home and sleep in peace. We're with you, not against you."

The old one smiled, and his stooped shoulders appeared to straighten a mite, as if a great burden had been lifted from them. "Son, I've one request," he said meekly. "Grant me that as a favor. Beat me! Beat me black and blue so that I'll have something to show I am not in league with you."

"He alone can grant that request," said Badjad sullenly, looking at the leader.

"I understand your point," Mustafa smiled, "and I am sure you will find a way by yourself."

CHAPTER 18

The raid on the village alarmed the surrounding country. Until this time, the government had made no serious attempt to wipe out the bandits by sending regular troops against them. However, the willingness of the villages to offer tribute was a challenge that no government could ignore.

This was cause for thought and action. Small, poorly disciplined units of militants were hardly a match for the outlaws. Soon Mustafa was informed that the government was assembling troops. He anticipated this and established counter measures. He had fortified and provisioned a number of strongholds so that if the bandits were chased from one, another would be ready.

Antsy, but vigilant, the outlaws in their dugout counted the uneventful days going by. Some of the men lay on their backs gazing at the ceiling of the dugout. Others cooked, sewed, or cleaned their weapons. Then, a sentinel walked directly up to the leader.

"Mustafa," he said in a low voice. "Soldiers are at the foot of the mountain."

Without comment, the leader stood up and walked to the wall to pick up his rifle and telescope. He stood before Badjad.

"Come along if you want to," he said.

They followed the sentinel with the ever-faithful Dio close behind them. From the lookout, Mustafa observed the troops in the valley, then passed the telescope to Badjad.

After a few moments of observation, Badjad remarked, "My estimate of their number is far less than we thought, but this might be just a detachment.

They're heading for the village at the foothill. The army always does things that way. We can avoid them, but I hate to send them back without giving them something to remember."

Mustafa smiled but made no comment. They stood watching for a while, and then headed back to their dugout. Orders were given to put out fires and double the sentries. Mustafa walked over to the Albanian, who was cleaning a portable machine gun purchased from a corrupt officer.

"With any luck, Hazim, we may get a chance to use it," he hinted.

Hazim's white teeth gleamed in his brown face. "Good! Things were getting dull since the gendarmes decided to keep their distance."

Two eventless days went by. From their lookout, the outlaws detected movements of the troops, but the soldiers were in no hurry; why should they be? They were far away from the lice-infested barracks and watery barley soup.

About midnight, Mustafa and four of his men, including his lieutenant, started toward the valley. They went down almost to the lowland. Finally, they stopped at the crest of a small hill to watch and listen. It did not take them long to discover that the troops were on the move, intending to hold the ways out from the mountains under cover of darkness.

"They will move at dawn," Mustafa speculated.

"Will you let them?" Badjad asked.

"We will see how persistent they are. But, we will show them it won't be easy. From their position there is only one way to get through. We will let them in partway and no further."

"Splendid," whispered Badjad, grasping the leader's arm.

Less than a mile ahead, behind the foothill where the troops were situated, the trap was set. The outlaw positioned his men on the steep, bushy cliffs over the trail. As Mustafa had anticipated, the troops moved in. There was no opposition until the vanguard of the troops contacted Mustafa at the point where he had taken his position. Then all hell broke loose. The surprised soldiers turned back. Badjad, who had played his role perfectly, started from the rear. With the deafening rat-a-tat of machine guns filling the air, the battle did not last long. The troops moved out to reposition themselves. They were at a disadvantage for a reason that, in other circumstances, would have been advantageous: their number. They could not make a move without tipping off the phantom foe.

As for the outlaws, their job was done; it was time to disappear. Badjad was the last one to get back to the dugout. Mustafa looked inquiringly at him.

"No one's missing. I left a few behind as lookouts," he said, laying down his machine gun. He crouched down, wiping his perspiration with a large red handkerchief. "Do you have you a cigarette?"

Dio supplied the cigarettes he personally rolled.

"When I left, the soldiers were halfway to the village with their tails tucked between their legs. I believe they have had enough to call it a day," reflected Badjad, ejecting jets of smoke from his nose.

"They'll return," commented Mustafa.

"The poor devils," Badjad muttered.

Mustafa gave a low, sardonic laugh. "I wager that, right at this moment, the commandant is boasting how many of us he killed, while licking his wounds at the same time."

A rude note coming out of Dio's curled lips made the men look at him. "I'm just a peasant listening," he snapped.

"If you were a peasant listening, you wouldn't sound that way," remarked Mustafa. "However, let's not take the commandant and his boast lightly. I think we should give him reason to make good on his boasts. We're leaving this place."

"They will never get in here—unless we leave it open, Mustafa," said Badjad.

"Let them have some fun," the leader replied.

"What about our provisions?" asked Dio.

"We have plenty stored in other places, but we'll take along what we want," said Mustafa. "We can make this game more interesting."

"I see your point," said Badjad. "Have them spread out."

"That, we will see."

That evening the outlaws vacated their dugout and moved to the other side of the mountain. Wiser through experience, the troops gradually worked upward. It had taken them two days to get up to the abandoned dugout.

Days went by, but the soldiers were reluctant to come out to hunt the bandits. Who could blame them? Badjad returned from his observation tower and sat beside the Mustafa without comment.

"They are still there?" commented the leader.

Badjad nodded.

"I think we've let them enjoy it long enough."

"I agree with you. You wouldn't have extended the invitation if you had thought they would be such obliging guests. But, surely you aren't thinking of chasing them out?"

"Only a fool outnumbered ten to one would try that, Badjad, but we could force them to move around."

"I understand. Get into the valley, scare people, make a noise and let the world know that we're still alive."

"That's exactly what I had in mind."

At dusk, the bandits descended to the plain. The news of raids spread like wildfire. The commandant of the troops, who had proclaimed that the bandits were bottled up in the mountains and would not take long to whip, had to act. He sent half the troops to the plains to chase them. Contrary to expectations, the bandits were not elusive this time. They encountered the troops at times and places least expected: at the bridge of a river, in a narrow pass, or at the entrance of a village. These skirmishes were short but costly engagements for the troops. The last entanglement of the seven weeks' contest between the soldiers and the bandits ended with an episode that firmly established Daly Mustafa as a supreme military strategist. He appeared to deliberately trap some of his men by the troops upon a hill, knowing that the troops would advance. At night he struck the enemy from the rear.

In such a situation any good soldier realizes that the salvation of his men lies in an orderly retreat. But in this case it was impossible to stop the rush to safety.

The soldiers were still present but not eager to continue the pursuit, while the outlaws watched them retreat from their strongold. They could have given them more trouble, but Mustafa, despite his reputed viciousness and infamy, let the soldiers go.

The pursuit of the Mad One had cost the Turkish government many casualties, while the losses for the outlaws were only about a dozen dead and wounded.

In the ensuing weeks, the outlaws enjoyed the fruits of their victory by taking time to rest and eat well. Then the Turkish government tried again. The force they assigned this time was larger, but that was not a reason for the outlaws to worry. However, they soon learned that the new commander was wiser. He never attempted to engage with the outlaws in places that were advantageous to them. Instead, he tried to block the outlets from the mountains, thinking that sooner or later they must get down to the valley for food. The outlaws changed their tactics, too. They always kept at a safe distance and attacked the soldiers at times and places least expected, giving the impression that they were everywhere. As the winter wore on, the task for the soldiers became more difficult.

Finally, Mustafa received a message from the commander, who offered liberal terms, including a pardon if he would surrender. But that did not fool Mustafa. Finally a compromise was reached between the outlaw and his pursuer. Mustafa agreed to stop raiding farms and villages, to let the mails alone, and to show more respect for the lives of government officers and soldiers.

In return, the commander agreed to pull out the troops. However, they wanted to keep the appearance that they were still after the outlaws. Both sides agreed not to cross each other's paths.

Here is how they agreed to this strange pact: As pressure from the soldiers was being lifted, it wasn't unusual for Daly Mustafa and his band to visit a friendly village and spend the greater part of the day there. A few hours after their departure, the soldiers arrived. The headman of the village was tortured unmercifully. Upon getting information on which direction the bandits took, the soldiers left hastily, but took the opposite direction—suspicious, no doubt, that the peasant had given them the wrong direction.

As the Turkish government seemed unconcerned, the outlaws enjoyed a peculiar sort of freedom. The peasants were friendly. Badjad's doctrine—we're for you, not against you—spread slowly but surely. It became common for the outlaws to be self-invited guests of a village. On these occasions, the strict orders were that the peasants should be treated kindly and nothing more should be demanded of them than they were willing to offer.

They stayed a whole day at a village whose head, a liberal man, they trusted. To make it easy, the outlaws were distributed among the families.

Mustafa, Badjad, and several others were drinking and telling stories at the house of the headman. Dio went out to gather the men. Mustafa was in a good mood. Dio walked in; he looked grave.

"The men are outside and ready," he mumbled.

"All right, but why the gloom, Dio? Come out with it."

"Nothing—I will tell you later." He drained the cup the host had offered him and gazed at the leader with glassy eyes full of hurt.

"You will tell me now," said the leader in a low voice.

"One of the men has betrayed you, Mustafa," he muttered.

The leader looked at those around him. The enjoyable repast suddenly took on the semblance of a judgment session.

"My esteemed guest and friend," remarked the host, sitting across from him. "My only wish is that nothing of importance has befallen you to mar this happy occasion."

"There is nothing that you should be concerned about," answered the outlaw placidly. "I would like a little privacy. Could you arrange that?"

"Of course," responded the host.

Mustafa and his two attendants followed their host to a small interior room that was furnished elegantly with soft cushions and homespun rugs.

The host stood by the door while the three settled down on the cushions. Mustafa looked at his host.

"I have the feeling that this is something we cannot keep from you," he said. Then he turned to Dio. "Go on—tell me everything."

Dio hesitated. "If I could only have kept my mouth shut," he muttered to himself. His self-reproach was replaced with a sudden determination. He straightened up. "Here it is. A short while ago I was told that a peasant wanted to see you, Mustafa. I wanted to know why. He refused to talk to me, and then changed his mind. This is what he had to say." He paused again, then continued in a whisper. "Mustafa, the traitor—who is lodging at his house—has attacked his wife and threatened her if she talks."

"How did the peasant find out?" asked Badjad acidly.

"He told me that his wife acted peculiarly. He found a few pieces of gold and jewelry and the woman told him the whole story."

"So, the harlot sold her charms for a few baubles, eh? Either that, or that is how her seducer bought her silence," said Mustafa. He looked at Dio and demanded harshly, "Who's the wretch that broke our code and betrayed me?"

"That's the worst of it," Dio growled. "He isn't a newcomer."

"I feared as much," commented Badjad.

"Bring him and the peasant in," commanded the leader.

Dio walked out. The host moved closer to the leader of the outlaws and sat before him.

"That sounds bad," he said in a low, shaky voice. "It can happen with young men. Maybe it isn't as bad as it appears to be, and the wench herself caused it. I'm sure that the peasant can be pacified, and the sordid story won't leave these four walls."

Mustafa's eyes were cold, his voice stern. "We will see," he muttered. "But we cannot compromise our creed. One unscrupulous enough to break his oath is capable of greater treachery." He looked at Badjad. "But don't misunderstand me. I'm not passing judgment. We all are involved. The men should know and decide."

The culprit was led into the room, with Dio behind him. One look and the faces of the two outlaw chiefs turned milky white. Badjad's hand went to his forehead. His choked voice cried, "Osman, you rogue..."

Mustafa stared at him tight-lipped, his eyes cold and without expression. Yes, it was Osman, the Georgian, one of Badjad's original companions. "Osman, do you know why you're here?" came Badjad's angry voice.

"Yes," answered the accused.

"Did you do it?"

"Yes."

The silence was deadly. An admission of guilt, with no defense. All that was left was to impose the penalty. The accused stood there calmly with a faraway look in his eyes.

"Talk, Osman, talk," cried Badjad, "for my sake, for the sake of the time we've been together. Did you force her? Did you threaten her?"

A diminutive, middle-aged peasant in rags was then pushed into the room with the door closed tight behind him. He stood with his hands clasped together at his waist, his yellow fox eyes shifting guiltily from accuser to accuser.

"You lowdown scum! I should have known better," cried the host. Then he whispered pleadingly, "Mustafa, his wife is a bitch, believe me. I'll drive them out of this village."

"What she is, or what you would do, does not concern me," Mustafa grumbled. After a second's hesitation, he turned to the peasant. "Now that you are here, what do you have to tell me?" he asked in a low, deadly voice.

It was a simple demand, but the diminutive man shook in his boots.

"Nothing, master, nothing!" cried the man. "I was just afraid."

"Afraid of what, your cur? No one with me will soil his hands with your filthy blood. Are you still afraid?"

The man had fallen down to the outlaw's feet, but he was kicked away.

"Did your wife tell you that she was paid? Do you want more? Osman, empty your money belt in his lap."

The man made anxious sounds that were not words. His arms waved in the air over his head. The gold pieces rolled all over the room.

"Disarm him, Badjad," Mustafa commanded harshly. "Dio, tell the men we're leaving." He looked at his host. "Take this traitor out of my sight before I, too, forget ..."

"Mustafa, Kurban, don't go hard with him," pleaded the host on his knees, hands clasped. "He isn't the guilty one. It's my fault for sending him to that house." He looked in the direction where the disarmed outlaw stood beside Badjad. "Son, why did you let that ..." He turned to the leader, pleading, "Mustafa?"

"I have no voice in the matter, that much I want you to know," retorted the leader as he stepped out of the room.

It was a long, sad march back to their stronghold. One of them walked alone, disarmed, head hung low, his shame a fate worse than death. The men knew that Osman had done wrong, but they dared not speculate among themselves. A life was at stake, the life of one they all loved; one who was part of them.

They gathered around their leader; some of the men were getting restless. Their eyes were glued on the humiliated outlaw standing pale-faced before them. Badjad's hard, relentless voice spoke up.

"What's wrong, Mustafa?"

"You will hear it," declared the leader coldly, "but I have one request. Think of him as one of your kinsmen before passing judgment. Osman has broken his oath. He attacked the woman of the house."

A mingled chorus of mumbles, shouts, and curses responded. Mustafa held up his hand.

"His fate is in your hands," he said in a grim voice.

"He must die!" voiced several of the men.

"We want to know more about it!" shouted another, standing up.

Mustafa looked at Badjad standing beside him.

"Osman alone can tell you what you want to know," said Badjad, "but he refuses to talk except to admit it and that he paid the woman. The issue is—did he do it against her will? If not, why did she bring it out into the open? She alone can make that clear, but will a good woman admit her vice in public?"

"You said she was paid. Did she accept her fee?" asked another.

"Yes, and the story is that her husband found the gold and wormed out a confession from her," Badjad answered.

"Is he an honest man?" cried one.

Mustafa shook his head. "The headman of the village doesn't think so. He swore that he would drive them out of the village."

"He must talk; make him talk!" the men shouted.

Still another voice, even louder, proclaimed, "He has broken his oath! Get rid of him, Mustafa!"

The leader's hand went up again.

"Not as long as someone wants to hear him. Are there any among you who think Osman can be forgiven?"

There was only grim silence. The men looked at each other, but no one dared to raise his voice.

"This might be your last word, Osman. The men who fought with you, who were willing to die for you, demand that you talk. You owe it to them," said the leader, looking at him.

Osman raised his head. His voice was low and calm. "Just one thing. I prefer death to living in disgrace. Now that I've betrayed you, one thing I ask: Forgive me after I'm gone."

"Wait!" cried Badjad, jumping to his feet. "Our code says, if one seduces a woman *against* her will, but did Osman really break his oath? Was it against her will? On the other hand, if our having affairs with women constitute a betrayal regardless, then I want to confess now that I'm guilty of the same crime. The difference is that in my case the woman wouldn't accept gold, or let the world know of the affair. I challenge anyone to come forward and say that he wouldn't be tempted by any woman who was willing."

He paused and waited. A long moment passed. No one stepped forward. Badjad continued in a humble voice, and turned toward the leader. "But I know Osman and beg him to answer. If he won't, he alone must decide his fate."

He checked his rifle, and handed it to the leader. Mustafa stared at it as though it were a strange object. The men moved away. Osman stood alone at a distance. The youthful leader of the outlaws had lived more than his share of sad moments, but this was the saddest he had known. To kill someone who was like a part of him; was this the price he must pay for being the leader? The condemned man's form swam in front of him. He tried to grasp the gun, but it slipped from his fingers to the grass.

"I can't do it. Don't ask me why. I just want to tell you this. Fate has been good to me. I haven't been put to the test of facing a woman in that way."

The men shouted their approval. Dio rose to lead Osman away. Badjad stood still as a statue, staring at the leader. Could it be that he, too, was human? He quickly recovered from his reverie.

"You justify my faith, Mustafa," he whispered.

"You saved him, Badjad," the leader whispered back.

CHAPTER 19

The forest glowed in autumn colors. Nights were getting chilly. It was time for the outlaws to get their dugouts ready and store provisions for the winter, but no one wanted to think about it. They felt that their days of being outlaws were numbered. The Turkish government tottered on its last leg. Large numbers of deserters roved around the countryside. The changing situation demanded some solution if the discontented hordes were not to turn against one another.

Mustafa received a message urging him to attend a meeting in a mountain village far away from his region, adding that if he could not attend personally, it was imperative for him to be represented. The message was signed by Mustafa Kemal, a competent Turkish general that had suddenly appeared on the scene and was quickly becoming an authority in open revolt against the government. His aim as a true patriot was to salvage whatever he could from the disastrous defeat by the Central Powers and establish a liberal, democratic form of government. He was willing to sit side by side with the vilest ruffian, who for a price would cut his own mother's throat, to discuss and adopt a course of action to save the country.

Had Mustafa the outlaw been a Turk, the part he would have played was obvious. But, he did not want to see any kind of Turkish government survive. However, others felt differently and saw an opportunity to restore Turkey's reputation. Badjad was one. Therefore, it was agreed that he would represent the band of Daly Mustafa at the rebel convention.

During Badjad's absence, things changed quickly. The Turkish army was totally disorganized and on the run. English and Greek troops landed on the Mediterranean shore and pushed inward, unopposed. The southern front had collapsed completely. Five thousand Armenian volunteers, most of whom enlisted from the United States and fought under the French flag, pushed northward at an incredibly fast pace. Mustafa thought of joining these volunteers. He knew that this would be acceptable to the Christian members of the band, but what about Badjad and the others?

Sensing the termination of their dubious careers, the men were in a lighthearted mood. They were justified since they could look forward to an automatic pardon. Very soon, with money in their belts, they would leave their hideouts and live as gentlemen with a checkered past.

Badjad came back. He spoke enthusiastically about the meeting and Mustafa Kemal, reporting what was said and what they hoped to accomplish. Mustafa listened intently, catching now and then Badjad's inquiring glance. The rule of drinking in moderation at all times was overlooked. The men spoke freely and laughed heartily. The intangible chain that had bound them together began to loosen. They drank to Dio's last toast, vowing eternal comradeship. Badjad and Mustafa moved away. Dio refilled his cup and repeated the toast all over by himself.

At an isolated cove, the two warriors sat leaning against the rocks. The night was chilly. Badjad's hand rested gently upon the shoulder of the leader.

"What's your plan, Mustafa?"

The leader turned his head and met Badjad's look with a friendly smile. Words were not necessary.

"While you were away, I was thinking, Badjad. What would you do if you were me?"

Badjad hesitated a moment before whispering, "I hope I have not done something you wouldn't approve of."

Mustafa observed his confederate's forehead, wrinkled and careworn. "No, Badjad, when I asked you to go, I wanted you to act as you wished. Please speak freely."

"The man I saw and talked to is a good man," said Badjad, "honest, wise, and unprejudiced, with one purpose, and that is to free the country from the cruel elements in the government. He isn't going to oppose the occupation of the Allies, but he will not lay down his arms until he has kicked out the Sultan from his throne. What I saw convinced me that he'll do it. Soldiers and militants are now on our side. He told me to remain where we are. We'll be fed and supported once the people learn what we stand for."

Badjad paused, grasped his companion's hand, and added, "Mustafa, believe me, knowing what you are, you would not be looked upon any differently from me."

"I believe it," answered Mustafa in a sullen manner. "But he cannot speak for those around him, just as I cannot speak for those who are with me."

They looked sullen. There was nothing more to be said. They had reached a crossroads where, despite their personal feelings, they must go their own ways.

"I do understand," said Badjad. "You have a country of your own. Though it isn't the one where you were born, your people are there and you want to be with them. Maybe it's best to end our friendship this way. Now that we have lived and fought together, we may help others to understand and hate no more." He extended his hand. "I've said this once, and now I want to repeat it: May we remain true to ourselves, wherever our paths lead, Mustafa. Now, tell me about your plans."

"I'm thinking of traveling south to surrender to the English. I cannot ask you to do that; your job isn't yet finished."

"There would be many who would want to do that," Badjad reflected.

"We'll make it optional. Those who want to remain with you will do so; others yearning for a peaceful life will come with me."

"That's fair. I hope you don't mind my staying until the last moment."

"Thank you, Badjad. It will lessen the sadness of parting."

The journey south was uneventful; the troops who had abandoned their ranks did not look for trouble as they found their way home. Mustafa was at peace; he had fulfilled what he thought of as his mission. The end of the insidious Turkish government was what he had hoped to see.

He and the men, including Badjad, were in the vicinity of a city, a short way from Smyrna by train, when the news of the armistice reached them. Constantinople and other large ports were in the hands of the Allies. A few days later, British troops entered the city.

In their mountain hideaway overlooking this ancient, scenic city, Mustafa stood before the men who had learned to honor and respect him. He looked humble. They had never seen him appear that way. He spoke, but it wasn't the unflinching, commanding voice familiar to all.

"Whatever you have done, or undone, ends here," he said softly. "From here on it's up to you. I'm offering you two choices. One, to carry on with Badjad to liberate the country. Two, to do what I've decided—surrender to the English, then go wherever you want to go. This is all I have to say. I know Badjad would like to say a few words, too."

"Those who remain with me will no longer be looked upon as outlaws or bandits, but as patriots," Badjad proclaimed. "We aim to overthrow the corrupt government, then make an honorable peace. Mustafa and I understand each other well. I want you all to know that. Though circumstances have forced us to part, our hearts will always be together. That's all I have to say. Now it's up to you."

None of the men asked questions. They milled around, talking in whispers individually or in groups. A dozen, including the Georgian and the Albanian, were among those who wanted to stay with Badjad. The majority, however, felt they had had enough of it and decided to go with their leader who had promised them a chance to live a normal life. The pact of brotherhood in arms, which was the only life that held them together, ended.

Now the leader's true identity was no longer a secret. He announced it to all and expressed the desire to be called by his real name, Zaven, adding to it the qualifying title Sivasly, meaning one from Sivas.

To those who had lived the kind of rough-and-tumble life that had made them immune to sentimentality, the parting scene was touching.

While pressing Badjad's hand for the last farewell, Zaven fondly stroked the barrel of his Luger and vowed in a low voice, "I will keep this forever as a token of our comradeship and our shared ideals."

"I hope it will bring you luck," said Badjad.

After waiting a few days in the mountains above the city, Zaven dispatched a note to the British commander, together with a brief description of himself and his men. Now that he had indirectly helped the Allied cause in a small way and victory was attained, he would lay down his arms if the safety of his men was granted. Several days later, he received a reply. It was very complimentary, assuring him safe conduct. He was directed to come down from the hills and was offered transportation anywhere he and his men wished to go.

The next day, in a colorful procession, Zaven and his men marched into the train station. The English commander received them warmly. Here the outlaws were disarmed, but as a reward for his efforts, Zaven was allowed to keep his beloved Luger. A passenger wagon specially reserved for the outlaws waited to take them to Smyrna. The men crowded in. Zaven was the last to enter with his British escort. As he watched the men sitting in silence, he felt a mixture of both contentment and remorse. Contented because he had kept them alive; remorseful because the appearance that had made people shake with fear at their defiant looks, their weather-beaten faces, and the crisscross stains on their jackets left by the cartridge belts was now gone.

Smyrna was a cosmopolitan city, second in size and wealth only to Constantinople. The train bringing the disarmed outlaws stopped at the big station. The platform swarmed with curious spectators, most of them Armenians. They had come to catch a glimpse of the notorious bandits of Bursa, especially the Mad One, who had turned out to be an Armenian. Zaven stood on the platform with his escort beside him. First he heard a noisy cheer, then the shouting of his real name. Who had told them? It didn't matter. He had nothing to hide any more. The English troops on guard opened a narrow path through the spectators. Did his appearance disappoint them? Zaven was tall, broad-shouldered, good-looking, and well mannered—a far cry from the demon they might have imagined. He made no response, and with downcast eyes followed his escort through the sea of people's hands touching him as he went to the waiting carriages outside.

A small, exclusive hotel overlooking the Mediterranean was reserved for him and his men. He was received by the British High Command, who seemed pleased with him. They had tea together. The commander had reassured his pledge of sending him and his men anywhere they wished to go. But that could wait.

He joined the men in the main salon of the hotel. A noisy, carefree party was in full swing. Women in scanty silk dresses with powdered cheeks and penciled-on eyebrows mingled in the crowd. Dio was in his glory with two of them at his side. Two years without a woman's touch was a long, long time. Zaven gazed at him and walked in the other direction. An attractive brunette sat alone in the corner. Zaven caught the naughty twinkle in her large brown eyes and turned away, but the woman sauntered toward him with a tiger's grace. It would be improper for him to walk away.

"I was waiting for you," she whispered, moving embarrassingly close, her strong perfume tickling Zaven's nose.

"Why for me?" he questioned casually. "There are so many others around."

"But there's only one you. I watched you from the window when you stepped out of the carriage. I knew then and there I wanted you."

Zaven smiled at her. Maybe she was a bit audacious, but she had charm. "That I can see," he whispered. "Do you always get what you want?"

"Yes, I'm used to it and it has spoiled me."

Dio, who by that time had realized that Zaven had appeared, was on his feet.

"Your place is reserved," he said. He paused, looked around, and added in a lower voice, "All this was arranged before we got here. Hope you won't mind."

"Mind what? We all are free."

They walked to the table. Women sang and danced; men drank and watched them. Zaven laughed at the spicy jokes of a plump, not-too-young woman who had introduced herself as the matron. The woman who had followed Zaven was sitting close to him and still lingered over her second glass. She didn't finish it. She rose, bent over Zaven, and whispered in his ear, "I'm going upstairs. Please don't keep me waiting long."

Zaven looked puzzled. Even that seemed prearranged. Well, he supposed he had to sleep somewhere. He wasn't in a hurry to leave, but the place was getting empty. Dio had gone; perhaps he had a bit too much to drink but would be all right. The musicians left, too. He was practically all by himself.

The pageboy approached and asked him if he wished to be shown to his room. Zaven answered that he did. He followed the boy two flights up and was pointed out a door bearing the number 14. He opened it. There she was, lounging on the settee, in a transparent black nightgown. Never before had he seen such a sight. She rose, walked to him, and put her arms around him. Zaven felt his manhood stirring as the woman nuzzled his neck. Her exotic perfume was intoxicating.

"What's your name?" he asked.

"Shooshan."

"Why, that's an Armenian name."

"And I'm Armenian."

Zaven's whole body froze. He pushed her away.

"Are you from Smyrna?"

"No, I'm from the interior. We were deported. I was brought here by a Turk."

"Did you have to do this? Thousands of others preferred death." Zaven had felt desire, but the woman's decision to live by prostitution suddenly infuriated him. She opened the closet, put on her robe, and walked to the door.

"Wait," said Zaven, walking over to her with a few gold pieces in his palm.

"You better give it to the matron, so that she won't be cheated. You won't see me any more," she whimpered as she closed the door behind her.

Zaven walked to the window. He looked out at the gray Mediterranean with the distant masthead light of a solitary sailboat winking in the dark. He looked and thought, and tried to find an answer to what was happening. He had no wish and no reason to hurt her. She was a woman; he was a man. Was it the fact that she was an Armenian when he expected a Turk that had turned him to ice? The lure of a city of vice that had kept the men together for a while faded away. Their number gradually dwindled. One or two left every day. It seemed that everyone had someone they pined to see and somewhere to go. Zaven had no one and no place to go. The four that still hung around him apparently felt the same as he did. They were Dio, his inseparable friend, Eremia the boy from his hometown, and two others who had been with him from the beginning. He pondered over the problem of reinventing himself. He received two enticing propositions: one, to become a partner in an exporting business; and another to buy an exclusive cafe. Dio was sold on that last idea; perhaps he figured that the drinks would always be on the house. The publisher of the Armenian daily newspaper suggested that he go to Adana.

The French government had taken over this region and was gathering Armenian refugees here for the purpose of founding a new colony. The idea had appealed to Zaven, but he wanted to know more about it. The information he sought came from an official source and he decided to go to Adana.

The four who would not let him slip away from their sight dawdled about lazily in his room. Dio was humming a ballad. His voice was obnoxious and Zaven had to put up with it.

"What are you so happy about?" asked Zaven curtly.

"And why not?" commented Dio. "Nothing to do, no place to go; that suits me just fine."

"This might spoil your fun, but I want you to know that you'll be going places soon. Or at least I will, if you find it hard to part from your harem."

"My poor butterflies. This'll break their hearts," Dio grinned.

"Not their hearts, but their pockets. Have you any more jewels left?"

The others laughed. Dio glared at them, then he, too, laughed.

"Where are we going, Zaven?" asked Eremia.

"I'm going to Adana, but I don't want you to feel that you have to come with me. I mean it. I never know what I may do next. You seem to be happy here."

Dio stared at him. "Oh Gabriel, blow thy horn, here I come!" he cried, raising his arms.

"Even he will have a hard time in your case," smiled Zaven.

Eremia just looked at him.

"All right, all right. I should have known better. I take it back. Get ready, we're leaving soon," said Zaven.

They readily obtained passports for five to Adana through the British commander, who handed Zaven a letter of introduction, addressed to the French occupation command, along with the train tickets. "I could use a good man like you here myself," sighed the commander, "but I think you will do better there for the cause of your people."

The journey to Adana would have been quiet and pleasant if Dio had behaved as a respectable passenger. When the train stopped at a junction to transfer the passengers to another train, a number of Armenians also on their way to Adana boarded the train. It didn't take long for the gregarious Dio to get acquainted with the new arrivals. Most of them had lived in the town through the war. One of them, a talkative, middle-aged fellow, stated that the Turks spared him because he happened to be the only tailor in the city. The way he talked indicated that his pretense of accepting Mohammedanism hadn't helped him much.

The tailor shared the interesting tidbit that on the same train were two Turks who had played an important role during the deportation. One was the mayor of the city; the other was the commissar of the police. While the tailor gave vivid and gruesome accounts of their nasty work, Zaven observed Dio's face. It boded no good for the subjects under discussion.

"Where are they going?" he asked.

"I don't know," replied the tailor. "They are likely to get off somewhere along the road. Since the English arrived, they think it will be safer to move away."

Dio was rubbing his nose. "Listen," he said in a voice that made the tailor regret not keeping his mouth shut, "the first place the train stops, you're coming out with me to show me where and who they are."

At the next stop, Dio and the tailor went out. When they returned, Zaven saw a peculiar look of contentment on Dio's face.

"Did you find your Turkish friends?" asked Zaven.

Dio pouted his lips and rubbed his nose.

The next morning there was a hushed murmur among the passengers. Two persons were missing from the train: the mayor and his companion. There were no clues, and no one had any idea how, when, or where they had disappeared. The best answer appeared to be that the two had stopped off at a small station at night unnoticed. Dio sat opposite Zaven, looking like a contented cat after a full meal.

"Dio, your friends are gone," remarked Zaven casually.

"Ya," he grunted.

"I'm curious to know how they could have disappeared so quietly."

Dio leaned forward. "The poor devils had the bad habit of leaving their window open, so they fell out."

"Both?"

"Yes, and by chance the accident happened when the train was going through a tunnel."

CHAPTER 20

"Adana, all out!" the conductor yelled.

It was a busy station. Zaven stood by the window and watched the bustle outside, while his companions looked around to make sure nothing was left behind. Dio opened the door of the compartment to remind him that they were getting off. They stepped out onto the platform. It was a big place with high skylights, but it wasn't the architecture that interested Zaven. It was the people. All around him he saw Armenian faces; men, women, and children—well-dressed and shabbily dressed, healthy and weak. These were the survivors of the calamity. He was happy to see them alive and together. A few paces away stood two soldiers in French uniform, speaking Armenian. He was ecstatic. He felt like rushing up to them with outstretched arms just to let them know that he, too, was an Armenian. Then, two ragged little boys with brown, intelligent eyes were standing in front of him.

"Will you let us carry your luggage, sir?" inquired the older one who couldn't have been more than twelve.

Something about the young boy startled Zaven. He looked at him and was reminded of his own youth, which seemed like many years ago. Then, as if he had just awakened from a dream, his mind darted ahead to their future, and to his own.

"Sure, son," he said.

Dio glanced at them and helped each one shoulder a small case. They followed their budding porters out of the station. The carriage drivers, too, were Armenians. One carriage would have done, but Zaven called for two.

"What's your name, son?" Zaven asked the older boy before taking his place in the carriage.

"Haik Mooradian, sir."

"My name is Aram Sarian," said the younger one, who did not wish to be left out.

"Where are you from?"

"I'm from Sivas. Aram is from Arapker," answered the older boy.

Zaven tried hard to remember if he knew any family with the name Mooradian. Yes, he knew one, but there were many Mooradians in Sivas.

"Where do you live?" Zaven asked.

"There," answered the boy, pointing to a cluster of box-like shanties along the railroad track half a mile away.

"Have you been here long?"

"Only a month. The English brought us here from the desert. We were there with the Bedouins."

"I suppose your mother is around?"

"Haik's mother is," answered the younger one.

"My mother died; I'm with my grandmother."

Zaven gave each one two gold coins. The boys gazed excitedly at the glittering pieces.

"These are gold, sir. Must be worth a lot," mumbled Haik.

Zaven patted his head. "It's yours, son. Now run along and don't lose them."

The boys ran happily toward the barracks. At that moment, Zaven made up his mind where to go first.

The carriage driver had watched and listened to the exchange between Zaven and the boys. He stared at the impressive-looking young man in fur hat, cavalry breeches, gray jacket, and shiny high boots, who was so liberal with his gold. He couldn't be a refugee, or an enterprising businessman. Who was he then?

"I hope you don't mind my being curious, sir," said the driver. "We don't often see people like you getting off here."

"My name is Zaven, and I'm from Sivas."

The driver was rubbing his forehead. The name seemed to register, but he wasn't sure. He looked sheepishly at his customers, who had already taken their places in his carriage.

"Ever hear the name of Daly Mustafa?" remarked Dio.

"The bandit of Bursa!" exclaimed the driver with an awed expression that amused Zaven.

"Take us to a good Armenian hotel," Zaven ordered.

"I know just the place," said the driver, smiling to himself.

Twenty minutes later, the carriage stopped in front of a four-story brick building. The driver dropped the reins and dashed into the building. He soon returned, accompanied by an elderly, fat-faced man who walked right up to Zaven, who stood by the carriage. He grasped his arm and exclaimed, smiling with glee, "Welcome, Daly Mustafa, the one and only! The place is yours. I will be offended if you don't take advantage of my hospitality."

"Daly Mustafa is dead," said Zaven quietly. "But Zaven is here to stay."

"Zaven then," shouted the overly sentimental hotel owner. The proprietor's fuss over the comfort of his extraordinary guests matched his enthusiasm. He showed them the rooms, and then went to town to supervise the preparation of the meal. He was back soon with a bottle of cognac.

"For two days you're my guest, Zaven," said the man, filling the glasses. "After that, if you insist on paying, I won't object."

"Can you afford that?"

"I can, and I will be honored. I came here from Aleppo two short months ago and am doing very well. The Turks started moving when the Armenian volunteers arrived. They are still moving out. You will find some in the slums of the city, but these are the ones who have done no harm. After six hundred years of slavery, Adana once more will become a small Armenia. You and others like you will lay the foundation, Zaven. Already we have a National Committee set up by the French. I hope you won't mind that I sent word to the Chairman that you're here."

Zaven's face flushed. Things were happening so fast.

"Thank you," he said. "But the first thing I want to do is to visit the barracks."

"Oh, yes, the refugees. We have thousands of them and they're bringing more and more each day."

"Who is taking care of them?" asked Zaven.

"The French are helping, but the National Committee is looking after them. Don't let that worry you. They're all right."

But were they all right? The images of two timid, undernourished boys in rags, barely into their adolescence but emotionally grown up, haunted him.

The next morning Zaven visited the barracks, which had been built in a hurry. His particular interest was to find someone who could give him information on his family. He found Haik. After calming the boy's fright, he asked him if he would take him to his mother. Haik's mother was a woman in her early thirties, attractive in spite of her rags. The tiny tattoo marks on her forehead, souvenirs from the Bedouins, gave her a mysterious charm. Zaven sat alone with her in an isolated corner while his companions each found someone they could talk with.

"I know your mother well, Zaven," she said in a soft, faraway voice. "She joined our caravan after you were separated."

Zaven looked at her humbly. The defiant look of the outlaw was gone. He could read in her eyes the awful words that she hesitated to say.

"She was one of the few buried decently," she said. "I saw it with my own eyes. That should give you some consolation."

"What became of my sister and the others?" asked Zaven, as though he had heard nothing.

"While camping on the banks of Euphalatus, she and your cousin Rose disappeared. We never saw them again."

"What about the baby?"

"I don't know, Zaven. Your sister had him with her all the time."

"How did you manage yourself, Sona?"

"You don't want me to go into that, do you?" she murmured pleadingly.

"No, Sona, I suppose not. Tell me, are you all right now? Suppose I get a place in the city? You can look after me and my companions."

"Please don't, Zaven. To be a help to you, and to be with you, is something I dared not even dream. But you belong to all of us. You don't want me to be selfish. All things considered, I am well, and I am happy here. And happier now, in seeing you."

"But if there is anything you want, tell me. I'll be hurt if you don't."

"I will, Zaven, I will. I promise you that. For the present we're getting reasonably good food and have a place to sleep. The gold pieces you gave to Haik will last us a long time."

Zaven produced a few more gold pieces.

Sona gently pushed his hand away. "I don't need them, and I won't accept them."

"I want you to take them and give them to those in need," Zaven insisted.

"Yes, I will do that. Thank you, Zaven."

Weary and brokenhearted, Zaven returned to his hotel; yet he felt strangely relieved. He began to feel a new inspiration. What could he do for those in the barracks? But this was not a personal problem, nor a national one. It was in the hands of the Allied Powers. Could he in his small way help the cause?

That night Zaven and his companions sought relaxation at a coffeehouse run by an ex-outlaw by the name of Erevant. Their appearance caused something of a stir, for it was not the sort of place one could walk into casually. Zaven carried a silver-handled whip, and the shape of a Luger bulged inside his pocket.

"Erevant, a table for the Sivasly," cried the hotel owner, who had insisted on accompanying them. Everyone started, and the proprietor, a tall, hard-looking man, came forward in a hurry. He extended his hand and led Zaven to a table that was quickly emptied.

"You measure up to your fame," declared the ex-outlaw.

The attendants of the coffeehouse gathered around them. Zaven observed their faces. They didn't look any different from those he had known so well in the mountains of Bursa. He saw possibilities.

The next morning Zaven opened his eyes reluctantly. It was an ordinary hotel room, but the atmosphere was comfortable. His companions, though each had his own room, were in the habit of hanging around his room. But they were not there. It must be late—later than he thought. Had he slept that long? They left the coffeehouse long after midnight. He had talked more than he usually did. His head was a bit heavy; cold water would fix that. The door opened gently. He saw Dio's face sticking out behind it.

"Come in, you old drunk," cried Zaven.

"Sorry to disturb your beauty sleep, but it's long past noon. Aren't you going to eat?"

"Food ... *ugh*," said Zaven, pretending to retch. "I doubt if I could keep anything down."

"I can see that," grinned Dio. "But you have an appointment. Have you forgotten that, too?"

"Oh, yes, I'll be down soon. You go ahead and eat. A cup of coffee is all I want."

"Don't you want to shave?"

"Yes, I can manage it myself."

"You're going to see an important man and you won't look handsome with a patch on your cheek."

"If my cheek has ever been patched, it has been your doing, you clumsy butcher. Go on. I'll meet you downstairs."

Zaven shaved himself, taking extra pains to groom his clipped mustache. He was proud of it, as it gave him the look of maturity beyond his years. He walked downstairs. Dio was ready. He drank his coffee and ate a crisp piece of bread. Then they walked to the waiting carriage.

"Take us to the headquarters of The National Committee," said Zaven to the driver, as they got into the carriage.

The National Committee organized by the Armenian nationals scattered around the world had picked a textile factory for its headquarters. The largest amount of financial aid came from the United States. The Allied Powers recognized the Committee in an official capacity as a governing body of the Armenian colony already established. They found the double gate wide open. The carriage drove into the courtyard and stopped by the winding railed stairway. Zaven stepped out.

"Should I wait, Sivasly?" asked the driver. "This isn't my carriage; I only drive it."

"Yes, wait," said Zaven curtly.

An officer in French uniform met the two ex-outlaws at the top of the stairway.

"The Sivasly, I assume," he said, offering his hand.

Zaven nodded and shook.

"Mr. Melikian is expecting you."

They walked through a long corridor with doors on either side. Their escort stopped before the door at the very end and tapped gently. A pleasant voice from within invited them to enter. The escort stood aside. Zaven and Dio walked in. A pale-faced man with a neatly groomed gray beard and sympathetic eyes emerged from behind a large desk. He grabbed the young outlaw's hand and led him to the chair close to his desk.

"We're proud of what you have done, Zaven, and are looking forward to bigger and more useful deeds from you," he began. "Now that we're bringing here all those who have survived, you and others like you can do your part. Let me explain why we're here and what we aim to do. For the moment, the civilian authority of this city and the surrounding places is still in the hands of the Turks. But the French government gradually intends to place this authority in our hands.

"Though no definite treaty has been signed yet, the Powers have agreed that Adana should become an Armenian colony under the protectorate of France. The most important thing during this period of uncertainty is for us to show that we deserve the grant. We already have many here. Some of them are behaving badly; that will harm us. I have this to ask of you, and I know that you are the one to do it. I want you to group these men around you and stop their vile escapades of raids and killing until we have them usefully engaged."

"It's a touchy job. I won't give promises, but I'll try my best," Zaven declared.

"That's all I wanted to hear. In the meantime, we will try to be helpful and eliminate the cause of this lawlessness. I want you to find out, Zaven, and report to me." He hesitated a moment, looked inquiringly at the young outlaw, and then added, "By the way, how are you situated?"

Zaven smiled. "You don't have to worry about us."

He left the Chairman of The National Committee with a heavy heart. Yes, the man was right. People demanding self-rule must prove that they are capable of it. Every misdemeanor would go against them and their cause.

Zaven told the driver to take them to Erevant's, which he had made a sort of headquarters. An ex-outlaw who had operated in the section of Ourfa pulled his chair beside him.

"Sivasly, I cannot remain idle much longer," he blurted out. "Money is going fast. The men are getting restless. So much is going on, but I've kept my hands clean. I'm telling you this because I don't want to do anything behind your back."

"It's good you feel that way," answered Zaven. "Tell your men to sit tight a little while. We may find a way to help those who are in the barracks."

That evening, Zaven left early. Dio went with him.

"A quiet evening with the two of us alone. I like nothing better," said Dio, walking to the closet.

Zaven smiled. "Pull my trunk out, please, before you come out with the bottle."

Dio stared at him sheepishly.

"I'm going to see the French commander tomorrow," added Zaven.

Dio had the trunk out. Zaven opened it and from under the folds of his clothes pulled out the letter given to him by the British commander.

"We must do something to take the men out of the city and away from temptations."

"Right," Dio agreed. "I was approached by someone to join a raid on a farm not far from the city. A Turk who is playing the part of an informer gave a tip that several rich natives with tin cans full of gold are staying on the farm before leaving for a place where they will be safe."

"What did you tell him?"

"I told him to see you."

"The only one who spoke to me did not mention anything like that."

"It wasn't him or any of his men," declared Dio.

Dio filled the glass and handed it to Zaven. "I don't like it," Zaven muttered, "but it's too late for you to do anything about it."

The next day Zaven was on his way to see the French commander. After a short wait he was introduced to the commander by the attending sergeant, who happened to be an Armenian. Zaven saluted smartly, trying to show that an outlaw could also be a soldier. The commander looked pleased. He read the letter presented to him and looked straight at the young outlaw standing at attention before him. He muttered a few words in French and lit a cigarette. His sharp, penetrating glance electrified Zaven. Zaven looked at the attending sergeant standing beside him and barely heard the commander whisper in his ears, "Rather young, but he may turn out to be the very devil I'm looking for." He spoke again, this time addressing Zaven directly.

"I want you to organize a band of Armenian scouts in the service of France. Can you do it?" asked the commander?

"Yes," Zaven answered without hesitation.

The commander explained, "We need about fifty scouts, and I want to make sure that they are the right kind. They'll receive monthly salaries, uniforms, and armament. It has to be a mounted detachment, but I cannot supply the horses."

"I believe we can manage it, sir," was Zaven's answer.

"You'll have the rank of a lieutenant. Other details concerning your duties will be given you when you are ready."

Eager to tell the good news, Zaven hurried to the café.

"You can easily muster two hundred volunteers, Zaven," said Erevant.

"Yes, but we must select them carefully. I don't want money hounds."

With the aid of Erevant and others whom he could trust, Zaven selected the men to his satisfaction. A few lacked the experience, but they had spirit. Now the big problem was getting horses. Zaven and Dio contributed all they had, but it was not enough. Only a few of the men selected could provide their own mounts. Besides, there were other needs, such as pistols and cartridge belts. The National Committee promised some assistance, but this, too, was not enough. Zaven was forced to borrow from Erevant and others.

It had taken almost a week to select the men and get prepared. Zaven went to see the French commander to receive his commission and the details of his duties. It would take several days to have their uniforms ready: khaki breeches and short-belted jackets with the French military insignia sewn on the collar.

His duties were to act as vanguard for the regular troops and be ready at short notice to go anywhere. He would take his orders from the local French officer, wherever he happened to be. He was on his way out when the commander called him back.

"Just one thing more, lieutenant," said the commander in a stern voice. "There will be occasions when you must collaborate with the Turkish soldiers. I hope you and your men will not allow prejudice to interfere with your duties. We are here to maintain law and order. Remember, from now on you are under military discipline. I'm giving you the chance to reject this service if, in your heart, you find it difficult to be tolerant."

"I understand, sir," said Zaven. "I bear no grudge against people. I want to see them live in peace."

"I'm glad to hear that. You've done that in the past, and I'm sure you'll do it again."

Everything was ready. Having a choice of rifles, Zaven selected the German Mauser repeating rifle for the men. He was to leave Adana the following morning for his temporary headquarters, a small Turkish town about twenty-five miles from the city. He was not in uniform yet, and sat alone at the café. The place was strikingly empty that evening; even Dio wanted to be on his own. A big man with a massive mustache, twisted into elaborate curls on the ends, entered and approached Zaven.

"It's you I'm looking for, Sivasly," said the man.

"Indeed. And why?" Zaven asked.

"It'll take too long to tell. If you would follow me ..."

Zaven did not like the uncertainty of his request. The man was a stranger, but he was an Armenian, probably one of the troops. Though suspicious, he followed him out into the street.

The man led Zaven to the Armenian quarters, then into an old, dilapidated house. The ground floor was dark and dismal. A crumbling staircase led to the second story. The guide, however, went down toward the cellar, and there, trussed up like a pair of fowls headed for the butcher's block, were two Turks lying on the damp floor.

"Who on earth are they?" Zaven asked.

"Spies," the man answered laconically. "We got them. Here they are. You have to decide what to do with them."

What could he do? Were they really spies? How could he find out, and if he did, what then? He was an officer now. He couldn't do anything to jeopardize his career at the very start. He realized one thought above all: The French must not learn about it.

"We cannot let them loose. You'll find my driver in front of the café. Go on and come back with him."

The man walked out. Zaven closed the door behind him, walked over to the captives, and stood over them.

"What business brought you to this part of the city?" Zaven asked harshly.

"We didn't come here, master, we were forced here," answered one.

"Why? It won't make any difference, so you might as well tell me the truth."

The men began to beg. That infuriated Zaven.

"Just one thing, master," pleaded the prisoner, "don't you really know why we are here?"

Zaven's look was scornful.

"You asked for the truth," continued the man, "and here it is. We are merchants. We sold all we had to go away and had a large amount of cash on us. We were trapped in here. They took our money."

Zaven walked out and took the stairway to the second floor. Two women, one elderly, the other young, along with a frightened-looking man and two children, clustered in the dark together. As Zaven stood in the doorway, the old woman rose, and then fell at his feet.

"My son," she cried, "what are you going to do with them?"

"Don't worry, they won't be here long. But I warn you not to breathe a word. Go to bed and forget all about it."

He went to the courtyard and waited for the mustachioed man to return with the carriage. He smoked half a dozen cigarettes and still no sign of them. It shouldn't have taken that long. He was getting impatient; then he became suspicious. If what the trussed-up Turk had said was true—which appeared likely now—the man who had brought him there might never return.

It was not yet past midnight. He must get rid of the prisoners. He debated over the safest and easiest way. He believed that the captives were innocent, but could he let them go? He walked out into the street. It was quiet. Who would dare be out at night in the streets where corpses were found lying in the gutters every morning?

He walked to the street corner where he saw three figures advancing sluggishly toward him. They must be the patrol, undoubtedly Armenians. He stood there and waited. The patrol approached. He recognized the leader, a volunteer from America.

"Hey, what's cookin', Sivasly?" asked the Yank in a jaunty tone.

"Nothing serious. I just want you to hang around this corner and let no one enter this street until I return with a carriage."

The American got closer and whispered in Zaven's ear, "Ah, so there is something cookin', eh? Well, you better finish it up before my relief comes. We'll keep an eye on things for you here."

"Thanks," said Zaven. A short time later he found his carriage.

"What happened? Where did you go? Erevant told me where you were," said the driver excitedly, "and I thought I better stick around."

"I sent someone after you. Did you see him?" asked Zaven.

"I haven't seen anyone."

"All right, let's go."

On the way back to the dismal shanty, Zaven did not speak a word. The driver stole occasional glimpses at him, but dared not speak. The carriage made a sharp turn and entered the narrow street, barely wide enough to drive through.

A figure emerged from a sheltered doorway. It was the leader of the patrol, who poked his head into the carriage and whispered, "All right, Sivasly. I'm leaving now. The coast is clear."

The carriage moved on slowly and stopped in front of the house. Zaven jumped out.

"Do you need me?" asked the driver.

"No, you stay out here and mind the horses."

He pushed the gate open and walked straight to the basement. The Turkish merchants were still there, bound and miserable. Zaven struck a match, found a candle, and lit it. The unlucky ones followed each of his moves. He stood over them.

"I'm going to be a fool and do what you would least expect," he said in a grim voice. "I'll let you live, but for your own good I advise you to keep your mouths shut."

"We will not talk, master!" cried one of the captives.

"You still want to leave the city?"

"Yes, master."

"All right, I'll get you out."

Zaven drew a glittering double-edged dagger that he carried in his boot. The helpless man quivered. Zaven smiled contemptuously.

"Don't get excited. I won't cut your throats, even though it would be the easiest and safest way to get rid of you."

While he was cutting the ropes, one of the men brushed his lips gently on the back of his hand. Zaven snapped at him and the man regretted his gesture.

"Don't overdo it. I despise life because of your kind."

He loosened their feet, but kept their hands tied. Then he went to the door, opened it, and signaled them to walk out. The men were hesitant to enter the waiting carriage. The driver glanced at them and turned his inquisitive eyes to Zaven.

"Drive out of the city," ordered Zaven.

The carriage rumbled through the deserted streets, passed by the last dwelling, and kept on going for several miles. Finally, it stopped at a secluded grove. Zaven got out.

He loosened their hands, let the ecstatic Turks go, and then jumped into the carriage. The driver looked at him, puzzled but relieved.

The trick played on him had enraged Zaven so much that he found an excuse to stay in the city for the day. In the afternoon, he was in the coffeehouse with Dio and some others. The stranger who had led Zaven to the captured Turks appeared in the doorway. He looked at Zaven, inched forward slowly, and slipped his hand into his pocket. With trembling fingers, he drew out a fat roll of bank notes and placed it before Zaven.

"Here, Sivasly," he said. "This is yours."

Zaven sat there quietly, staring at him. The man was becoming uncomfortable. Great beads of sweat broke out on his broad, oily forehead and rolled down his fat jowls into his elaborate mustache.

"About last night," he went on. "I'm sorry I couldn't get back. I was followed and had to shake them off."

"You're a liar!" Zaven roared. "You were no more followed than I was. What's this, my butcher's fee?"

He flung the money back at him, sprang up, and put his whip into action, savagely beating the man, who at last managed to break away and ran out, screaming like a woman.

"Erevant, do you know him?" Zaven asked.

"He's been around, but I really don't know much about him, Zaven."

"It's your business to know who your customers are. I'm holding you responsible for him."

Erevant looked in the direction of two-hard-looking thugs sitting in the corner. They left the place. The following morning a body bearing the description of the man Zaven had beaten was found floating in the river with a bullet hole in his head.

CHAPTER 21

It was a sight that caused Armenian hearts to rejoice: Sixty Armenian mounted scouts paraded down the main street en route to their designated post. The sidewalks were crowded. The young, eye-catching leader mounted on a spirited gray mare led the procession. Dio and the outlaw from Ourfa, his two subordinates, rode behind him. For a moment the parade came to a standstill by the notorious café. A wild cheer filled the air as the servers, led by the wily proprietor, rushed out to say goodbye. Zaven raised his arm and waved. Erevant dashed out in front of the cavalcade, brandishing a bottle.

"Will the commander grant me the favor of offering the men a drink?" he asked.

Zaven shook his head.

"Between the two of us, then," suggested the ex-outlaw.

Zaven shook his head again and spurred his mount, leaving the dejected Erevant in a cloud of dust.

They rode for most of the day through vast and fertile plains, stopping at the villages intermittently and making themselves self-invited guests. The men's spirits were high; Zaven was excited at the prospect of a meaningful career ahead of him.

At dusk they reached their destination. It was a scenic little town of five thousand nestled in the foothills of the mountains. The officer of the Turkish guard stationed in the town escorted them to their headquarters, which was an old inn. Zaven found himself in a difficult situation at the very start. The soldiers were also in the service of France. So, they might well go on joint expeditions, which was not a happy thought. The following morning Zaven presented himself to the French occupation officer, a major who had lost one arm in combat. Zaven was somewhat relieved by the major's statement that he and his men were part of the French Army.

Weeks went by, and all was well. Although incredible, it seemed that the Turks had humbly resigned themselves to their new fate. But Zaven was not convinced. Could this be the quiet before the storm? Regardless, it suited him because the men needed training.

One day Zaven was at the training field. One of his aides, an accomplished horseman, was showing the men how to pick up something from the ground while riding at a gallop and how to cling to the side of the horse to become a smaller target. The major's orderly appeared on the field. Zaven rode up to him.

"The major wishes to see you, sir," was the message.

"Now?" Zaven asked.

"Yes, sir."

Zaven rode alone to the villa on the hill overlooking the town. Its former occupant, the German liaison officer, had left it intact. The major, a confirmed bachelor, loved luxury. Cooks, chambermaids, and guards swarmed all over the place. Zaven tied his horse outside the main entrance, acknowledging the salute of the posted guard, and walked in. The door of the major's private room was partly open. He stood by the window, turned, and stepped forward. Zaven saluted and tried not to stare at the major's left shoulder, against which the long, empty sleeve of his uniform shirt was pinned up. The missing arm caused him to stand slightly off kilter, but otherwise he seemed healthy enough.

"I've received an order from the Commanding General," said the major, grabbing Zaven's arm with his preternaturally strong right hand and closing the door. "You're to leave for Adana immediately. I believe the Commandant wants you to enlarge your forces. Soon we will extend our occupation zone. We want men we trust. A train going to Adana will arrive within an hour. I want you to be on it."

"I haven't much time then."

"Yes, good luck. Take two men along with you."

With Dio and another man, Zaven rode to the station, which was about a mile away. They barely made the train. Three others, who had accompanied them to the station, led the horses back. The train was packed with troops and passengers, most of them Armenian refugees finally liberated from the Bedouins. They squeezed into a wagon.

The train was slow-moving and took almost three hours to make the twenty or so miles. After arriving Zaven and his two companions took a carriage and went directly to Erevant's, who had prospered greatly. He had bought the whole building, enlarged his café, and converted the upper stories into a hotel. Zaven congratulated the clever ex-outlaw. After reporting to the French military headquarters, he visited the barracks. The size and numbers had increased. There were private homes next to the hastily put together square wooden shacks for the men. He was pleased to learn that Sona had left for the United States just a few days before.

While sitting in the café in a lighthearted mood, Zaven was startled by a man stalking into the large, smoke-filled room. Zaven gazed at him, scrutinizing every move of the approaching figure and every line of the stern face. He froze. Was he dreaming, or by some strange event had he leaped backward through the years? His brain whirled along with the smoke clouds in the saloon. The figure now stood in front of him; he felt as if a cool wind had swept across his face and then he realized that this was no dream. The figure was real: It was Hagop, the man who had made him what he was!

Zaven rose, dazed, took a step forward, and stood speechless. Hagop was looking at him stupefied, no less overcome. For a moment the two stood there staring at each other.

"Why, Zaven, it is you!" shouted Hagop, throwing his arms around him. "What are you doing here? And in that uniform!"

"Yes, it's me, serving France."

The occupants of the café gathered around them. The two men sat down. There was so much to say, enough to keep them talking for days and nights. Erevant sent the overcurious audience back to their seats and stood there with two glasses in his hand.

"Thank you, Erevant, now I am the happiest man in the world," Zaven cried.

"I share your happiness," said Erevant, patting Zaven's shoulder, "and will do my part." He filled the glasses, raised his and shouted, "To this happy reunion!"

"After I sent you off, I cursed myself a thousand times," said Hagop, lighting a cigarette. "Now, tell me what happened to you."

"A great deal," smiled Zaven, and launched into a long, mesmerizing account of his adventures that had every head in the café—especially Erevant's—craning every which way to eavesdrop.

Hagop listened without interrupting him.

"I always believed that you would pull through," he said. "I came here and found my wife and you, too, Zaven."

"That calls for a drink. For finding your wife, I mean. What about your little boy?"

"He died," Hagop answered sadly.

Erevant came to announce everything was prepared and ready upstairs in a private room. They followed him. One look at the lavish table and the sizzling roast in the center was proof enough that Erevant knew his business. Five of them, including the host, took their places around the table. Now it was Hagop's turn to tell his story.

They ate, drank, and listened. Hagop had waited for Zaven three days in the mountains, then had given up hope and moved on. After several scrambles with the soldiers , he succeeded in crossing the border. In Armenia he served under the celebrated warrior, General Antranig, an outlaw himself. In the regular army Hagop distinguished himself and gained the rank of captain. Things were quiet in Armenia. After learning that France was gathering Armenian refugees in Adana, Hagop had taken a leave of absence and came here hoping to find his family.

"Do you have to return?" asked Zaven.

"No, I don't have to, now that we are together again. But that is how I feel." He looked at Zaven and smiled.

"That is the nicest thing that could happen to me," replied Zaven, pressing Hagop's arm.

"Will you have me in your group then?"

"I will have you as my leader."

"From what I've heard of the reputation of the bandit of Bursa, I feel inferior compared to him."

"Once a leader, always a leader," Zaven declared. "And you could not have come at a more opportune time. The French want to enlarge the corps of scouts. That's why I'm here. And I was feeling that the job was getting to be too big for me."

"You said that very nicely, Zaven," Hagop smiled. "I would be happy to join you."

"We will serve together, and for the good of all concerned, let me handle it my way, Captain Hagop."

Hagop shrugged his shoulders.

The glasses were emptied and refilled over and over. Hagop could take his liquor, but he became very animated. He hurled the last glass he had emptied against the fireplace.

"I want to tell you this," he said in a grim voice, "whatever the Turks did to us, we did the same to them and more. So, everything is even. Now there is work to be done, and Adana is closer to my heart than Armenia."

CHAPTER 22

Hagop was introduced to the French commandant. Zaven didn't have any problem convincing the commandant that Hagop, a former outlaw and now a captain, was the right man to command an enlarged corps of scouts. Recruiting and equipping the volunteers fell upon Hagop's shoulders. Zaven had no reasons to stay in Adana. Hagop accompanied him to the station and waited on the platform until the train pulled out.

When he arrived in Smyrna, Zaven saw through the window several of his men huddled on the platform when the train stopped. How did they know that he would be on that train? He stepped out. The men slowly walked over to him. They greeted him, but it was perfunctory—not the kind of greeting Zaven expected. He looked at them. They looked grim.

"Is all well?" he asked.

"Didn't you receive a telegram?" answered one.

"What telegram?"

The men looked at each other.

"What's wrong? Come out with it!" he barked.

"There has been an accident," blurted one.

"What sort of accident?"

"Kevork killed himself, but before doing so he killed two soldiers."

Zaven's lips tightened. His face showed rage more than grief. No one else got out of the train. They walked stiffly toward their horses and mounted. Zaven turned to the man riding beside him.

"How did it happen?"

"Kevork was in a tavern last night. Two soldiers insulted him. Kevork shot them on the spot. The other customers ran for their lives. Kevork barricaded himself in the store. We went after him. He had to either kill himself or some of us."

After a moment's silence Zaven grumbled, "Fool, but brave enough to end it that way."

They stopped momentarily at the gate of the inn. The others rode in, but Zaven headed for the major's quarters. To face him would be difficult. He ignored the salute of the guard by the door. Then he nearly overlooked the formality of being admitted. The tactful noncom covered the error.

"Yes, lieutenant," he said in a loud voice, "the major is expecting you."

Zaven threw him a casual glance, and walked in. His salute was of the matter-of-fact variety. They gazed at each other for a while in silence.

"Hope you enjoyed your trip, lieutenant," said the major. "I deeply regret that this unpleasant situation forced me to call you back. How far did you get?"

"All is done, sir. I learned about your telegram when I stepped off the train here."

The major went to his chair. "Sit down, Zaven," he said. "You have my heartfelt condolences. I want you to know that I understand fully what occurred. Had you been here, it might not have happened. But, no man is bigger than the job entrusted to him."

Zaven's pressed his fingers to his forehead. The major watched him sympathetically.

"I understand, sir," said Zaven. "I promise on behalf of myself and my men, you will receive our wholehearted cooperation."

"The case is closed, but I wanted to hear you say that, as a precautionary measure. While the tempers are still high, I advise you to keep calm."

"Yes, sir."

"Now, tell me what you did in Adana."

"Soon you will have eighty more scouts, and a new commanding officer."

"A new commanding officer," repeated the major. "As I remember you were sent there to recruit men. I'm satisfied with my officer in command. If there were to be changes, I expect to know."

"I'm sure you will receive a full report on that matter, sir."

"And what would you be doing in the meantime?" asked the major, looking directly at Zaven.

"Still serving France as a loyal subordinate, sir, if you will have me," Zaven replied quickly.

The major pounded the desk with his fist. "Who did that? I thought all was arranged. I will have something to say about it."

"There has been no interference, sir. As a matter of fact, it was I who recommended strongly that Captain Hagop should be the one in command."

"Who is this captain you're speaking about?" the major asked in a measured voice.

"He is someone who made me what I am. He fought his way through the lines and joined the regular Armenian forces in the Caucasus. He got his release and came to Adana hoping to find his family."

"Did he have any luck?"

"Yes, he found his wife."

The major rose and circled once around the room. He stopped behind the desk, and looked directly at Zaven. "Won't finding his wife make things different?"

"No, sir. He was born a fighter. Nothing will stop him."

"You're a bigger man that I thought, lieutenant. If it is your doing, it must be right. I won't keep you any longer."

Simultaneously with the arrival of Captain Hagop came the news that the bandits who had not appeared on the scene during the winter months were on a rampage. They had blocked a road and killed several Christian travelers. Hagop was ordered to go after them.

After a day's ride, the scouts reached the small Armenian town of Kessab, close to the Mediterranean shore. It was a picturesque little town famous for its orange groves, nestled in the foothills of the Taurus mountain range. Here they joined a mixed force of twenty-five hundred made up of Turkish soldiers, along with French, and Hindu, supplied by England as a gesture of collaboration. It was a formidable force to move against the elusive bandits in the mountains. To Zaven, it was a similar, ludicrous story. No one understood the situation better than Hagop and Zaven. What success had the Turkish Army had chasing them? Left to their own devices, Hagop and Zaven would have divided their men between them, and slipped quickly into the mountains to kill the bandits or die. But governments do things differently. Now there was a potent force set on certain victory. Hagop and Zaven looked at each other. If they had anything to worry about, it was the presence of the Turkish soldiers. If the occasion arose, which side would they take? But Hagop was not one who would take a chance. He instructed his men never to let Turks get behind them whenever there was the likelihood of action.

The combined force commanded by a French colonel halted at the entrance of the narrow trail that wound through the ravine leading to the interior of the densely wooded mountains. Twenty men waiting in ambush on the slopes could do a lot of damage. Aware of this, the colonel discussed the situation with his staff.

Hagop turned to his lieutenant. "We'd better lead them into the mountains. We can do it in a way that no sane outlaw would take the risk of showing that he is around."

Zaven nodded. Hagop approached the colonel. "Sir, will you allow me to clear the trail?" he asked.

The officer accepted the offer without hesitation.

"I'll start alone," said Hagop. "When I advance about a hundred feet, you tell someone to follow me, and so on, one man at a time, until you get my signal that all is clear. If the bandits are in hiding there, they cannot kill more than one or two of us."

Nothing happened. Zaven received the message and informed the colonel that all was well.

For days the force carried on a diligent but hopeless search for the outlaws. The closest they came to finding them was the discovery of one of their strongholds, and from all appearances the bandits had made a hurried departure. Half a warm calf was left behind.

Then a message came that the bandits had moved down into the plains and raided several villages. The French colonel ordered the mounted detachments, who had left their mounts at the base, to descend to the plains and pursue the bandits while the rest of the force would hold the trails and prevent the bandits from retreating into the mountains. A detachment of the French troops, the Turkish soldiers, and the scouts was sent to the plains. Zaven was amused; how familiar this was to him.

A young French captain was in command. For several days they roamed in the fields, showing up belatedly at the places where the outlaws were reported to be. One morning, while on the course of this wild goose chase, they met a Turkish officer hobbling along. He was unarmed and his clothes were ragged and torn. Zaven knew him—his name was Bakier, and they had exchanged harsh words over the Kevork incident. Bakier's story was that the bandits had caught him and his men at a farmhouse early that morning. After an hour's battle, during which he lost more than half his men, he was forced to surrender, but he managed to escape. Zaven looked at Hagop. To them, the tale sounded pretty thin.

"A commendable exploit, Bakier," snapped Zaven. Then in a low undertone, he added, "But tell us, why did they let you loose?"

Bakier turned red. "I wish you had been with me, lieutenant, or perhaps I should address you by a more fitting name, Daly Mustafa."

Zaven smiled sardonically. Some fifty Turks had joined the bandit, or perhaps a more fitting title, the outlaw, for the cause. But why was Bakier let loose?

"When did you make your escape?" asked the French captain.

"Less than two hours ago, sir," Bakier replied. "The bandits can't be far away. If we hurry, we might overtake them. I will direct you if I am permitted."

Perhaps it was Zaven's skeptical look that raised suspicion in the French captain's mind, for he thought a moment, then said, "You need rest, lieutenant. I will return you to Osmaniieh. Captain Hagop, I want you to assign one of your men to accompany the lieutenant—and you, too, Captain Bakier." He addressed the commander of the soldiers: "I want you to provide a horse and assign three of your men as escorts."

Hagop looked at Zaven in dismay. This was bad. One Armenian with four Turks set for a long journey through a territory swarming with outlaws.

"I can't ask anyone to go along with those bastards," Hagop whispered.

"You don't need to ask. I'm going," Zaven replied.

"You're not," Hagop frowned.

"Don't worry," Zaven smiled.

Hagop's angry look suddenly disappeared when he saw Dio pushing his way through the crowd.

"Go ahead, you two," Hagop mumbled as he turned away.

When Zaven and Dio rode in the direction of the four Turks, Bakier seemed to be the one least surprised. What a break this was for him. The French captain looked puzzled. He might have realized his error, but it would be worse to try to change it.

"Well, it'll be nice to have your company, lieutenant," said Bakier haughtily, "but don't you think that you might be missed?"

"Oh, they'll get along without me," Zaven smiled. "It is much more important to me to see that you get to Osmaniieh safe and sound."

Zaven rode by Bakier. Dio fell back, letting the other three Turks ahead of him. Bakier noted this maneuver and shrugged his shoulders while riding along. He scanned the hills as if expecting someone. Then he threw a sideways glance at Zaven, watching him like a hawk with a frigid smile. They were riding through a small village midway in their journey. The Turks halted by the side of a gate and prepared to dismount.

"What's on your minds?" Zaven asked harshly.

"We're looking for food and something to drink," answered Bakier.

"Stay in your saddles. I'll have it brought if needed."

"He's looking for trouble," one of the soldiers muttered.

"True enough," cried Zaven, "and it's you who will get it if you don't follow orders."

"Oh, come on, let's move," mumbled another, urging his horse forward.

In an hour they would reach Osmaniieh. The danger of encountering the outlaws at this point was very slim. This had been Zaven's main worry while riding along the narrow roads and through the slopes. The remaining part of the journey ran through the plains. He seemed greatly relieved.

Suddenly, Bakier turned his horse and faced him, pointing at Zaven's hat, to which was fastened a silver insignia designating his office and origin.

"That badge on your hat," he said, "betrays you. I would advise you to take it off. I have a hunch that the bandits are lurking about. Should they attack, our only chance will be to surrender. But then, they would not need a second guess to identify you after seeing that thing."

Bakier moved forward. Zaven remained motionless, staring at him. Behind them Dio had already leveled his rifle.

"Be careful," warned Zaven. "In spite of how I feel, I still want to take you alive to Osmaniieh."

Bakier stiffened. What did he have on his mind? The three soldiers turned to see what was happening. A glimpse of Zaven's cold, expressionless face left no doubt that their lives, to him, were as insignificant as the whispering breeze. They dropped their heads, spurred their mounts, and moved on.

"I meant no wrong," Bakier apologized.

Zaven laughed. "Now move on," he commanded, "and pray that we don't meet your patrons. I'm not one to take chances."

Bakier moved forward. Zaven stayed behind him.

"I want to be straight with you," said the Turk. "When the peasants informed us that the outlaws had surrounded the place, my men refused to fight. They disarmed me and sent me out to find you."

"To lead us into a trap," Zaven growled.

"No," Bakier protested. "Believe me, they made me do it."

"Move on, you have said enough," Zaven commanded.

They rode directly to the headquarters of the major. Zaven was closeted with the French officer for about fifteen minutes. When he came out, he found Dio waiting alone.

"Two soldiers took him out of my hands, and the others were ordered to report to their barracks and remain there until further orders," said Dio.

Zaven mounted his horse and looked at his watch. "We have a couple of hours' daylight," he said. "What about starting the trip back right away?"

"Suits me, but not before I moisten my parched throat. What about the guards? Aren't you supposed to take them along?"

"No, I told the major that I would feel safer without them."

They went to their favorite cafe, operated by a good-natured Arab. The place looked empty. They settled down, ordered anisette, barbecued mutton, and freshly made salad. The bottle of anisette was soon half empty, but it took time to make fresh salad and barbecue mutton. The chubby Arab had just placed the sizzling meat before the customers when they all turned toward the door, which opened with an ominous screech. One of the guards who had made the trip appeared in the doorway. He hesitated a moment, then walked directly toward Zaven, who, somewhat surprised, responded to the guard's salute with a nod and invited him to take a seat.

"Thank you, sir," replied the guard, drawing up a chair.

"Care for a drink?"

The guard's eager eyes answered, and Zaven asked for another glass.

After draining his glass in one gulp, the guard spoke.

"Sir," he said, "I've really come here to square myself with you. In the first place, I want you to know that I am an Arab and care no more for the Turks than you do. Next, I want you to know that they had ideas, but should anything have happened, you would have found out where my sympathies lay."

Zaven smiled. "And ... your name?"

"Ihmed, sir."

"Listen, Ihmed, all is over. I've arranged it so that you can stay here."

"Would you trust me, sir, if I give you my word of honor?"

Zaven looked hard and long at him.

"Don't leave me here, sir. Trust me. My village is on the way. The last time I saw my family was two months ago. Allah alone knows when I may see them again."

Dio's quick, penetrating glance and nod answered Zaven's question about the Arab's honesty.

"May my head be forfeited if I have treachery in my heart," he went on, adding pleadingly, "Say that you'll be my guest for the night."

"Are you married, Ihmed?"

"Yes. I have a wife and two children. One I haven't even seen yet."

"You must have missed your wife badly, Ihmed," Dio interjected, jauntily filling the guard's glass. "How did you get in this pickle?"

"I volunteered. My father can handle the farm, and the money I earn serves us well."

"I accept the invitation," declared Zaven. "We'll start soon after eating."

"I wish you would leave some room for my wife's cooking, sir. She's a good cook."

"I've no doubt, and we'll look forward to taking a second supper at your home," smiled Zaven. "In the meantime, share this meal with us."

"Thank you, sir."

"Where's your horse?"

"Right outside. I gave the excuse to come down here to eat."

"On our way, we'll drop off to tell them that you are coming with me."

They were on the verge of leaving the place when a Turkish policeman aimlessly walked in. He lingered around, threw a sidelong glance at Zaven and his companions, exchanged a few meaningless words with the proprietor, then stepped out. Zaven did not like the man. When they came out of the café, he saw him again, but tried to dismiss his suspicions.

The journey proved to be a pleasant one. Though it wasn't news to Zaven, Ihmed gave him some inside information about the loyalty of the Turkish mercenaries in the service of the French.

At dusk they reached the village, a wretched-looking place, composed of not more than twenty-five clay huts. Ihmed's house was a one-story, rambling affair, with a sandy flat roof, encircled by a wooden fence, forming a sort of courtyard. They rode in through a wide opening that served as a gate. Ihmed's father, an elderly, simple-looking peasant, greeted them enthusiastically. Contrary to custom, the wife, her few weeks' old baby, and a half-naked three-year-old boy, were introduced. The delicious meal prepared by Ihmed's wife lived up to her husband's accolades. Afterwards, they chatted for a while; the old man did most of the talking. He told about his woes, about the menace of outlaws, and elaborated upon the political situation and his views. He seemed to believe that the country would be much better under the mandate of France. The young woman entered the room with a bulky mattress upon her shoulder.

"Ihmed," said Zaven, "if it isn't too much trouble, have our bed prepared on the roof."

Ihmed smiled. "You don't take chances, do you, sir? I don't blame you for that."

The guard rose. He could do the job better than his wife. When Zaven and Dio climbed up on the roof, they found two mattresses spread side by side in the middle.

The night was full of mystery; the moon was high in a cloudless sky and the refreshing breeze delighted their senses. The whole world seemed to be at peace. Not a sound disturbed the stillness, but they couldn't, or dared not, sleep. Instead they lay silently on their beds.

The moon faded away, leaving a purplish streak behind it. It was dark, but their eyes became accustomed to the darkness. Suddenly, Dio sat up, looked around, and then crept to the edge of the roof. Zaven watched him. There hadn't been any sign whatsoever to justify their uneasiness. It was instinct, perhaps a sixth sense that people like them possess. In the dusk, they could discern the outline of a form moving toward the house. They were ready. They hadn't even taken off their boots nor loosened their cartridge belts. Dio turned to Zaven, and crouched beside him.

"Can you make out their number?" whispered Zaven.

"No, but they're armed and getting closer," replied Dio.

"We will let them get closer—as close as possible."

"Should we warn Ihmed?"

"No time, the dog will do that."

They looked at their horses. A pair of spirited thoroughbreds, trained to complement the temperament of their masters, stood below them, skittishly stamping the ground with their great hooves.

"They're restless," commented Dio.

"Their instinct is stronger than ours, Dio," Zaven remarked.

"What about that good-for-nothing mongrel lying by the gate? Two of them are nearly on top of him, and still not a yelp."

Dio hadn't quite finished his words when the big dog sprang up, growled between his gnashing teeth, and leaped forward. A shining object in the shape of a cutlass swayed in the darkness. The dog, with a pathetic whine, fell flat.

"See," whispered Zaven, "the mongrel had sense. We'll wait until they get into the courtyard. They seem sure of themselves, and that faint yelp won't waken anyone. We'll use grenades. That will stop them long enough for us to get on our horses."

A sudden explosion disturbed the quietness of the night, followed by the appearance of two mounted figures dashing through the courtyard. Two figures, standing numb by the gate, toppled into the dust under the blows of swords. There followed gunfire, but the riders didn't even take the trouble to look back. They were in the open, flying like arrows in the dark. The guns kept on booming, but the echo was getting weaker and weaker. Who were the bullets aimed at? They paused and looked back; it was incredible that they could have covered so much distance in such a short time.

The echo of the shot was barely audible, but the place they had left behind was in flames. Was it the grenade that had done it? Anyway, that was immaterial. True enough, there was Ihmed, the old man, the wife, and the children, but they had no time to think about them. They had a job ahead, and the job was to join Hagop. There was no use planning on charting a course; just do one thing at a time and cover as much ground as they could before sunrise, which wasn't far off.

Zaven rode up close beside Dio, tapped his shoulder, and said, "It could have been worse."

CHAPTER 23

Captain Hagop was pleasantly surprised that Zaven and Dio were back in time to share the meal with him.

"So, you think they took it out on the poor guard and his family?" reflected Hagop.

"Looked that way," Zaven replied.

"You have to report it, but before you do, I want to finish this meal in peace."

When Zaven reported the incident to the French captain, he was ordered to return with the captain and his troops to the scene of the crime. This time, however, the guards were left behind. They reached the village late that night and found life normal there, except that a hut was burned to the ground. No one could tell what became of the occupants. The glib tale that bandits had burned the house couldn't be verified, though the captain tried. Zaven knew how to force the villagers to tell what they knew, but in this situation he could not do it.

After several weeks of chasing the outlaws, the troops were gradually disengaged, even though not a single outlaw was killed or captured.

Soon after, a small French railway outpost about fifty miles north in the vicinity of the town of Bakcha was attacked. Six soldiers were murdered. Hagop was ordered to send half his men to Bakcha, and Zaven, with sixty men, was assigned to this new post.

Toward noon, halfway along the road to Bakcha, Zaven and his men, with Dio and Eremia among them, reached a farm. It appeared to be prosperous, with a large home and open courtyard, and a number of sheep and cows grazing in a nearby field. Zaven dismounted and went in search of the master, planning to have him feed his men and see to their tired horses. The men, sensing the leader's intentions, wasted no time and dismounted.

"Well," chuckled Dio, "they're leaving our host no alternative."

"I hope these men can afford it," commented Zaven.

"That's his worry," retorted Dio. "I only hope that he has some barley for the horses."

As he swung the gate open, the farmer came into sight from a corner of the house. He was an old man and did not look healthy. Zaven's appearance seemed to have frightened him, but after staring at the hard-looking young officer and his tough subordinate armed to his teeth, he managed to bow ridiculously.

"At your service, Master," he mumbled in a quivering voice.

"Grandfather, we've been riding since sunrise. Some bread and pilaf will do us good. In addition, if you can spare a little grain for our horses, we'll be grateful and pay for it."

"Genuine hospitality accepts no compensation, Master," said the old peasant, bowing again. "What I have is yours, and the fact I have served you is my reward."

"I will remember that," Zaven declared ceremoniously.

At that moment two young boys with closely shave heads, and clad in long blue cotton trousers that could have stood laundering, ran into the courtyard.

"Cool off the commandant's horse," ordered the old man. He turned to Zaven and added, "May Allah preserve your steed from the evil eye. He is a fine animal, Master."

Zaven thanked the obsequious farmer and walked with him into the courtyard, where they stopped at a portico. Presently, two women, wrapped in customary flowing charkhas, arrived with loads of mattresses and pillows.

While they waited, the portico was transformed into an inviting place for rest. The women disappeared as quickly as they had appeared. Dio stayed behind to send out the sentinels. The old farmer, his hands crossed upon his abdomen, stood at the entrance. Zaven sat on the mattresses, looked at the old man, and asked courteously, "Whose hospitality am I enjoying?"

"Hussein, the Lame, your servant," answered the peasant with a bow.

"Well, Hussein, come and sit with me," said Zaven, which was a command, not an invitation.

The old man hesitated. He had extended time-honored affability to his guest but the law of the land, as he knew it, would not give him the right to sit with an officer. He obeyed by squatting on the boards. Zaven shook his head, pointing to the mattress. The old man submitted timidly and took his place beside his guest. Zaven offered him a cigarette.

"Hussein, I've no doubt that you know why I am here. Have the bandits troubled you?" he asked quietly.

"Allah be praised, Master, so far I am spared from the scourge of the scoundrels."

He avoided Zaven's eyes, and glanced uneasily about him. It was obvious to Zaven that bandits or outlaws would not miss a bountiful farm like this.

"Hussien," urged Zaven, "tell me again, have you seen the bandits?"

"Indeed, no," mumbled the old man, but he looked alarmed.

"The last time you saw them," Zaven hinted slyly, "how many were they?"

"That I don't know. But I've heard that there are hundreds."

He exaggerated the numbers. Why? This was not a good sign.

From the very start, while the old man hobbled ahead of him, Zaven had made certain deductions. He was comparatively well-to-do, a regional leader. Therefore, he could not remain aloof. How well did he know the outlaws? Zaven wanted to find out.

"You seem to know more than you pretend," he snapped. Then he made a wild guess. "Was it not you who sent word to Osmaniieh some weeks ago that bandits had raided your place? Be careful, Hussien, I know more than you think."

"No, no!" cried the old man. "As Allah is my witness, I have no cause to hide anything. My daily prayers are for peace."

"Your information will do more good than your prayers. Come, you're an honest man. You would not lie and be foolish."

"Forgive me, Master, I was afraid."

"Afraid of what?" said Zaven, looking sharply at the old man.

"Believe me, Master, I had no desire to shelter the knaves who raided my place, took my money, two of my horses, and ordered six of my best sheep killed and fried."

"That I understand," Zaven grunted.

Two large copper trays containing more variety of food than Zaven expected were laid down before him. Zaven tried hard to have his host share the meal with him, but no use. The old man was really worried. When Zaven finished eating, the old man set the copper washing pan before him and began pouring water on Zaven's hands. The dishes were cleared. The old man stood by the entrance of the portico with his hands crossed upon his abdomen. Dio came to report that the men had finished eating and were ready to depart.

Zaven turned to the old man, looked straight into his eyes, and said softly, "You are coming with me."

The old man fell at his feet, pleading.

"Take him away, Dio," was the curt command.

Dio and the old peasant emerged from the stables; the latter was perched on a lean mule. He looked pitiful. Zaven spurred his mount and moved ahead. At sundown they were at the outskirts of Bakcha, a little town with flat-roofed dwellings in the mountains. To the left was the fabled high peak, Ararat, lording over the famous pass of Amanus. They attracted considerable attention as they rode through the dusty streets. Presently, they were met by a French noncom who directed them to their quarters. This was a long, one-story stone building used as a school for the Armenian children before the deportation. It included a large hall and two small rooms. Zaven occupied one of them.

The French commanding officer, a captain, stepped over the conventional official line to express how pleased he was to have Zaven on his side. His brief outline of the situation indicated that things around Bakcha were very grim. Zaven would have more or less a free rein to deal with the situation as he thought best. He liked that. He thanked the captain, told him that he would do all he could, and left without mentioning that he had a prisoner.

Back at his quarters, the hustle of settling down had ended. Zaven walked through the length of the hall where the men lounged on their blankets with colorful tapestry saddlebags serving as pillows. He cast a sideways glance at the old man sitting cross-legged in the corner, looking miserable and afraid. He walked into his room. Eremia had prepared his place. To his surprise he had a mattress and a hard pillow. Zaven smiled.

"While you were away, we had visitors," said Eremia.

"Visitors? Isn't this a bit premature?" Zaven mumbled.

"I didn't expect them, either, but they were the welcoming committee of Armenians, including children. You should have seen their faces, Zaven. One of the women ran back and brought the mattress and the pillow for you."

"That's very nice, but I can do without it. Where's Dio?"

"He walked out with them."

"Didn't he resist the temptation?" Zaven frowned.

"He tried, but they wouldn't listen. They told us that ever since they returned back to their homes, they have been waiting for this day."

Zaven relaxed on the mattress. He was tired, but his tiredness wasn't physical. He looked at Eremia, whose friendly countenance had suddenly become sullen.

"Heaven help us not to let them down," muttered Zaven. Then, in a clearer voice, he added, "How many families came back to their homes?"

"About twenty-five or thirty."

"I was told that once more than half of the town's population was Armenian; that makes it roughly one out of ten coming back."

Dio returned, accompanied by several members of the self-appointed reception committee, who in all probability had taken the last morsel from their pantries to supply a meal for those they revered.

A large, hand-painted tablecloth was spread in the middle of the floor in the hall. Food and drinks were arranged on it. Zaven acknowledged the greeting and tried to dispel the anxiety of the returning Armenians with reassuring words, but he had no appetite, nor was he in a celebratory mood. His distracted voice and reluctance to join in the frivolity made it clear to everyone that he had serious things on his mind. He walked back to his room; Dio followed him.

"I understand, Zaven," he said in an apologetic voice, "but I could not refuse them."

"All right, make it short," Zaven said sternly.

Dio walked out. Soon all was quiet. The rustic kerosene lamp on the wall cast its dingy yellow rays, giving the small room an eerie look. Dio pushed the trembling old peasant into the room. He flopped upon his knees before the young officer.

"Hussien," Zaven addressed him gently but firmly, "I have eaten of your salt and meat ; therefore, I all the more loathe to handle you roughly. At least I have not handed you over to the French, who would have sent you to heaven knows where. You have certain information I want."

"I'll tell you all I know, sir," the old man answered pleadingly, but he found no sign of mercy in the officer's eyes.

"How many bandits were there when they came to your place?" Zaven asked.

"On my oath, I don't know," mumbled the old man.

"Listen, you old ass, so far I've tried to be good to you. But my patience has its limit." He stood up and seized him by the shoulders. "Tell me, how many?"

The old peasant still remained obdurate. He shook his head. "That I do not know." Then, looking up at Zaven, he murmured, "I didn't count them."

"You're lying!" shouted Zaven, but inwardly he was relieved to see that the old man was weakening. He nodded to Dio, who walked out and momentarily returned, accompanied by two big brutes, one of them carrying a heavy knotted stick and a rifle.

Now Zaven was doubly sure that the old man knew all he expected of him. His problem was to make him talk without actually hurting him. First he must eliminate any hope that, deep down, he was not as ruthless as he looked.

The old man looked dazed as Dio ordered him to take off his sandals and stockings. Again the unfortunate man looked pleadingly at Zaven.

"Stretch him out!" Zaven shouted.

"You would not beat an old man, would you, son?" he whimpered.

"I'll thrash you as far as death's door if you don't talk."

"Son, don't do it. You're brave and young. Don't soil your hands in this fashion."

"You can save yourself; this is my last warning. I will make you talk. Yes, even if I have to break every rotten bone in your body. Don't toy with my patience."

The men were ready to work on him. The old man was convinced, and his will broke. Sobs choked him as he cried, "Let me be, let me be! Allah won't permit me to die this way. I'm too old. Only let me be, and I'll tell you all I know."

"Go on," Zaven shouted. "How many came to your place?"

"About twenty-five."

"You must have known some of them. Give us their names."

"I know none of them."

"Hussien, if I tell them to go on, you will not sit up again."

He was not given time to consider the point. One of the men had him on his back with his feet pushed up and tied with a rope. "Stop!" he cried. "Stop!"

"Their names," Zaven urged. "Give me their names!"

He gave some names. Zaven quickly wrote them down on a sheet of paper. Now that he had loosened the old man's tongue, he had to press on until he had drained every bit of information out of him. It was a grinding ordeal. However, before Zaven was finished with him, he had thirty names on his list. On the surface they were ordinary peasants trying hard to extract a living out of their worn-out lands.

"Now, Hussien," Zaven said, "I have the names. Tell me where I will find them."

The old man hesitated, but it was too late to stop now. His will was broken. He shook all over and gazed at the Mad One through rheumy eyes wide with terror.

"They are from the village of Kazul-Dash," he gasped.

Zaven was through with him. He had all the information he needed, and he felt some measure of gratitude toward the man and rewarded him with a cigarette.

"I will leave soon, but the others will see that you are set free in the morning." He turned to Dio, saying, "Bring in that blacksmith who supplied you with the booze. He ought to know his way around."

"Son," said the old man solicitously, appearing to have regained his composure. What he had gone through had been purely mental torture; physically he was untouched. "What I've told you this night must never come out."

"That's entirely up to you. No others but your family know that I've brought you here. However, if you want to be sure, I can send you away where you will be safe."

"No, son, no one knows about my coming, and as for my family, they will keep their tongues still."

"Good," Zaven declared.

"Will you let me go now?" asked the old man in a pleading voice.

"That is unwise. Wait until morning," Zaven said indifferently.

Dio walked in with the blacksmith behind him. The short, chubby man, who had been talkative and jubilant, now looked grim. He had surmised what kind of a man this youthful leader was. He admired him; with him around he felt safe, but he was scared to be close to him.

"Sit down," Zaven said in a friendly manner. "First I want to tell you that I wouldn't have asked you to come if I didn't really need you. Don't be alarmed. If there was any danger, I wouldn't be here."

The blacksmith's face brightened a bit. "If there's a-anything I can d-do ..." he stammered.

"How far is the village Kuzul-Dash from here?" Zaven asked pointedly.

"That notorious place? It should be turned into ashes along with everyone in it. Why, even before the war the men from there never did an honest day's work, but robbed and plundered the neighboring villages."

"I suspected that. Who knows, we may take your advice. But you haven't answered my question."

"Oh, yes, it's about ten miles from here, deep in the mountains."

"Can you take us there tonight? Not through the roads, but by a roundabout way so that we'll be there before daybreak."

The blacksmith pondered a moment. "Yes, I can," he mumbled, "but we have to go on foot."

"I'm aware of that, and I intend to make it a complete surprise. Have you ever used a rifle?" asked Zaven, smiling.

"I do fairly well with a shotgun," answered the blacksmith.

"You'll do all right," said Zaven. He turned to Dio. "Give him a rifle."

"I should have brought my dagger," the blacksmith lamented.

Zaven laughed. "You won't get the chance to use it, so don't get excited. Just take us there as quietly as you can."

Those who anticipated a good night's sleep after the day's ride were sorely disappointed, when Zaven ordered all but five to get ready.

"Take an opposite direction at the start," said Zaven to his guide, standing beside him.

"I understand," the blacksmith consented.

It wasn't an easy march through the narrow trail. They stumbled over the rocks and exposed roots, and were slapped by hanging branches. When they reached the top of a barren, rocky peak, they saw a deep valley before them. The blacksmith touched Zaven's arm and pointed out the village down below. "This is it," he said.

"We made it in good time," Zaven commented. "Let's relax a bit."

Legs outstretched, his back against a massive rock, Zaven watched the magnificent spectacle of the sunrise through the mountains. For the moment his mind was completely detached from the impending task. He hadn't yet decided how to tackle it. Whatever he did would be impulsive, and he hoped that it would be successful. He stood up and raised his arm.

"We will surround the village," he cried, addressing his men, "but don't get too close to the houses and don't let anyone get out. This is all I can say for now."

He started descending, while the men spread out in all directions. The howling and barking of the vigilant dogs signalled to the villagers that something strange was going when Zaven and six others appeared in the narrow street.

A gate opened halfway. A head appeared and disappeared behind it. Zaven walked to it and pounded with his heavy boots.

"Come on out! You, the son of a jackass!" he shouted. "If you don't want me to knock off that fat head of yours."

There was no answer. He was on the verge of breaking the gate off its hinges when it opened. A trembling, half-dressed, middle-aged man faced Zaven. He wanted to say something, but he stuttered.

"All right," Zaven interrupted in a softer voice. "I am an officer. Take me to the Muhtar."

"That I will, sir. Please forgive my doubts. If you will give me time to put something on ..."

He was not long, as there was not much that he had put on—baggy breeches and a sleeveless jacket.

The Muhtar's house was the best in the village. Zaven pounded on the door with his fists. In a few moments, a bright-eyed boy in his early teens opened the door. He gazed at the unexpected visitors in bewilderment.

"The commandant wishes to see your father," mumbled the escort.

"My father sleeps," the boy replied. "But if you'll allow me a few minutes ..."

The boy went back inside, closing the door behind him. Zaven waited uneasily, surveying the situation. So far, so good. Suddenly, two distinct shots reverberated in the peaceful morning air. Zaven looked at Dio. He assumed the Muhtar had ordered the firing to either frighten or kill Zaven. Zaven and Dio flattened themselves against the wall. He waited. The shots were not repeated. It was a relief. Dio wanted to ask something, but Zaven's eyes gave the answer. The Muhtar had to be reminded that they were still there waiting for him. This time Dio went into action, using the butt of his rifle. If the shots had not awakened everyone in the village, this pounding should.

It didn't take long for the door to open. A man with the keen, temperate face of a mature diplomat stood there. He saluted with traditional courtesy.

"These are bad times. I pray that you come with good tidings, sir," uttered the Muhtar, nervously stroking his graying mustache.

"Good, Mahmud," Zaven replied. The headman of the village looked surprised at being addressed by his name.

"Your mounts, sir. I must see that they are attended to."

"We came by foot, and my men are outside the village. I regret to say that they have orders to shoot anyone attempting to get out without my consent."

The Muhtar stared at Zaven with alarm and said nothing.

"Send word to everyone," Zaven continued, "to gather at your house as soon as possible. I have a message for all of you."

"Kurban," said the Muhtar in a cordial voice, "if some evil-minded one intimated that you may find those you are looking for here, you were misinformed. No, I am not going to deny they have been here, but believe me, we had little to say about the matter. There are no soldiers, no troops here. We cannot stop them."

Zaven left two men outside and, with the rest of his troops in tow, followed the Muhtar. They ascended a stone stairway leading to the flat roof in the center of an ample cabin. In keeping with the dignity of its owner, the large room was furnished more elaborately than is customary in small villages. There were fine woven rugs scattered about the floor, as well as soft mattresses for the indolent. The long, hard pillows, with embroidered cases, did not belong there, but the things that struck Zaven's eyes most were the two silver candlesticks placed on the mantelpiece. No doubt, these once were the property of an Armenian church. The Muhtar noticed Zaven's interest.

"These are my most prized possessions, Commandant. They were given to me by a cherished friend."

"Undoubtedly your cherished friend was an Armenian priest, and you couldn't save his life," Zaven scoffed. Then, changing his tone, he added, "Now, let's get down to business. Yes, you're right: I was informed that those I seek are here. I want every grown male summoned here, and be quick about it!"

"Yes, sir," replied the Muhtar weakly.

"Go ahead!" Zaven commanded tersely.

The Muhtar walked out. Zaven paced around the place. Every article he observed and touched reminded him of some poor Armenian, but this was not the time for sentimental thoughts. He had decided on the course of action and did not know how it would end. He walked out on the roof. It was the highest one in the village. From there he could see in all directions. Everything was quiet—depressingly quiet. In the distance, around the village, he could vaguely see men crouched behind the rocks and bushes. That was all well and good, but one thing bothered him: the shots. He did not want to hear another shot. He lingered a little while longer and looked about, attempting to catch some signs. Nothing to worry about. He walked into the room and sat down. He was tired, really tired.

The Muhtar returned. With him came some sixty or seventy frightened peasants, who crowded into the room.

"Are you sure no men have been left out?" Zaven asked.

"They are all here," the Muhtar reassured him.

"You'll forgive me for doubting your word, but I will have to make sure of that. Dio, go out with the Muhtar and make a thorough search of every house in the village. Bring everyone here, also every gun you find."

Twenty-five more men, a dozen rifles, and a large number of small guns were sent in by Dio and his search party. Again Zaven was assured under oath that all the adult males of the village were in the room, but it was Dio's nod that satisfied him.

Now that the villagers were gathered in the room, Zaven wanted to play it safe. He sent a man out to bring in half of his men from outside the village.

"Now," he said, walking toward the door, "my orders are to search every house for concealed weapons. You," ordered Zaven to the closest peasant, "come forward!"

Dio searched him. Of course, he didn't expect to find anything. During the process, Zaven asked the man's name. Sure enough, he was one of those on the list. Zaven had taken pains to memorize every name. Dio received Zaven's signal and knew what to do with him.

The plan worked well enough, but he had only picked half of them. Were the others really not in the room? He had to make sure. He took out his list and checked the names he had already picked. Then he turned to the Muhtar and started reading the names. "These are the men I want, Mahmud. I know that they are in this room. Show me."

A spasm of pain crossed the Muhtar's face. His son's name was on that list, too.

"Sir," he said after a long pause, "whoever gave you the names is a traitor. We are a peace-loving people. Those men are not from this village."

"We will see, but before I go any further, I want you to know this. I was assigned this job. Though my orders are to arrest these men on any pretext, I could wipe out this whole village from the map. I will give you two minutes to think it over."

Complete silence; eyes staring at him. Was the Mad One bluffing?

"Come, we have no time to waste," Zaven said loud enough for everyone to hear.

When the last of his men had filed out, Zaven turned and locked the door behind him. At that instant, the men inside cried out.

"What are you going to do with us?"

"Burn you like rats!" Zaven shouted.

One voice rose above the frenzied shouting: "Let us out! Let us out! The men you want are here!"

Zaven opened the door. An old man who had been hammering upon it collapsed at his feet.

"Allah be praised for showing you the way of mercy," he sobbed. "It is not right that the just should suffer along with the guilty. I'll show you."

Twenty-five men were all placed under arrest, and two more who tried to get out were in safe hands, one wounded.

That the job was done without violence was beyond Zaven's wildest expectations. The prisoners were tied. Zaven and his men took the weapons and ammunition and started out.

They arrived in Bakcha late in the afternoon. Zaven personally took the captives to headquarters.

"What is this rabble?" the captain asked in amazement.

"Members of the band," answered Zaven. "I was informed that they were in a village not far from here. As it was too late to report to you, I took it upon myself to go after them. No incident to report, captain. They're yours."

The captain laughed. "You've lived up to your reputation, lieutenant."

CHAPTER 24

The revolt against the French occupation, which at first was sporadic, grew to alarming proportions. Peasants and outlaws were united for the common cause. Until this time, Marash, a city of some forty thousand inhabitants under British occupation, was to be turned over to the French. Two battalions were consigned to go there. Zaven's unenviable role was to act as vanguard.

The men were in high spirits and unconcerned with the risks of their mission. They left at night, several hours ahead of the troops; their objective was to cover a dangerous mountain pass. It was done without hindrance, and they moved on ahead of the troops. An uninterrupted eighteen-hour march brought them to Marash.

They found that the British forces had left the city. There was a jubilant reception by the committee representing the three thousand Armenian nationals who had drifted back into the city after the British occupation. The American Mission had established an orphanage for the girls found in the Mohammedan homes. Most of them were taken away by force.

The arrival of Zaven and his men was hailed with joy. Festive scenes greeted the scouts; parties were organized in their honor. The French colonel permitted Zaven to set up his quarters in the Armenian district.

Zaven spent over a week in complete rest, after which Hagop arrived along with two thousand reinforcements. Zaven was happy about his friend's advent, but they quartered separately for strategic reasons. The church and the district surrounding it, where most of the Armenian families lived, were Zaven's particular responsibility. Never before had these uprooted people felt so secure in their homes. Zaven wished he could assure them that they could remain permanently in this city.

Here Zaven met a man with whom he became very friendly. A watchmaker by trade, he, too, was from Sivas. His name was Hachik, and he had been picked up from the deportation caravan because the city of Marash needed a watchmaker. His wife, his mother, and his ten-year-old son were with him. He asked Zaven many times to spend a night at his home, but Zaven had declined the invitations because of his duties.

While strolling through the marketplace with Hagop, they visited the watchmaker. He welcomed them warmly and ordered coffee. They sipped their coffee leisurely, smoked their cigarettes, and watched the men and animals milling about outside. It was the busiest site of the bazaar, with low-roofed stores lining either side of the street. A middle-aged man with sharp green eyes like a reptile and a painstakingly-groomed mustache entered the store. His broad shoulders fairly filled the doorframe. He was well dressed in semi-western style clothing and carried a silver-handled whip. He gave the traditional salute, the open palm touching his chest, then his forehead.

"Forgive my intrusion," he said in a caustic manner that left no doubt he thought his august presence was a blessing on the humble shop.

Hagop and Zaven looked at each other. The man turned to the watchmaker. "Is my watch ready?" he asked haughtily.

"It is, sir," replied Hachik, reaching into the sideboard to pick up a heavy gold watch from its hook.

The man took his watch, repeated the salute, and walked out.

"Important-looking man," Zaven commented.

"He is the former Commissar of Internal Security," Hachik said scornfully.

"What is he doing now?" Hagop asked.

Hachik hesitated. "Nothing—he is wealthy and influential."

"His influence … is it good or bad?" Zaven asked.

Hachik thought again. "Bad, very bad, from our point of view. I've been in this store nearly five years. I was here when there were no more than fifty Armenians in this city. Most of them changed their names and vowed publicly that they were confirmed Mussulmen attending the mosque twice a day. I didn't do that; I didn't have to. Men like him wouldn't let me breathe a moment if I wasn't needed. I want to tell you this. The Turks in this city are not as timid as they used to be when the British were here. It's beyond me to figure it out. The French have five times their force in and around the city; the British never had more than two companies at a time. Did the Turks respect the British more? I don't know!"

"How did the British handle the situation?" Zaven asked.

"They paid well and conscripted about three hundred Turkish soldiers who kept things in order the way the British wanted."

Both Hagop and Zaven knew about these soldiers. They were quartered in the fort at the northern edge of the city. The colonel did not quite know what to do with them. He had ordered them to carry on as before, but these guardians of law and order seemed touchy and did not want meddlers.

As they were about to leave, Hachik again urged Zaven to be his guest for the night. Zaven was about to offer the usual excuse when Hagop interrupted.

"It's time for you to have a night off," he said. "You won't be far from your quarters. I'll drop in and tell the men that they have to do without you for the night."

This time Zaven didn't offer any argument. Hachik closed his store earlier than usual and Zaven left with him.

It was a cozy little two-story house at the side of a slanting hill where the indispensable watchmaker from Sivas and his family lived. The first floor, paved with marble, was a combination courtyard and hallway, with a room in the rear used as a kitchen. All the other rooms were on the second floor. The parlor was large and furnished in good taste. Hachik introduced Zaven to the family. The old lady embraced and kissed Zaven. The young wife did not dare go that far, but her greeting was warm just the same. The young boy looked frightened. Zaven patted his head and offered him the insignia that was on his hat. The boy's face glowed with delight.

The table was set in the parlor. The Marash wine, which was famous around the world, loosened Zaven's tongue and held the family spellbound. Long after the coffee had been served, he was still talking. Finally, he leaned back in his chair and apologized.

"Why, Zaven," Hachik protested. "You don't know how long I've been waiting to hear all this. There's also another reason you may think of me as a bit overzealous."

Zaven looked at his countryman, whose face betrayed his struggle to remain an amiable host even as anxiety gnawed at him.

"That man who came to the store just before we left," the watchmaker went on. "He's keeping a young Armenian girl in his home. When he snatched her away she was not more than twelve. Though he already has three wives, he took her, too, as a wife about a year ago."

"Did the British know about this?" Zaven asked.

"Yes, I told them; they took the girl away from him and placed her in an orphanage. She was there only a week; she slipped out and returned to him. She was found and brought back. This time she stayed only three days. Feeling that he had done all he could do, the English commander did not bother anymore. Today she lives with him, seemingly content."

Hackik stared at Zaven, marveling at how one's personality could change so quickly and completely. For the first time since he had known Zaven, he saw the look of a ruthless man who has no regard for human life. Now that he read the answer to his unspoken question—would he rescue the poor concubine?—in Zaven's cold, piercing eyes, he wished that he hadn't said anything about the girl.

"If she can find it in her to care for that kind of a wretch," Zaven grunted, "I have no patience with her kind."

"Please don't be so hasty, Zaven," pleaded Hachik. "This girl is from our own town. It is possible that you know her from the old days, for she comes from your part of the city. Her name is Veronica Seropian. It's just possible she had good reason for going back to him. He is still dangerous. I beg you to have a talk with her before drawing any conclusions."

"Just as you say. But nothing she can do or say will change my feelings. My only concern is that she may get in my way."

"She won't get in your way; that I can assure you. But the problem is, how are we going to arrange it so that you can see her? At one time, before she was placed in the orphanage, my wife could visit her, but now no one is allowed in the house."

"Frankly, Hachik, I am not too keen about seeing that girl," Zaven said coldly, "regardless of who she is or where she comes from. All I want is certain information and I'm sure you can give it to me."

Hachik looked worried. What information was expected of him? How did Zaven intend to handle the case? By himself or through the French? He wanted to free the girl and give her the chance to live with her own people. True, he despised her abductor. He had committed enough crimes to deserve the worst, but he wanted to have him pay the penalty publicly, through the law.

The young wife, who apparently was eavesdropping, walked in. "Perhaps I can arrange for you to see this girl," she said in a shy but confident voice.

Hachik frowned; he did not like her interruption. "You go along and attend to your dishes," he grunted.

The wife shrugged her shoulders. "Thought I could be helpful," she mumbled as she walked away, but Zaven called her back.

"What have you in mind, Satenic?" he asked.

She ignored her husband's scowl and sat on a stool facing Zaven. "On her way to the bath house," she said, "Veronica always drops in for a chat with me. We could arrange for Zaven to be here on one of these occasions. An ambush, as it were."

(It is not generally known that the houses in the cities of Asia Minor at that time had no bathrooms; men and women who wished to keep clean had

to periodically attend public bath houses and remain there the greater portion of the day. Zaven remembered going with his mother when he was a little boy, and then going with his father. It was like a holiday to him.)

"See, Hachik?" Zaven chuckled. "You have a clever wife! But as for talking to her, I doubt if it would do any good."

"I'm almost certain that after meeting her you'll learn that she isn't as bad as she sounds," Hachik said. He turned to his wife and asked, "How are you going to arrange it?"

"That's my concern," she replied saucily. "I've given Zaven my promise. Veronica will be here." With that, she left the room.

Hachik had an inviting bed with clean white sheets prepared for Zaven in the parlor. It was the nicest bed he had lain on for a long time. But he could not sleep. Thoughts, irrelevant and trivial, turned over and over in his mind. He tried hard to bring back all the memories of the days in Sivas, to see if he could remember the family name Seropian. It sounded familiar. Veronica? The name did not ring a bell. She must be a few years younger than him. What would she look like? Would she recognize him? What would he say to her? What would she think of him? His mind raced with scenarios. He got up several times to smoke. That was a relief.

A few days later Hachik told Zaven that Satenic had arranged everything. In the meantime, Zaven had consulted with Hagop, who agreed with him that the former Commissar of Internal Security should receive his righteous punishment without fuss.

On the appointed day, Zaven made his way to Hachik's house. He was led to the familiar room, where a small table was set with relishes and drinks. He was left alone. He smoked and paced around the room. The cuckoo clock whirred open and the ridiculous little bird whistled ten times.

The door opened. Satenic stood in the doorway. "She's coming up the road," she announced and walked downstairs.

Soon he heard the voices of two women from the adjoining room. He was a little perturbed, thinking he had agreed to meet this frivolous creature. Pride, honor, and decency were shattered for one who had taken advantage of her own people. What good could be accomplished by seeing her? But it was too late. He would make the best of the situation.

Satenic appeared again, alone. "She's ready for you now. I told her that you are her cousin. She's frightened. Please be kind to her, Zaven."

"The best I can do is arrange a safe refuge for her," he said.

He followed his hostess into the next room. The girl sat on the couch. Scarcely more than a schoolgirl, she was wholesomely pretty and had a slender figure. She was dressed in a pink skirt and a light blue embroidered blouse. Her long dark hair hung in braids upon which small gold coins on chains were cleverly inserted. She gazed with astonishment at Zaven, trying to figure out from where this cousin of hers had so suddenly appeared. A second and more probing look made her realize that this supposed cousin of hers was not an ordinary man, but rather an important officer. She was shocked.

"This is Zaven, Veronica," Satenic said. The girl gave no sign that she had heard a word.

"I wish you well, Veronica," Zaven greeted her gently. "Please forgive me. I wanted to see you in case I remembered you from Sivas. Our house was opposite the American School, not far from where you lived. Don't let my looks upset you. I'm just an officer in the service of France. I'm here to help you if I can."

Still she said nothing and played with her fingers, like a child in the doldrums.

"Have you anything to say?" Zaven asked in a sympathetic voice.

She nodded, motioning him to sit down on the couch beside her and whispered, "I'm sorry, but you surprised me. I dared not dream that some day I would meet someone like you."

"They didn't kill all of us," Zaven said grimly. "Some of us remained to avenge those who died with their hands tied."

"Satenic told me a little about you," she said in a shocked voice. "It frightened me; you can understand that. But now, I want you to tell me more. Tell me about yourself and what you have done, if you want me to walk out of this house holding my head high."

Her voice and the way she had said it made Zaven ashamed of his thoughts. He could not look at her. Beneath that servile existence lived a proud spirit, waiting for the day to vindicate itself. How dearly she had paid. Death would have been the easier way out, as many others, including his own sister, had done. He was at a loss for words.

"There isn't much to tell," he blurted out. "Frankly, I'm here to seek your consent to do away with the fiend who has you in his clutches."

"Am I worth the risk?"

"That is what I live for. But tell me: Do you care for him?"

Veronica evaded the question. "It's good of you to seek me out." She paused. "No doubt you know my story, and of course you despise me."

"You aren't making it easy for me, Veronica," Zaven said softly. "Can't you understand why I had to see you? As for this man, he must pay for his crimes, whether you agree with me or not."

"What do you want me to say? What do you want me to do?"

"Tell me that you hate him and that there was a reason for you to return to him."

"If I told you that I did not care, would you believe me? The English didn't save me when they put me in the orphanage. The man would have taken me back as long as I was within his long reach. He is wicked and powerful. And right at this moment he is plotting yet another vile scheme. When I went back, I did not think of myself but of those who were in the orphanage. Their lives were in danger every moment I was there."

She began sobbing. Zaven was deeply moved; he moved closer and sympathetically patted her shoulder. Evidently, this man was a bigger menace than he had thought. He would like to know about his activities, and how far he had progressed. But at this point, it did not matter as he had already made up his mind.

"Veronica," he whispered, "supposing I assure you that you will be safe from him forever, that no one will suffer on your account—will you do as I say?"

"Tell me how," she challenged, sitting up straight and looking into his eyes.

He leaned toward her. The temptation to throw his arms around her was great, but he suppressed his feelings.

"Tomorrow night," he said in a low voice, "with a few of my men, I propose to enter your house. I will take you away and make sure you are safe and happy. Please accept me as a brother, and to me you'll be the dearest sister I have ever had."

She touched Zaven's hand, pressing it gratefully as she nodded her consent. Her eyes flashed; the hopelessness was gone. She would make the beast pay and no one would suffer on her account. She looked defiant and no longer shameful. For the first time she imagined that she could find happiness.

"Can this be true?" she whispered in a scarcely audible voice.

"Very true," he said, "as you will soon see. But there are a few things I'd like to know. Is there a dog in the house?"

Veronica shook her head. "He despises dogs."

"As much as they despise him, no doubt," Zaven snorted.

For the first time he saw her smile.

"Does he keep the house guarded?"

She thought a moment. "He has a bodyguard and a valet, but both go to sleep in his part of the house soon after he is in bed."

"Can you manage to leave the front door open after everyone has gone to bed?"

She thought again. "Yes, we all sleep in separate rooms. It won't be out of the ordinary for me to come out of my room on some pretext."

"Good. How many people are in the house?"

"Six other women besides me. Three of them are his other wives. Two are servants, and there is also his young niece." She looked earnestly into Zaven's eyes and said in a slow, measured tone: "She's the only one I care for. I don't want anything to happen to her."

Zaven smiled. "Don't worry; nothing is going to happen to her." Sensing that this casual promise didn't satisfy Veronica, he added, "Women will not be touched. Anyway, how old is this niece of his you seem so concerned about?"

"About my age."

Zaven gently pressed her hand and smiled. "Rest assured, none of them will be harmed. We may tie and gag them for safety, but that is all. You and the three men will be the only ones coming out of the house. And now, if you'll just let me have a rough outline of the rooms."

Veronica mapped out each room in detail and disclosed who slept where. "You won't find his part of the house locked, but some of the women lock the doors from the inside when they go to bed. You may find Zohra's locked."

"Is that the niece's name?" Zaven smiled.

"Yes," replied Veronica.

"You have to convince her to open the door then," Zaven said gently. "And I hope you won't object if we tie her up, too."

There was a knock on the door. Satenic looked in through the half opening, and then entered. She looked very satisfied. Zaven was sure she had been eavesdropping again. She settled down in a chair facing them.

"I wish I knew what you two have been talking about all this time," she said innocently.

"You know all too well," said Zaven. "These walls are thin, and your ears are big."

Satenic's mouth dropped open but she did not fight the accusation. She took a moment to gather her thoughts and began, "I, too, have a confession to make. Even my husband doesn't know about this. But now it must come out. I have been partly responsible for Veronica's misbehavior. I was the one who urged her to return to him, because the fiend, knowing how close we two were, threatened me, and I know he had the power and the means to carry out his threats. I pleaded with her to go back and stay with him for a little while until we all could arrange our escape to Adana. As a matter of fact, Zaven, we had practically completed our plans when you arrived here. That fiend trusts my husband and me—not that he thinks we're grateful for saving us, but because he's so sure that we will never go against him. We aren't afraid of him anymore."

"You've played your hand masterfully, Satenic," commented Zaven.

"Now we must go to the bath house," she said, standing up.

Zaven pressed Veronica's hand and rose. "Tomorrow night, then?" he whispered. The girl nodded meekly.

Turning to Satenic, he asked, "Is the coast clear?"

"Yes, I've seen to it. You have to use the garden door, back of the house. No one will see you until you get down to the main street."

Veronica jumped to her feet. "Tell me first," she said, "what time will it be?"

"Two hours after midnight," replied Zaven and hurried away.

CHAPTER 25

The dimly lit community hall looked out of character contrasted with the rows of blankets stretched on the floor and the walls decorated with armaments. Hagop was the central figure. Zaven stood in the doorway. His presence, even though felt, had not caused any concern.

He advanced toward Hagop with contentment in his eyes. Hagop looked at him and asked intimately, "Any luck?"

"Better than I expected. She is not what I feared she might be. Not by a long way."

"Pretty?"

"Yes, and very charming, but it was not her looks that interested me."

"I know that. Tell me more," Hagop smiled.

When Zaven finished, Hagop commented, "All that sounds good. I wish I could be with you, but one of us must say in the background in case something goes wrong. So, it's up to you. But this much I want to say. You must do it swiftly and in strict secrecy."

Zaven nodded confidently.

"How many men would you need?"

"Nine should be enough," replied Zaven.

They lit their cigarettes.

"Dio, Eremia, and Sarkis will be three of them," Hagop said, puffing on his cigarette.

"Right. I don't care who the others are."

"Have you seen the house?"

"Yes, and I have its layout. Here, take a look."

Hagop studied the rough pencil sketches in silence for a few moments. "Not bad," he commented, handing the paper back. "The house looks isolated and seems at the outskirts, but you cannot drive a carriage up to it. It will attract attention."

"Yes," Zaven agreed. "I had thought of that. We'll take the carriage up to the street. I will not get in, and we will have the route covered all the way. It should be simple with Veronica's help. Six will handle it. Those left in the house must be bound and gagged and put in a locked room."

"Sounds good," Hagop reflected. "What about Veronica?"

"I will take care of her as long as she needs me."

"Suppose she wants your name, what then?" Hagop speculated, gazing intently at Zaven. The cold-blooded outlaw, now a respected officer, was a handsome young man, muscular and agile. The thin clipped mustache lent him a sophisticated air and his sensitive brown eyes would attract any young women who saw him.

"I see that beneath that hard exterior you bear soft feelings," Zaven chided Hagop. "But to me, women are only delicate and pretty things to look at and to admire, but never to get close enough to touch, for what I am makes my touch poisonous."

"How right you are," Hagop said solemnly. "I touched one. She was fool enough to marry me. What sort of life has she? She gets upset every time I see her long enough just to say goodbye."

Two hours after midnight nine men, three in uniform and the rest disguised in native garb, slipped out of the heavy iron gate of the church. A carriage was waiting outside. The ones in uniforms got in the carriage and the others followed it at a safe distance. The carriage stopped at the foot of a narrow cobblestone street. The men in uniforms got out and scattered. Zaven alone stood by the carriage when the six in disguise approached him.

"Remember, Dio," he whispered, "the women are not to be harmed. Bring only Veronica and the men out. The job should be done in less than half an hour, and no thieving."

Dio and those with him started up the narrow street. Zaven watched them until they were out of sight. He walked up to one of the uniformed men, who stood in a doorway. "Go to the carriage," he said. "I am going to take a walk up the street."

He had not gone too far when a voice, close to the wall at a corner, whispered, "Is that you, Zaven?" He paused; the man walked up to him. "Hagop ordered us out," he said. "Your path is well covered."

Zaven nodded and walked along, stopping here and there, watching for lights in the windows and investigating the streets crossing the route. All was well; deathly quiet. He was satisfied. By the time he got back to the carriage, he discovered that it was already loaded. It had taken less time than he had anticipated.

He signaled the men in disguise to move on. He climbed beside the driver, waited a moment or so until the men were well ahead, and ordered the driver to start.

Some time later the carriage stopped in a dark and narrow lane lined with trees. Zaven jumped down, pulled at the canvas covering the back, and helped Veronica down. He loosened her gag and untied her hands.

"Zaven!" she cried, and threw her arms around him.

"Hush," he whispered.

Sarkis, one of the men in disguise, was a bold man in his early thirties, a former outlaw who had spent the war years in the mountains with half a dozen followers. He had built a reputation for himself as daring and ruthless.

Sarkis violently shoved the nightshirt-clad figure. Zaven remained motionless and stared at the man, who, in defiance of his grim predicament, tried to maintain his dignity. Zaven walked up to him and jerked the gag roughly from his clamped jaws. He looked straight into Zaven's eyes.

"I believe we have met before," he mumbled.

Zaven said nothing.

"You're a responsible officer. May I ask what this means?"

"Sorry to have disturbed you, Commissar," Zaven taunted, "but I thought it only fair to tell you that you're here to pay your debt. This is not exactly the kind of justice written in the law, but it's the kind I know."

"W-what do you m-mean?" the Commissar stammered.

"Isn't it obvious?" growled Zaven.

The Commissar's bodyguard and valet, who were still in the carriage, were pushed outside. To Zaven's utter amazement there was a third figure: a female, graceful and pretty. She trembled behind the inadequate shield of a silk nightdress. Zaven went up to her, caught her by the shoulders, and turned her around. Her charm and her innocent, tantalizing eyes left him breathless. He was ashamed of himself and his brutality and angry that she was there to see it.

He turned to Dio and asked harshly, "I thought I made it clear only Veronica and the men of the household were to be removed. Who put this girl in the carriage?"

Dio shook his head. "I didn't know she was in there," he mumbled.

Zaven turned to the girl, but she had slipped away and found shelter in Veronica's arms.

Veronica stood up, facing him squarely. "Zaven," she said, "you know who she is—Zohra. I love her as a sister. She has been the only bright side of my tormented life. If you have any concern for me, and for the cause you told me you live for, you will think of her as you think of me."

"She does not need to be afraid," Zaven said calmly and turned toward the prisoners. "You have heard the saying, 'an eye for an eye, a tooth for a tooth'? Its significance will not, therefore, be lost upon you now." He turned to Dio and barked, "Take them away! Make it quick and noiseless. Take Sarkis and some of the other men."

Dio hesitated a moment and glanced at Sarkis, who looked away guiltily.

Before he was led away, the Commissar took several cautious steps to face Zaven and said coldly, "When I saw you at the watchmaker's, whom I made the mistake of letting live this long, I thought that you were a cur, but I got careless. That passage you quoted just now is from the devil's book, which seems to have a hand in this. In another day or two, the two of us might have been playing reverse roles."

"I was aware of that," Zaven sneered. "Now there will be three less to deal with."

"What are you going to do with these two?" sneered the Commissar, pointing to the two girls locked in each other's arms. "One, who is your kind and has served you so well, will do all right. But, what about the other? She's delectable. I had my eye on her, too, but I waited too long."

A couple of sharp slaps cut the man's words short. During his turbulent career, Zaven had seen behavior of all types, but this was beyond the pale. Coveting one's own niece? This wanton lasciviousness would not go unpunished.

"Dio, make this bastard's final moments as painful as you can," Zaven said flatly.

The valet, a shifty-looking man, pleaded for his life, offering himself as a witness to expose his master's crimes and treacheries. Zaven ignored him; he was dragged away. The bodyguard, a huge but stupid hulk, spat at his captors and was rewarded with a rifle butt to the head. It took three of Zaven's stoutest men to drag his limp body away.

While justice was being meted out somewhere deep in the forest, Zaven nervously paced back and forth. Eremia had stayed behind. He was talking to Veronica. Zaven watched them from a distance and noticed that they had much in common to talk about. He was pleased. Zohra, in Veronica's arms, was crying her heart out. Eremia had tried to reassure her, but to no avail. Angrily, Zaven loosened his cartridge belt and removed his jacket, tossing it toward Veronica.

"Wrap her up," he commanded, "and tell her to keep quiet."

His brusqueness intensified the girl's weeping. Veronica looked at him reproachfully. "That is not like you, Zaven. I know she should not be here, but you cannot hold that against her. If you harm her in any way, you might as well get rid of me here and now."

"It isn't that," he replied calmly. "She is all right. No harm will come to her. But a man I trusted betrayed me. Eremia, did you know anything about this?" he asked vehemently.

"Yes, I knew, but by then it was too late for me to do anything, and it wouldn't have helped had I told you about it. This is more than a simple disobedience. For his sake, I hope Sarkis can explain."

Cocooned in Zaven's warm jacket, Zohra grew quieter. He walked over to her. "I'm not as wretched as you may think," he said softly. "I'm sorry that these things must be. You heard him; he was your uncle, but he exposed himself at the end. Even you must accept that he had outlived his foul life. Someone had to stop him and that someone happened to be me. Now, tell me how you got into the carriage."

Her fear subsided somewhat, and if she shrank from him, it was more from sorrow than from fear. Zohra sobbed. "The man who was in the carriage carried me out from the house."

"How did it happen?"

"I woke up to find him standing above me, with a dagger in his hand. He told me to keep quiet. Then he wrapped me up in a blanket, and that's all."

Zaven walked away. Sarkis might have been ruthless and loose, but he was not treacherous. Zaven could not imagine what had possessed him to act that way. He never suspected Sarkis of being the kind to take revenge on an innocent girl. What then? Not that Zohra's presence was anything more than a nuisance. Even though she was Turkish, Zaven would never harm a woman, and after the defense Veronica had made on her behalf, to hurt her in any way was out of the question.

Dio and the others were back, but Sarkis lagged behind.

"Sarkis," Zaven called, "come here!" Hesitatingly, he walked up. "I thought I told you that no women other than Veronica were to be taken out of the house. Why, then, did you bring this one?"

Sarkis looked at his leader with guilty eyes, reluctant to talk.

"Speak!" Zaven shouted. The men gathered around, looking astonished.

They had never heard Zaven talk that way to one of them.

"Zaven," said Sarkis, "aren't you making a lot of fuss over a Turkish wench? Is there any wrong in reciprocating blood for blood and insult for insult? Of course, if you don't believe in that, get rid of her. It's all the same to me." He shrugged his shoulders.

"You miserable wretch!" Zaven cried in rage. Scarcely knowing what he was doing, he advanced toward Sarkis, who jumped back a pace or two.

"Zaven," Sarkis warned in a bitter voice, "if you lay a hand on me, I'll kill you."

Zaven was beyond reasoning. Again he moved toward him, and simultaneously Sarkis dropped his hand to his belt. A bullet whizzed by Zaven's ear. Within seconds, Sarkis was lying on the ground with Eremia on top of him holding a dagger at his throat. That was enough to bring Zaven to his senses. He was grateful to Eremia for his quick action on the spur of the moment. All that was said and done seemed insignificant now. Two comrades, either of whom would have died for the other, were at each other's throats over nothing more than a woman, and a Turkish one at that.

Zaven drew wearily aside. "Leave him alone, Eremia." He looked at Sarkis and said, "Get up and finish the job. Maybe I deserve no less."

"Are you mad?" Dio exclaimed. "The man's a traitor! He would have killed you if ... I won't let him get away with it."

"Leave him alone," Zaven repeated calmly.

Sarkis rose. "I did betray you," he said. "I deserve what you said. I would rather die than be disgraced."

"The fault is mine. I lost my head. Let's forget it. Just one thing, we all must remember that while we seek vengeance, we will have no part in dishonor. This has been and always will be the key to whatever we do."

Sarkis hung his head. "I don't know what made me do it. But now she's here," he moaned.

Zaven looked across at the girl. She was aware of her peril, yet her eyes seemed to say she trusted him. Zaven spoke to her, almost in a pleading tone.

"You shouldn't have seen this, Zohra," he said. "The sensible way out is to do away with you. But that I cannot do. It is too much to ask; nevertheless, will you promise not to betray me?"

She hesitated and covered her face with her hands. Everyone looked at her, weighing, no doubt, the sanity of their leader's proposition. To their credit no one spoke.

Zohra raised her head and whispered, "I cannot go back, and you cannot send me back, now that I know who and what you are. What I say or do will not alter my being an outcast. I prefer death rather than to return and face what's in store for me. As for what has been done, it would be hypocrisy on my part to express sorrow. You heard him. He killed his own brother so that he could have his wife. This woman was my mother, who put an end to her miseries by taking poison. I shuddered every time he had his eyes on me. It would have been in keeping with the rest of his ways, but I had resolved not to be helpless and die my mother's way. Please don't ask me to go back. If I'm allowed to stay with the one who has been a sister to me, I'll be content, and you'll have nothing to worry about. If that won't do ..."

Weeping bitterly, she fell into Veronica's arms again.

"If I agree to let you stay, could you accept the conditions?" asked Zaven.

"You mean become a Christian?"

"No, not that. But for your own safety, you would have to pretend, for a while at least, until things could be arranged for you."

"Yes, I will!" she cried. Zaven caught her eyes. He believed her.

As darkness faded, the carriage stood before the gate of the scouts' headquarters. The two girls were helped to the ground and taken into the building. Hagop was in the courtyard.

"And who, Zaven," he asked in a perplexed manner, "may be the beautiful one? I mean, the one wearing your jacket?"

"An innocent bystander," answered Zaven curtly.

Hagop looked angry. "She'll be troublesome. Fool that you are, your virtue will be the death of us. We might manage Veronica, but her—a Turk!"

"I prefer not to discuss her. But let me be very clear, no one will lay a finger on her so long as I live."

Grumbling, Hagop went indoors with Zaven following behind. The two were alone in a small, comfortable room containing a bed on elevated boards and a table and two chairs. This was Hagop's private office and chamber. Zaven closed the door behind him. Hagop looked at him; the anger was gone. He sat down on his bed with Zaven sitting down in a chair facing him.

"You'll hear about it eventually," Zaven said in a measured voice. "It's better that you hear it from me. She was taken out of the house against my orders. I learned about it too late. I had an unpleasant incident with Sarkis, who brought her out. The other alternative was to kill her, and I don't think you could have done that, either."

"Perhaps not," muttered Hagop.

"She's innocent, and has good reason to hate the man she had to live with."

"So, you intend to give her comfort and security?"

"I have no such thoughts," Zaven protested. "You know me better than that."

"Yes, I do, and I'm going say the same words you said to me. Remember? 'Beneath that hard exterior you bear soft feelings.'"

Zaven was silent. Hagop smiled. He walked to him and gently grasped his arms. "I want you to know that I understand, Zaven. I'm sorry I acted badly; let's forget her for the moment. I'll have a good talk with her. Tell me what happened."

Zaven told him the story.

"Can you still trust Sarkis?" asked Hagop.

"I believe I do. It was one of those situations where tempers were high and we weren't thinking. For that I take the blame. You talk to him and find out for your own satisfaction."

Zaven had been up most of the night, but when he lay down, he couldn't sleep. He had many sleepless nights, but not while lying down and trying hard to rest his tired body and weary mind. And his thoughts were not what he expected—they were of Zohra.

In the morning he finished his tour of inspection. A dark cloud seemed to hang over the city. Zaven walked past the house where Zohra and Veronica were sheltered. He paused momentarily, walked back to the door, and knocked lightly. He had no reason to visit them, but he had an inner urge to see Zohra. She opened the door and stood motionless for a moment looking at him. He couldn't find any words. She had impulsively drawn close, almost touching him. She wore a light violet gown, a perfect fit that accentuated her petite figure most alluringly. Her appearance, too, had changed. That frightened, beseeching look was gone. There was a spark in her eyes, the anticipation of happiness. She invited him in.

"Thank you," said Zaven. Veronica and Mother Sara, whose face reflected her wisdom, met him in the parlor.

"Isn't she lovely?" whispered Mother Sara, the patroness.

Zaven's face flushed; Zohra turned away. Veronica walked over to him, took his arm, and led him to the sofa. She asked kindly, "Have you eaten yet?"

"No, but I haven't any time. I just dropped in to see how you were."

"I'll prepare something," Zohra said, throwing a quick glance at him, and walked toward the kitchen.

"I'll help you, Zohra," said Veronica and followed her.

Mother Sara, with an inscrutable smile in her eyes, watched him in silence for a while. Zaven felt uneasy. She moved to the sofa and touched his hand.

"Had I been born thirty years earlier, I, too, would have felt the way they do, for you are a most handsome rogue, if I may be so bold as to say it. However, you're lucky, my son. One has accepted you and loves you as a brother. But the other one, maybe you should have killed her. Ah, but she has fallen in love with you. That I know, son; take my word for it."

Zaven hesitated. He couldn't deny what he was feeling for Zohra; remaining aloof from her was a torment he could scarcely bear. "I'm very much concerned with her welfare, Mother Sara," he said pensively, "and I'll do all that is in my power to help her readjust herself."

"She already has, son; she has no life outside of you."

"Has she said that to you?"

"She didn't have to. You didn't have to speak, either, because I know what's in your heart. Sometimes love happens that way, and people who feel it, the way you two do, don't have to say a word. Their every move, every gesture, every breath is the echo of their heartbeat. Marry her."

"That's crazy! Who am I? What sort of life could I offer her? I'll die before disrupting her life again."

"You can only disrupt her life—nay, you will destroy it—by being blind enough to reject her. Listen to me, son, when a woman truly loves, a moment's bliss is an eternity to her, as is even a moment away from her beloved. The man you love and respect had a long talk with her, then he talked to me. I discovered that he too has a heart."

"You mean Captain Hagop," Zaven mumbled.

Mother Sara nodded.

The girls walked in with trays in their hands. Veronica seemed light-hearted and carefree. Zohra's face showed deep anxiety. Zaven glanced at the trays. There were good things to eat, but he wasn't hungry.

"Zohra asked me to pick out a romantic Christian name for her," Mother Sara remarked blithely.

"She has a beautiful name," protested Zaven. "I don't want to know her by any other."

Zohra's eyes met his. What felt like electricity went through him. He lowered his eyes. He wondered what she would have done if they were alone.

"Eremia left a short while before you came in," Veronica said lightly. "I remember him before he went to Constantinople. I was in pigtails then."

She paused. "He was very nice, but he seemed to take special pleasure in teasing me. He has been very kind to me, Zaven, and I do care for him."

"That's wonderful!" cried Zaven. "Nothing you could have said would have made me happier. Now that we have connected again, after what seems so long ago, I feel the two of us are like brothers.

"Has he talked to you?" Veronica asked airily.

"He will in his own time," replied Zaven.

"In that case, there's something you should know. This morning he gave me all his money, a sizeable amount, and asked me to save it for him. I didn't want to, but he said he doesn't want to carry it with him. I wanted you to know about it."

Zaven smiled. "The money is his, and I think he has done wisely. That reminds me. I, too, carry mine around with me. Perhaps I'd better let you keep mine also."

"Not I," Veronica said, casting her eyes on Zohra.

Zorha nudged her gently. Zaven rose. "May I use the other room for a moment?" he asked, walking away. He came out from the room carrying a leather money belt. He handed it to Zohra. "You keep it for me," he said. "I'll feel better."

It was bulky and heavy. Zohra let it drop in her lap. She raised her head and looked at him; then, in an emotional outburst, she sprang up and ran into the other room. Zaven felt bad. Had he hurt her? He looked at his belt coiled on the floor. Mother Sara walked over to him.

"Take it to her," she said, pressing his hand. "She is crying tears of happiness. She wants you there."

He walked hesitatingly toward the room. Face down upon a cushion, Zohra was crying. He stood there in silence for a while. His only experience with women who cried before him was to have them dragged away. But now it hurt him deeply to see her cry. He dropped to his knees. He touched her soft, fragrant hair tenderly.

"Zohra, look at me," he whispered. "Before you came into my life, I had nothing to live for. Now I have. I'll do anything to make you happy."

She raised her head and moved into his arms. "I want nothing, just you."

"You're adorable, but foolish. If that's all you want, this sordid, uncertain life of mine, it's yours."

Zohra pressed his lips with her fingertips. "I love you, and even before knowing that you existed, I dreamt about someone like you."

He kissed her hand and then her cheeks, and with his arms around her, lifted her to her feet. They stood facing each other. Zaven dried her tears using his handkerchief. Zohra took the money belt and tucked it under her pillow, and they walked out hand in hand.

CHAPTER 26

It was Friday, the day designated by Mohammed as the day of rest and worship. The sacred ritual of every Mussulman was to attend the midday prayer at the mosque. Accompanied by Eremia and three others, Zaven was exploring the marketplace, the nerve center of the city. An ominous quietness prevailed. Most of the stores were closed; Christians operated the few scattered ones that were open. The customary stands displaying food and assorted merchandise lined along the pavement were not to be seen.

Half an hour earlier, they had heard the Hodja's call from the minaret to all the faithful. As they approached the gate of the largest mosque, they heard a hysterical uproar. Soon after, a mob of fanatics armed with a hodgepodge collection of weapons rushed out of the mosque. The red flag with the white emblem of a half moon and star soared high in their midst as they cried out frantically, "Ai Allah! Ai Allah! Ai Allah!"

Zaven instructed Eremia and the others to stay behind, and he advanced alone toward the leader of the mob, a priest in his long green mantle and bright yellow turban.

"What has you set on the warpath, brother?" Zaven implored the fanatic.

The priest lowered his sword and peered at the officer beneath shaggy eyebrows. "Are you a Mussleman?" he inquired.

"Al-hamdu'ullah, such I was born," Zaven answered solemnly.

The priest glared at him suspiciously. Who was fooling whom! This colossal human wave would have swallowed Zaven and his men in seconds, and the worst they could do in retaliation was to kill a dozen; but, of course, the priest would be one of the first.

"Then join us, my son," bade the priest in a tempered voice. "It is the command of the Prophet to tear down the flag of infidels from the battlement of the fort and put our holy banner back in its place."

"Brother," Zaven laughed, "the fort is already in our hands. We may be in the service of the infidel, but at heart we serve a holy cause. Do not rush things. I'll go ahead and make certain that there will be no problems, which could be costly."

It worked. The priest halted his mob. Zaven quickly joined the others and they hurried back to their quarters.

In record time nearly a thousand Armenians crowded the courtyard within the high walls of the church. The gates were bolted, and the walls and windows fortified in a hurry. If the worst happened, fifty men would have to defend the frightening multitude against overwhelming odds. Zaven mingled with them, showering encouragement, attempting to pacify the frightened children; the response was prayers and blessings. A feeling of exultation possessed him. His devotion to the cause close to his heart left no room for personal feelings. Never before had he totally understood its meaning.

When he had done all that was expected of him, he thought of Zohra and Veronica, to whom he had given his room. They, too, must be consoled. He stood in front of the door, waiting. Did he look calm? He must try, and with that resolve he knocked on the door gently. Zohra opened it. Veronica was curled up on his bed. Mother Sara was engaged in arranging the satchels.

"What does all this mean, Zaven?" Zohra cried, throwing her arms around him.

"Just a precautionary measure," he replied calmly, closing the door behind him.

"If anything is going to happen, please don't hide it. It's better to know and face it, and then wait and see," commented Veronica.

"I'm not hiding anything. I only saw the mob on their way to the fort to pull down the French flag. I think they will do it. There are no French troops in the fort to stop them. They are fools but we cannot take chances."

"It is serious," sighed Zohra.

Zaven looked into her eyes, red from weeping.

"You have been crying again," he scolded her.

"I am with you now," she whispered, pressing her check against his. "Nothing else matters."

Night came. Contrary to all expectations not a single shot was fired. Undoubtedly the Hadja whom Zaven had momentarily stopped was disappointed at not finding him among the soldiers who welcomed him with open arms at the fort. It was difficult to concede that a great power like France could swallow such an insult, but the Turkish flag still soared. As for the soldiers, they bolstered rebel forces.

During the ensuing days, there was a kind of "wait-and-see" atmosphere in the city. The stores were closed and the streets were empty; it was the Turks who were in peril if the French cared to show them how her flag should be treated. But the French Commandant had taken an indifferent attitude.

Meanwhile, conditions in the Armenian Church were bad. Every last Armenian had taken refuge there, until there was hardly any room to move around.

Accompanied by half a dozen men, Zaven ventured out to survey the situation and find Hagop. His appearance on the deserted streets frightened those who prowled around. Hagop was delighted to see him. He commended him for his daring, but admonished him for taking such a risk. Here Zaven found the same conditions as those at his own quarters.

"What do you make of all this?" he asked when alone with Hagop.

"I can't tell you anything," Hagop replied hesitatingly. "I haven't received a word from the Commandant. But I expect to receive orders to transport those who are with us to a safer place. Then he can act. A city of this size cannot remain in this condition for any length of time. It looks to me as though the Commandant is the kind who would not stick his neck out. Maybe he is waiting for orders."

"I thought that someone in his position could deal with the situation as it demands," Zaven commented. "If he delays longer, he will regret it. The Turks are using every moment to prepare themselves."

Hagop blinked. "You're isolated in that church. How would you stand in case of sudden outbreak?"

"We'll manage," Zaven answered calmly.

"I wish we could group all of them in one place outside the city."

"That would help. Do we need the Commandant's approval for that?"

"No, if we can do it without mishap, which I doubt," Hagop blurted out sulkily.

They caught each other's eyes and made their way slowly through the crowd, stopping here and there to answer questions. When alone in the little room, they sighed with relief.

"I must get back quickly," Zaven said when they lit their cigarettes.

"Yes, but I'm not sure whether I should let you take the risk again," Hagop said, blowing coils of smoke through his nostrils.

Zaven laughed.

"The devil himself can't stop you; I'm aware of that," Hagop smiled. "The only thing I can do is to let you out with a few more than you came in with."

"I don't believe I'll need them. Six are as good as twelve."

Hagop shrugged his shoulders and walked to the window that opened onto the courtyard.

"Does your place look like this?" he asked.

Zaven nodded.

"How are Zohra and Veronica?" Hagop asked, in a nonchalant manner.

"They are all right—safe as the rest."

"I hope you've provided them with some privacy."

"They have my room."

"You know, I've had a long talk with Zohra. She's a good girl, and very sensible, which is more than I expected of her. What troubles me is that without you, she cannot exist. If you really care for her—and I think that you do—you have no alternative but to give her security and restore her self-respect. Don't let her down, Zaven. This bit of counsel coming from me may surprise you."

"I'll think about it when the time comes," Zaven replied curtly.

"One cannot set a time for such things, Zaven."

"But—"

"I want you to listen, Zaven," Hagop interrupted. "You cannot drag her along wherever you go. As things are, the only way you could give her security is by giving her your name. Then we can send both her and Veronica to Adana. They can stay with my wife. This situation—serving France to help our cause—looks dubious to me. We know little about the French policy and their occupational status. Things are getting more and more precarious each day. When we get out of this mess, I'm going to resign. I know you'll stick with me, and then we will be free to decide and act."

"I fully agree with you," Zaven replied seriously. "But I cannot ask Zohra to go to Adana. She has to decide it. I want her to be happy, but I don't want to control her life."

"She would go if you want her to go."

"I must leave," said Zaven, walking to the door.

"Be careful, and don't take chances again," Hagop cried after him.

What good had it done to see Hagop except to add an emotional twist to the impending crisis? Head down, careless, Zaven walked a dozen paces ahead of the alert men behind him, moving forward cautiously and hugging the walls. The door to a house about fifty feet ahead of them slammed shut. The noise spurred Zaven. What was going on behind those closed doors and shuttered windows?

Zaven dashed forward. The men behind him were taken by surprise. Eremia rushed up beside him. Zaven stopped in front of the heavy door that had just been slammed and pounded on it with the tip of his heavy boot. No answer.

"Open the door, you ass!" he shouted in an accent that no one would suspect was anything but Turkish.

A timorous woman's voice came from within. "I swear, master, there's no man in the house."

"Open it, woman! I just saw one going inside. We're here to protect you."

The door opened. A feeble, elderly woman enveloped in her black burka, exposing only her panicky eyes, faced Zaven.

"I want to talk to the man," Zaven said. "Who is he?"

"My husband, master."

"Tell him to come out; I assure you that no harm will come to him."

The woman hesitated. She was trying hard to make out who Zaven was, but did not dare to ask directly.

"Go, woman," commanded Zaven in a milder tone. "I've given you my word."

"Yes, master," she mumbled, as she marched into the house.

Zaven opened the door wide and stayed outside. The men positioned themselves on either side of the street. It had taken longer than Zaven expected for the man of the house to appear. He was contemplating forcing the issue by walking inside when a gray-bearded, conventionally-dressed man appeared in the hallway. Zaven was not particularly interested in this little mouse of a man's name, and used a different tack to start a conversation.

"And what do you do for a living?" he asked.

"I have a store in the covered market," the man answered timidly, his squeaky voice a perfect fit for his mousy manner.

"Why aren't you at your store?"

The man stared at him sheepishly.

"Tell me, little rat man!" demanded Zaven. "I'm trying to find out what's at the root of the fear that grips this town."

"People are panic-stricken in fear of a reprisal. Most of them went away;

only the old and feeble ones like me who would rather die in his home than become an outcast stayed behind."

Was the old man telling the truth? That did not matter.

"All right, go in then," ordered Zaven. "It isn't too late yet to save yourselves and your homes."

He turned to Eremia. "We're going to look around," he said nonchalantly.

Eremia looked at him, perplexed.

"Don't worry," Zaven added, "you'll be safe as anywhere else in this accursed city."

They roamed through the smutty alleys and lonely streets. They encountered several women and two men. Zaven stopped them all for questioning. What he learned from the little rat man, the others confirmed. They paused at the entrance of the covered market. The bare platforms and the emptiness of the narrow, low-roofed, tunnel-like place made it look eerie. The cobblestone streets were strewn with rubbish, and the foul odor of disuse clung to the heavy air. Zaven turned his head, threw a quick glance back, and moved on. Reluctant as the men behind him might have been, they followed him. He found a few stores that were looted. He stopped to look inside, but did not take the trouble to go in.

They emerged safe from the opposite end. Paved with white stones, the grand courtyard of the mosque appeared empty, even though it was close to midday prayer. Normally, the place would have swarmed like a beehive with the faithful cleaning themselves in the numerous tiny fountains lining the courtyard walls. Zaven ventured to walk in and look around while the others watched him through the large arched gate. He confirmed the mysterious fact: not a single soul was there.

"Eremia, Hagop does not know about this situation," he said. "Take two men along with you and report it to him. If trouble comes, it'll come from the outside. Come back if you want to, or stay with Hagop."

"I'll be back," Eremia blurted out, and signaled two men to follow him.

Zaven's reappearance stimulated some hope to the fugitives in the

Armenian Church. He smiled and gave words of reassurance to those who sought them, and walked directly toward his quarters. Zohra stood in the half-opened door. Though there were hundreds of eyes watching her, she did not care, and threw her arms around his neck, her toes barely touching the floor. Zaven caressed her silky dark hair, straightened her head, and looked into the dark, passionate wells of her eyes.

"All is well; all will be well," he whispered.

They walked into the small room.

"Where's Eremia?" Veronica asked, jumping up from the cushion.

Zaven smiled. "I sent him to Hagop with a message. Don't worry; he'll be back."

"What's going on outside, Zaven?" Zohra asked.

"Nothing; everything is quiet—ominously quiet. Most of the houses are empty. Those who are in them are old men, women, and children."

"What will the French do?"

"My guess is that they will not do anything—that is, if the people get back to their homes, restore the French flag at the fort, and attend to their own business."

"Do you really think that it'll end up that way, Zaven?" Zohra cried, grabbing his hand and pressing it against her cheeks.

"I wish I could say so definitely, Zohra."

It is human nature for people to cope with their circumstances, no matter how dismal; then, they look around for ways to improve their existence. This was what happened to the Armenians who initially rushed into the enclosure of the church. Now, some of them wanted to return to their homes. Most of them wished to get the things they needed. Zaven found it difficult to say no. They needed clothes, blankets, and—most of all—food. But he couldn't let them roam the streets without armed escorts. However, he thought that, by covering a small section at a time, this could be done.

He had just asked the priest to help him with his plan, when Eremia walked in to tell him that he had some unexpected visitors. A company of

French troops was lined up in the street. Eremia handed him the written message from Hagop instructing him to immediately transfer the refugees to the American Orphanage at the outskirts of the city.

For the refugees, this was not very cheerful news. They would rather have been left in the care of a small, lightly armed band of their own countrymen than five hundred troops. But, neither Hagop nor Zaven had any say in the matter. Two fair ladies, in particular, were going to be singularly depressed with the new arrangement. If Zaven had his way, he would not let the two out of his sight for even a moment. At any rate, he would be near.

Guarded by the troops and with scouts leading the way, the transfer of refugees from the church to the orphanage was accomplished without incident. Undoubtedly, malicious eyes peered at the procession through door cracks and window blinds; otherwise, a city of forty thousand had become a ghost town.

When the refugees were safely confined behind the high, strongly fortified walls, Zaven sought the supervisor, Ann Hadley. She was a gracious, kind-faced missioner who reminded Zaven of Miss Blake, the American missioner he greatly admired and respected. Both women had spent half their lives in Turkey and spoke the language like natives.

"I'm here to ask you a favor," he said gravely. "There are two girls, one of them you may recognize. She has been here before. The other one is not an Armenian, but very important to me. Could you provide a small quarter for these two so that they won't attract attention?"

Ann Hadley smiled and placed her hand gently upon his shoulder. "I understand," she said softly. "And you're Zaven, the famous one from Sivas. I know quite a bit about you. For twenty-five years I have lived in these parts to help and serve your people." She paused. "Maybe I, too, have some Armenian blood in me."

"Will you do it, then?"

"I'm flattered that I've not been ordered." She smiled. "Of course I'll do it. There is an adjoining room that I use for my study. The girls will have this room."

"I don't want to deprive you of your room," Zaven said apologetically.

The missionary just smiled. Zaven tapped the door; Eremia was waiting outside.

"Go and bring the girls here," he instructed.

"Have you time for some tea?" asked Miss Hadley.

"Thank you, I don't believe I do." Zaven walked to the window; the missioner settled down in a chair.

"Are you going to be with us?" she asked.

"I wish I could, but I have no say in the matter. Don't worry; you are well protected."

"Yes, but how will it end?"

"Your guess is as good as mine. But there's one thing I can assure you. Regardless of the outcome, this time the unlucky fugitives will not be left to the mercy of the enemy."

"I'm sure of that, but what a shame they must go through this."

Zaven's faraway look intimated that he hadn't even heard her last words. There was a gentle rap on the door. Miss Hadley went to answer it. Eremia and the two girls appeared in the doorway. They were courteously invited in. The supervisor gazed at Veronica in silence for a moment, then walked over to her and grasped her hands.

"I'm glad to see you back, my dear," she said gently, and turned to Zohra. "I'm happy to have you, too, my child. My only wish is that—"

"The supervisor has been kind enough to let you have a room of your own" Zaven interjected.

"I'm glad that I could help both of you," said Miss Hadley. "This is going to be your room, girls. Mine will be the adjoining one. The door is open if you wish to use it. I have a little work to attend to," she said and walked out.

"Oh, this is so nice. Thank you, Zaven," said Veronica. "I'm going to see the other room. Come with me, Eremia." She took Eremia's hand and led him into the adjoining room, giving Zaven and Zohra some privacy.

"I understand why we're here, Zaven," said Zohra. "My worry is, where are you going to be?"

"As close to you as I can, Zohra," he said in a soothing voice. "But I have to report to headquarters first. Still, I'm content; you will be much safer here than with me."

She wrung her hands in anguish. "I knew this would happen," she cried. "I am not afraid of death, but of something worse. Suppose they send you away, Zaven?"

"I'll be back. Nothing can separate us, Zohra."

That's what frightens me. This accursed land, these evil people." She pressed her head against his chest and whispered, "Promise me ..."

"What, Zohra?"

"Promise that you'll resign as soon as you can. We will leave this hateful land and find happiness where there is no hatred."

What could he say? What she asked meant giving up everything he had been living for. His fanatical ideas of killing the enemy had been replaced by a constructive purpose: to help his people. Was Zohra's influence stronger than his rededicated life? His hand involuntarily went to his forehead. He was conflicted, but he heard the words inside his head: Your allegiance now is to her. You have deprived her of all that was once hers. She comes before everything.

"Answer me, Zaven. Please, answer!"

Zohra's voice came to him as if from a great distance. He harked dreamily to the impassioned words gushing forth from the beautiful face.

"Haven't you evened the score yet? I know, my beloved, you have been wronged, terribly wronged. That's one of the reasons I feel about you the way I do, Zaven. But haven't you made them pay? Only say that you will resign when you can. I'll make you happy, believe me, my love."

Too confused to speak, and not knowing how to deal with his feelings, Zaven took her into his arms and pressed his lips to hers. "I love you,

Zohra," he whispered. "Nothing in this world comes before you."

There was a knock at the door. Dio burst into the room. "Zaven," he cried, "the men are on their way! You'll have to hurry!"

Scarcely daring to meet her eyes, he pressed her hand and blurted out in a husky voice, "Be brave, Zohra! I'll see you as soon as I can."

CHAPTER 27

The emptiness of the church depressed Zaven even more than when it was jammed with frightened people. At that time, there was hope that the tempest might pass and those who—after so much hardship—had reestablished their homes, might go back to them. Hagop stood alone in the doorway. Zaven walked over to him.

"This is a relief. They'll be all right until the French decide," Hagop commented.

"Where are the men?" Zaven asked.

"I was ordered to move into the inn, where our horses are."

"Sounds logical," Zaven muttered. "Anything else?"

"We are ordered to set up two patrols, one mounted for the outskirts of the city, the other to assist the troops patrolling the streets."

"That's all well and good, but it won't settle anything."

"True, but my guess is that there will be some action—first, an ultimatum to the rebels to return home and attend to their business and surrender the fort."

"And if the ultimatum is ignored?"

Hagop shrugged. "Do I have I a crystal ball?"

"Ah, I wish you did," sighed Zaven as three others emerged from the building and joined them. "Let's go!" he cried.

The inn was the best and the largest in the city, built in the conventional style. The ground floor was the stable, with rooms with doors opening on the glass-paneled porch on the second floor. For a change, the men could experience relative luxury. The beds were comfortable, and the large coffeehouse with its plentiful utensils and supplies that were left in the storeroom served them well. Best of all, drinks were on the house.

Zaven was in charge of the mounted group patrolling the outskirts. This was a twenty-four hour job. A schedule of six-hour stretches was established. It suited him, because he could stop at the orphanage to see Zohra.

The ultimatum giving the rebels twenty-four hours to return to their homes and attend to their business was issued. The stipulated time lapsed; if there had been any response, it was not what was expected or hoped for. Those in the city were prepared to defend themselves and the rebels outside realized that time was running out.

At dawn the following day, the six-man mounted patrol that Zaven led was surprised at the outskirts of the city. By the time the scouts positioned themselves defensively, the attackers had quickly retreated. It was a hit and run affair, but it cost Zaven dearly: his precious horse and two men perished, with one other man seriously wounded.

Zaven reported the incident to the French Commandant. Now the die was cast.

"At this point, Lieutenant, I want you to know the true facts of this situation," the Commandant declared gravely. "I have received definite orders. We are here only temporarily. This city is not within our occupational zone. We will leave soon after things are in order. However, we cannot leave behind those who are in the orphanage. I am instructed to establish order before I leave."

He sprang to his feet. "That I will do, and in the course of it teach a lesson to those who resist my orders. Don't risk your life and the lives of your men. Stay at your quarters. You'll hear from me soon."

"Yes, sir," Zaven said, turning toward the door. He hadn't yet closed it behind him when the Commandant called him back. Zaven stood at attention.

"Drop in at the stable and pick out a horse for yourself," said the Commandant kindly. "It will be yours, even if the animal happens to be mine."

"Thank you, sir."

"Too bad you lost your mount. A good horse is as close as a good friend."

"Sometimes closer," said Zaven as he took his leave.

Another incident occurred the same day that dispelled any remaining doubt. One of the patrols that had ventured close to the fort was fired upon. Four were killed, and several wounded.

The fort was the strategic point dominating the city and the countryside around it. The only approach was a narrow steep path winding its way through the walls of high cliffs.

A battalion with the scouts as auxiliaries was assigned to take the fort. They surrounded it and sent a messenger with a white flag to deliver the three-word ultimatum,"Surrender or perish." The answer was curt and defiant: "Come and take us!"

The shooting began, but no orders were given to storm the fort through the path. It would have been suicidal, and attempts to get closer would have been costly.

The following morning, the troops around the fort were badly jolted by the rebels within the city. It turned out to be a bloody skirmish. The troops withdrew in an orderly fashion. There was an attempt to take the inn occupied by the scouts. Those left behind defended it, but Hagop received orders to abandon the inn.

The clatter of hoofs over the cobblestone had brought curious faces to the windows. Were they thinking this was the final departure of the infidel Armenians? The scouts rode to the command post set upon a hill outside the city. The fighting was more than they had bargained for, as the Turks were well prepared. That night they attacked the orphanage and stormed several small outposts. The French troops defended the orphanage, but they did not take any further action in response.

The Commandant summoned Hagop. Zaven and the men waited anxiously for his return. They saw him walking with measured steps with his head lowered. Zaven went to meet him.

"What's the news?" he asked.

Hagop looked up, his face grim. "We're ordered to go to the orphanage," he said casually.

Zaven felt better, because nothing else mattered as long as he could be with Zohra.

"Oh, also," Hagop continued, "we're instructed to distribute arms to those who can shoot. Soon—but the Commandant did not say when—we will accompany the refugees to Adana."

"What about the situation here with the Turks?" Zaven asked. "Is the Commandant sneaking out?"

"I wouldn't put it that way, Zaven. The Commandant is not a coward, but he has his orders." Hagop paused, looked impassively at Zaven and added, "He will need to fight his way out."

Zaven understood and nodded. "Tell the men to get ready. We'll start right away."

Hagop deployed the men in a radius of two hundred yards from the orphanage, and lashed the horses along the wall outside. Then he and Zaven went in. Their appearance gave some hope and reassurance.

"Are you going to stay?" came the question from all directions.

Zaven looked up. Zohra was at the window, alone and apart. She had seen him. He made his way to her through the crowd. Hagop smiled.

"I'm going out. Don't be in any hurry," Hagop cried after him.

"I haven't seen you for three days," she protested, throwing her arms around him.

"I couldn't come, Zohra."

"You were in the middle of the fighting."

He smiled, caressing her hair.

"Not really. But I was defending the outskirts of the city, and I wasn't far from you. I died a thousand times ... from missing you."

She stepped back, scrutinized him from head to toe, and then walked to the sofa, her eyes glued upon him. Zaven hobbled over to her.

"You're wounded!" she cried frantically.

He laughed.

"Why are you limping then?"

"I took a spill and sprained my ankle. It happened when my horse was shot out from under me. The poor devil was killed."

"Are you telling me the truth?" she asked, jumping up.

"The very truth," smiled Zaven.

But she wanted to make sure. She ran her hand over his limbs. She smiled; there were no bandages, and she rested her head upon his chest.

"Where is Veronica?" he asked.

"She is out helping out by getting the food and supplies that we need. I wish I could do something, but I'm not allowed to go out."

"Miss Hadley is a kind and wise woman, Zohra."

"I know that."

Someone knocked at the door. Zohra went to open it. Ann Hadley walked in, with Veronica behind her.

"Sorry to intrude," she said courteously. "You may use the other room if you wish."

"Thank you, but I was just about to leave," Zaven answered.

"It is so heartening to have you with us. I hope you will stay until it is over. Yes, we're well defended, but your being here is different." The missioner went to the window, watched outside for a moment, then turned and added, "Zaven, what is going to happen?"

He hesitated. "We may take you to Adana," he said calmly. "That seems to be the best solution, but it is not yet definite."

"Then you will come with us?" cried Zohra.

"Yes, Zohra, I'll be with you."

"Is Eremia with you, too?" Veronica interrupted in an anxious voice.

"Yes," Zaven smiled.

"Will you send him in for a little while if you can spare him, Zaven?" Veronica requested.

"Of course. Don't worry. I must go now. If you want anything, send word through the guards at the gate."

That night the fighting began. The way it started indicated clearly that the Commandant had taken more than his pride and temperament could allow. Now that the city was abandoned by the troops, the rebels infiltrated it. Maybe this was what the Commandant waited for. The artillery barrage was unceasing. By midday the fort was leveled and the whole city was on fire. The outlying countryside within artillery range was smoldering in dust and smoke. Was this, Zaven pondered sardonically, the Commandant's idea of "teaching a lesson?"

Night fell, and all seemed to be quiet, although the evidence of the day's battle was very visible. By morning the troops had retaken the remains of the fort. In the city stray cats and dogs roamed the corpse-littered ruins. Hagop received the order to evacuate the orphanage. Two companies of troops were to accompany the scouts on this move, but the main reason for this was to deploy the troops at strategic points along the road to keep it open.

The order was passed on to the refugees; their reaction was mixed. Those who hadn't much to lose did not mind, but others who had to leave behind home, comfort, and economic security took it hard. Some of them were even inclined to stay behind and take their chances with the Turks, but moral sensibility and national pride overruled. There was no means of transportation; whatever they wanted, they had to carry on their backs. The hazardous, nonstop exodus was bound to be slow and trying, but the important thing was to take them safely to the junction of the train station and embark for Adana.

Zohra was the first to know. Zaven had his reasons. He was alone with her and needed to clear all doubts. Yes, they loved each other very much, but there were things stronger than love. He must make sure that if she wished to return to the roots of her heritage, then he would make certain that she would get there, at the risk of his own life. Only once did he look into her eyes, but he had not been able to put his thoughts into words and stood there in silence, staring into the distance. She grasped his clenched fists with both hands and pressed them to her lips.

"My own," she whispered, "I know your thoughts; you don't have to say them. And this is my answer: You are my world. I have no life without you. Now, what else do you want to say?" She kissed him quickly but lovingly.

"Nothing, Zohra, nothing. I was just wondering if you want something for the journey."

"You can get me a pair of strong shoes fit to walk in," she said, smiling, and gazed at her dainty slippers.

"I won't let you walk."

"We'll see. There will be others who need your horse more than I."

"Sturdy women's shoes may be a hard commodity to come by," Zaven mumbled helplessly, "but I'll try."

"Don't let that worry you, my love, I was only jesting," she smiled.

Zaven looked sheepish.

"When I get to Adana, will you be away for long?" she asked.

"I hope not, Zohra."

"You will resign as soon as you can?"

"Yes, Zohra, as soon as I can."

She kissed him again. They started toward the door.

"Oh, yes" he added. "Some of us may start a few hours ahead. I wanted you to know about it, but don't worry. I'll be with you the rest of the way. Anyway, my horse will be at your disposal."

"I told you I was walking, Zaven," Zohra said stubbornly.

"We'll see," he smiled.

Zaven, with forty men, started shortly after midnight to occupy the bridge over the river on the road out of the city. To their surprise they found the bridge undefended. They took their positions, and waited for the refugee caravan.

At daybreak they observed a large number of enemy bands that seemed to have learned belatedly about the evacuation and went to the bridge to make things difficult. The skirmish did not last long. Caught between the advance guards of the caravan and Zaven at the bridge, the enemy disappeared, leaving behind a large number of their own.

What sad memories this slow-moving procession of downcast fugitives brought to Zaven. But this time he played a different role. That alone consoled him. He spotted his horse, which he had selected from the Commandant's stable, but instead of Zohra, another woman with a child in front of her rode the noble beast. He saw Zohra walking a dozen paces behind with Veronica. She had seen him. Disregarding propriety, characteristic to the women of her caste, she dashed forward. He was proud of her.

"Nothing else matters," she whispered, as he enfolded her in his arms.

She carried a canvas sack. He glanced at her dainty feet and smiled to see she had secured a rugged pair of brogans for herself.

"You're wonderful!" he cried. "That little woman needed to ride, but surely you could have thrown that sack on the back of the saddle."

"It's light, Zaven. I don't mind."

He grabbed it from her shoulders.

"No, no!" she protested, "I won't take the chance of losing it. You have enough to carry."

Veronica had joined Eremia. Captain Hagop, who had watched the heart-warming scene of lovers reuniting from a distance, walked slowly toward them.

"The going should be smooth from here on," he said. "I want you to take charge of the caravan, Zaven. I'll head off."

Zohra smiled gratefully at the thoughtful captain, who nodded approvingly and went on his way.

"Now, go along, my precious; Veronica is waiting," Zaven said. "I may not always be around you, but my eyes will be on you." He turned to Dio standing several paces away and commanded, "See that the men are in position. I am going to wait here for the end."

The scouts were positioned several paces apart from each other and walked about fifty feet outside of the caravan, forming a mobile defensive chain. The last of the refugees, an old man who hobbled along with a cane, passed by. Zaven approached him.

"Do you want to ride for a while, father?" he asked.

"Thank you, son. I might be a bit slow, but I can walk. You'll find others who really need to ride."

Zaven instructed four of his men to stay at the rear. Behind them were the troops acting as rearguard. Then he moved on in long, loping strides, stopping now and then to talk to people who had problems. He saw a small child, filthy from continually tumbling into the dirt, being dragged along by his grim mother, oblivious to the boy's whimpering. He spotted a horse, one of theirs, ridden by an old woman. He picked up the exhausted child and placed him in the saddle in front of the old lady. The dazed mother watched him, at a loss for words.

At sunset they reached a good-sized village at the foot of a high mountain, the top of which was covered with snow glimmering under the sun's fading rays. They had passed the halfway mark of their destination. It was mid-November, and the evening had turned cold. The fugitives did not have much to keep themselves warm while they rested, and they needed the rest badly. Would it be wise to camp here overnight? Hagop and Zaven thought it would be all right, but the French officer in command thought differently. He wanted to keep on going. Several men were dispatched to survey the village. They returned with the news that they found only a small number of women and children in the houses.

Besides the need for rest, Zaven and Hagop reasoned it would be safer to travel by daylight. It was Hagop's job to get the French officer to see their point of view.

"There's that precarious ford not far ahead," Hagop said to Zaven. "It could be difficult to go through at night. I'm going to see that pigheaded Frenchman. I may be able to convince him that, for safety's sake, the ford should be held. We'll volunteer for the job."

"That should work," Zaven commented.

"You are staying. I'll see to it," Hagop declared.

Zaven looked at him inquiringly.

"This is not a gallant gesture." Hagop added. "You, too, need some rest. Besides, you are doing better with these people than I am."

After hearing Hagop out, the French officer in command agreed his suggestion was sound. A detachment of troops was to be posted at that point anyway. Hagop wanted fifty men to achieve their objective, and Zaven was left with the problem of finding places for the fugitives where they could be warm. He entered the village with half a dozen men. Most of the houses were unoccupied.

At another house he tried the door but found it bolted from the inside. He pounded on it with the butt of his rifle. There was no answer. He was sure that someone was inside, as the smoke from the chimney left no doubt.

"Open up!" he shouted angrily, and waited a moment. "Break it down!" he commanded his men.

The order was carried out using a heavy plank used as battering ram. Zaven cautiously stepped inside. Two soldiers sat by the fire, and a plump woman, pale as a ghost, stood against the wall, facing them.

The soldiers sprang to their feet. They knew Zaven, even though they were not of the regular army. They stood at attention.

"What are you doing here?" Zaven asked harshly in French.

"We asked her to give us something to eat," replied the soldier who seemed to be bolder of the two.

"Have you permission for that?" Zaven snapped.

There was no reply.

"As far as I know," Zaven continued, "you have no business to be here. Are you aware of the consequences if I report this?"

"Yes, sir, but we meant no harm," said the soldier meekly.

Zaven looked at the woman. She walked over and kneeled down in front of him, grasping his hand. But Zaven pulled it away.

"Get up! Did they harm you?"

"N-no, m-master," she faltered. "Allah sent you in t-time."

"Get out," Zaven shouted, turning to the soldiers, "before I lose my temper and spare you from the routine of a court martial!"

The soldiers picked up their rifles and scampered out quickly.

"Do you mind having some women at your house overnight?" asked Zaven.

"Anything to repay your kindness, master," said the woman.

"And if you offer them some hot soup, I'll appreciate it."

"I'll see to that, master."

Soon the refugees were allowed to go into the abandoned homes. Zaven, who understood the impulse of getting even, saw to it that no atrocities would be committed. He had each house guarded by his men. His orders were not to touch food that the villagers had left behind. Zohra, Veronica, Ann Hadley, and several others were housed with the woman Zaven had found.

Sporadic cracks of gunshots discharged accidentally or by trigger-happy novices were the only disturbances that night. Zaven slept a few hours outside the house where Zohra and the others stayed. The plump woman of the house had given him a warm comforter.

At sunrise the refugees resumed their slow march. Everything went more orderly than it had the previous day. The refugees seemed to have accepted their situation. They walked with vigor and without complaint, and the fear of being attacked diminished as they got closer to their destination.

Late that afternoon they reached the train junction. It was a small station, and a relatively large Turkish town was about a mile away.

Hagop had arrived a few hours ahead to make arrangements and, if possible, to have a train ready for the refugees. This would spare them from the cold of the night in the open. Zaven saw him standing at the door of the station house, and walked up to meet him.

"A train from Aleppo is due soon," Hagop said. "It might be full, but we will put on it as many as we can. Anyway, you will be on it; the rest will follow you on a special train. You won't need more than half a dozen men. I was told that all the trains are heavily guarded. Take Eremia and Dio along. This is an assignment, but I'll give you a week's leave of absence."

Zaven looked surprised. The refugees were all over the place.

"Let's go in," Hagop blurted. "There's a small room belonging to the officer in charge, an agreeable young lieutenant. He offered me the use of it."

It was a very small room with one high, square window. The furnishings comprised a cot, a rickety table, and a couple of old chairs. Hagop settled down in one of them. Zaven walked around and stood on tiptoe to watch out of the window. He saw Zohra standing on the platform. He turned and walked to the empty chair.

"What will you do after I'm on my way to Adana and the refugees are out of your hands?" Zaven asked.

"I am instructed to get back to Bakcha, and wait." Hagop looked pointedly at Zaven. "There won't be much to do; I can spare you for a week or more." He paused again. They lit their cigarettes. "Besides," he continued, "there are a few things I want you to do. We'll talk about them. But the first thing I want you to do is marry her."

Zaven looked surprised. "But—"

"Stop!" Hagop interrupted. "I know what you're going to say. I want to be present at your wedding more than anything else, but the real celebration can wait until we are free, and my opinion is that it won't be very long. Yes, I want you to marry her. You cannot leave her behind without giving her the security that your name alone can give. Do you understand that, Zaven?"

Zaven rose and paced around the room, then stood in front of his leader.

"You're right," he said. "Veronica might get along, but not Zohra."

"I think Eremia and Veronica will marry, too," Hagop reflected. After a pause, he added, "I want you to find out what is brewing in the political pot. We know little, if anything. I don't like the way the French are handling things. Yes, I want to be of help, but are we really helping?"

"It is a mess," Zaven agreed. "Why they don't take a firm stand against the Turks, I'll never understand."

"Maybe they can't. After all, how sure are they that these territories will remain in their hands? The British had Marash first. The way it looks, neither one wants the other to have it."

"Looks that way," Zaven muttered.

Zaven could read Hagop's expression, even though he hadn't yet spoken a word. "We must organize an independent force and show the world that the Turks can only be controlled by military strength, or they will take over whatever territory they want," Hagop said.

"I've thought of that," Zaven replied. "It won't be hard to gather five thousand men. A force of that size with spirit would raise havoc."

They heard the whistle of the train.

"Here it comes. We've got to get you on it," Hagop said, walking to the door. Zaven followed him, and stopped momentarily by Veronica and Zohra.

"We'll get on this one," he said softly. "Follow me." Zohra managed to suppress her joyous outburst. The train stopped; they walked over to it. The lieutenant in charge was there. Zaven was introduced to him.

"She looks pretty full to me," said the lieutenant, "but we must make room for the lieutenant and those with him."

There were several crowded passenger coaches, but most of the cars were freight cars full of troops and passengers. The sergeant in charge of guarding the train stepped down.

"The lieutenant is going to Adana along with some of these people," said the officer in charge.

"There isn't much room, sir," replied the sergeant.

"Move some passengers to the freight cars to make room"," commanded the officer.

The sergeant saluted and went back to carry out the difficult assignment. Zaven went over to Miss Hadley.

"We will get on this train," he said to her. "Some of us may be lucky enough to get into the coaches, but I want all of the girls to get on, even if they have to ride in the freight cars."

"I don't mind being with them in the cars, Zaven."

"I understand, but I want very much to have a few of you in my company."

Miss Hadley smiled. Zaven signaled those around him to follow; half a dozen people, including Zohra and Veronica, climbed up the steps. The rest of the refugees from the orphanage were trying to get on the train too. To stop the mad rush, Hagop stepped forward.

"We're only sending the girls from the orphanage in this train," he announced in a loud voice. "Zaven is going ahead to make arrangements for the rest of you. In a short while, you all will get on a special train, which is on its way. You'll be much more comfortable in it."

Some of the refugees who had actually boarded the train got down, but a few persistent ones stayed on.

Zaven examined the coach from the rear entrance. It was full with a mixture of civilian passengers and French officers. Every seat was taken, and a number of people stood in the aisle. He moved on slowly. Ann Hadley and the others followed close behind. A French captain acknowledged Zaven's salute and exchanged a few words with him. Then he made the gallant gesture of offering his seat to Miss Hadley. His companion, another officer, followed his example. Other officers fell in line.

All those who had entered the coach with Zaven had seats except Veronica and Zohra. Zaven's eyes rested on two fat, well-dressed men wearing fezzes. The captain noted the objects of Zaven's interest. He walked briskly over to the men and grabbed the shoulder of the one sitting on the aisle.

"Get up, you big fat pig, or I'll throw you out!" he shouted. "Civilized men won't let ladies stand."

The men smiled foolishly, got up, and moved to the next coach. The two girls sat down. Zaven smiled and moved to the rear. The captain followed him.

"Where are these people from?" the captain asked.

"From Marash," Zaven replied grimly.

"What's going on there?"

"Hell. We had to evacuate the civilians. I suppose troops will go, too. After the job is done."

They gazed at each other. The captain shook his head, but made no comment.

The train moved on slowly. The engineer could not take the chance of running it at full speed as he was not sure what lay ahead.

Shortly after midnight, Zaven had just walked past Zohra and Veronica, sleeping peacefully in their seats, when the train stopped with a sudden jerk. People were knocked out of their seats. Zaven rushed to the girls; they looked shocked, still half asleep.

"It's all right, stay low and keep away from the window," he said hastily, and went to the gate. They were in a gorge, a bad spot, but he couldn't see any sign of ambush over the cliffs. He walked through the coaches to the engine in front. The engineer, a calm, middle-aged Italian, spoke in Turkish.

"There's nothing to worry about," he said. "Just a few rails torn off. Lately I haven't completed a trip without experiencing something like this. The brakeman and his maintenance crew are fixing it. Won't take long."

In the early hours of the morning the train stopped at a small station close to Adana. Two men in scouts' uniforms got on board. They looked around with searching eyes. They had noticed the two fez-wearing gentlemen that had been reluctant to offer their seats to the ladies. Zaven approached them.

"Are you authorized for what you seem to be doing?" he asked.

"Yes, Sivasly," replied one, displaying the rank of sergeant. "We belong to the Security Corps, and we are taking charge now. These men are under suspicion. We're taking them in for questioning."

"Under the circumstances," Zaven reflected, "I have to take your word. But don't forget to see me in Adana."

"We will, Sivasly," smiled the man.

CHAPTER 28

The train stopped at the crowded station in Adana. Zaven got out first. He led Veronica and Zohra to the waiting room and told them to wait there until he returned to the train. It was awkward for the girls to jump down from the elevated ledge to the platform, but most of them gamely performed this bit of acrobatics with excited shrieks. The less daring were helped down from the platform by Zaven's men.

A police officer approached. His face seemed familiar to Zaven but he couldn't identify him by name. Zaven looked at him inquiringly.

"You seem to have forgotten me, Zaven," said the policeman in a friendly manner. "My name is Melkon; I am from Sivas. Now do you remember?"

"Oh, yes!" cried Zaven, extending his hand.

"Welcome to Adana," Melkon greeted him. "We were informed about the refugees from Marash and have prepared temporary quarters for them. Are they all on this train?"

"No, just the girls from the orphanage."

The policeman hesitated a moment. "The quarters prepared for the refugees are the barracks back of the station. But for the girls, if I am not mistaken, there is a special place in the city. We'd better find out."

"Let's do that," Zaven said. "They need rest, and a hot meal will do them good, too."

Melkon nodded sympathetically.

"There have been considerable changes since my last visit," said Zaven, noting the town's booming prosperity as they waded through the crowd.

"Yes, I saw you at Erevant's. I wasn't in this uniform then, and I wanted to be with you very much. But you left, and by the time Captain Hagop got down to my name, the quota was filled."

"If you want my opinion, I think you were lucky that it turned out that way."

"I don't know. I'm happy with my job and doing my part, but if you would have me, I would rather be with you."

"A couple of weeks with me and you'd change your mind, Melkon," Zaven smiled. "Anyway, what's the setup now?"

"Everything is in our hands," replied the policeman promptly. "The Turks left on their own accord. It was better that way."

They walked into the office of the stationmaster. Here Zaven was warmly received by a polished gentleman of middle age, who sounded as though he knew him from way back, although Zaven could not recall the acquaintanceship.

"I have to call the headquarters, with your leave," said Melkon.

"Go right ahead," the station manager replied in an airy manner and turned to Zaven.

The two chatted while the policeman talked on the telephone. Zaven received an invitation for dinner, but he could not accept it as he had too much to do.

"I thought so," the policeman said, replacing the receiver. "There is a special building ready for the girls in the city. A schoolhouse. A nice place with plenty of room. They're sending the trucks."

They walked out. Zohra and Veronica stood at the same spot where Zaven had left them. Their faces brightened when they saw him.

"These two are not going with the girls," said Zaven, turning to the policeman. "They have a place to go. Help me to get them there."

"Sure, Zaven."

"Do you know where Captain Hagop's wife lives?"

"Why, yes, I do."

"I would appreciate very much your finding a carriage to take them there."

"Of course, and someone to go along with them. I would like to do it myself."

"Can you?"

"Why not? It won't take long."

They walked out of the station. A taxi driver was helping a fare board his vehicle, a Ford Model T field ambulance that had been pressed into service as a taxi. The policeman whistled and called the driver by his name. Much to the annoyed fare's dismay, the driver turned him away. Zaven helped the girls into the taxi and the policemen took his place beside the driver.

"I'll join you as soon as I can," said Zaven, pressing Zohra's hand.

He met Miss Hadley in the station.

"All is well," he said. "You will have your own place in the city. The trucks will be here soon to take you there."

"Thank you, Zaven. That is nice," she smiled.

Five battered German trucks lined the street in front of the station and the girls were crowded tightly in them. Melkon was back and sat self-indulgently with Zaven in the lead truck.

The truck slowly rolled through the main street. People stopped to watch and wave their hands. But Zaven was interested in the sights around him. Adana had completely changed. The streets were cleaner. New stores of all kinds and descriptions had taken their place among the others. There were even sweet shops and cinemas. A dormant city had become a metropolis. New industries were established. The old knitting mills were in operation again. The population had tripled. New residential sections had sprung up and a feeling of security prevailed.

The schoolhouse, situated in the formerly Turkish district, was an ideal place for the girls. The gate was just wide enough for the trucks to drive through. Zaven, followed by Melkon and Miss Hadley, walked into the building. There were several large rooms on the first floor and smaller rooms on the second and third, but the rooms were bare.

"They are going to send the bedding and furniture soon," the policeman said. "Stoves and cooking utensils will come but may take a little time. In the meantime, food will be brought to you, madam, until you organize everything the way you want."

"One cannot ask for more," said Miss Hadley.

"The well is in the courtyard back of the building. Its water is pure," added the policeman. "Soon you will have some people to clean the place. I have assigned a soldier as permanent guard."

"Thank you for everything."

"I hope when I see you again, I will find you all settled," Zaven said.

"We'll do our best," responded Miss Hadley, as she shook Zaven's hand.

On their way out the policeman stopped to give some instructions to the soldier standing at the gate.

"Before we get back to the station, I want to see Erevant for rooms. I assume he still operates a hotel," Zaven said.

"Yes," replied the policeman. "The biggest and best in the city. It has everything, including dancing girls."

"He must be doing very well then," Zaven remarked.

"Yes, Zaven, he is a rich man."

"Good for him! After I get settled in, I'd like to drop in to see Zohra and Veronica."

"Very well," said Melkon. "The house is not far from Erevant's."

"I knew that Hagop's wife, Mariam, had moved from the place where I first saw her. It was at the other end of the city. She is fortunate to get one right in the center of things."

"That was one way for the government to show appreciation. She has a cozy little house and two women to help her."

"That is nice."

"We can wait for a taxi or a carriage," suggested Melkon. "This is a main street; one is bound to come along. Or, we can walk if you wish."

"I was cramped on the train," complained Zaven, grimacing and massaging his aching knees. "Walking will do me good, if you don't mind."

"Not at all."

"By the way, do you have a detachment of scouts or security guards—a so-called Security Corps—operating in the outer limits of the city?" Zaven asked.

"I don't know exactly what you have in mind, Zaven," the policeman replied in a somewhat confused voice. "Security is our responsibility, and there are the soldiers to assist us."

"What I mean is, is there a special unit in uniform such as I am wearing to screen the trains and pick up passengers for questioning?"

Melkon rubbed his chin thoughtfully. "Ah, I think I know what you're trying to find out. Tell me what happened. We are doing all we can to stop violence, but it takes time."

"I can appreciate that, Melkon. Here's why I ask: There were two men who said they were Security Corps who were going to question a couple of Turks on the train. Since there were French officers around me, it wouldn't have looked right if I had tried to find out then and there who they really were."

"I know exactly how you feel. We, too, have to overlook things for appearance's sake."

"They said they will see me, but if they don't, I hope to see them."

"The chances are that they will see you, Zaven. Some of them think that they are demigods and that every Armenian feels the same way as they do when it comes to the Turks."

They entered Erevant's. Every chair was occupied. Men with bold eyes and devil-may-care looks displayed their pistols openly. They laughed, shouted, and drank. The appearance of an authorized officer and a policeman did not disturb them a bit. The policeman stood close by the door. Zaven walked toward the counter.

"Where's Erevant?" he asked the man in a white apron standing behind the counter.

"Next door in his office, I believe," replied the man and called the boy serving the customers.

One of the noisy revelers, a man with fierce eyes and a jet-black moustache, jumped into Zaven's path and shouted drunkenly, "Join us for a drink, Sivasly!"

"Later," Zaven replied and followed the boy to the back room. Through a side door they entered a long corridor lined with doors on both sides. Zaven stopped momentarily to peer through the glass door at the overcrowded restaurant. A drink and a little frivolity would probably do him good, he reflected. But that could wait.

They stopped in front of a door. The boy knocked on it three times sharply. Erevant's forceful voice from within bade them enter. The former outlaw, now a respected civic leader and businessman, jumped up from his chair, grabbing Zaven's arms and giving him a vigorous shaking.

"Welcome, Zaven!" he shouted. "I hope this time you'll be here for good. Things are getting big. We need you."

"I can see that, Erevant. Things are certainly getting too big," Zaven intimated.

"We'll talk about that later," said Erevant. "Have you brought the boys along?"

"Only a few. We will be here for a week or so. All I want of you are five or six rooms, Erevant."

"You will have as many as you want!" He addressed the boy who stood by the door: "Send the steward to me."

"Haven't got time, Erevant," Zaven demurred. "I must get back to the train station."

"As you wish, Zaven. Duty comes first."

Erevant accompanied him out to the street, where a new Ford waited.

"This automobile is at your disposal, Zaven," he said airily.

"Thank you," smiled Zaven.

Mariam's house was convenient to everything. A peasant woman who was helping Mariam with the household duties opened the door. Melkon modestly remained in the hallway while Zaven followed the woman. He saw Zohra descending the stairway.

"Is all well?" he asked in a low voice.

"Yes, beloved. I am so happy," she said, throwing her arms around him.

"I want to make your happiness permanent, Zohra."

"Very thoughtful, my love, but I want to live for the moment while I have you all to myself."

Veronica, Mariam, and the other servant woman appeared at the head of the stairs. Zaven greeted them. Zohra emerged from his embrace with a kiss and began climbing the steps. They all went into a modestly furnished large room serving as a parlor.

"Welcome, Zaven," Mariam said. "Is Hagop coming too?"

"He will come as soon as I get back," replied Zaven.

"It has been long, very long," she whispered. "How is he?"

Zaven knew Mariam was subtly referring to her longing for her husband's touch. "Frisky and healthy as ever," Zaven smiled.

"I was told that Eremia is with you."

"Yes, Mariam."

"That's wonderful, Zaven. I am so happy. Happy for all of you."

"Thank you, Mariam."

"Zohra, will you help me prepare something? He must be hungry," Veronica said.

"I have not much time, Veronica."

"Surely you have time for a cup of coffee and a sandwich?" Zohra interjected. "You see, Zaven, we have everything."

He could not refuse her sweet smile. "All right. We must get back to the station before the train arrives," declared Zaven.

Veronica and Zohra left the room to prepare the light lunch. Zaven was alone with Mariam. She came and sat beside him on the sofa.

"Zaven," she said softly, taking his hand, "I admired you for what you were, but now I am proud of you. Zohra is a sweet girl and she loves you.

She will make you happy. What does Hagop think of her?"

"He will kill me," Zaven smiled, "should I dare to go back to him unmarried. Take care of her, Mariam, while I am away."

"I will look upon her as I would my own, Zaven."

"Thank you, Mariam."

"Zaven, will you and Hagop be back for good?" Mariam asked anxiously.

"I believe we will. There are things I must find out. Our work outside is finished. But we must make sure of that, and when the Captain gets here, he will make our release official."

"That's the best news you could have given me!" she cried.

"Mariam, the police officer has been very cooperative to me. Please ask him to come up," he said.

"Of course, Zaven. I know Melkon well. He is a good man."

Melkon came up and took a seat in the parlor. Zohra brought in his lunch and walked out of the room. Zaven wished that she could sit beside him while he sipped his coffee, but he wanted her to break away from her traditions in her own time. Melkon saw her as she walked out and was struck by her beauty.

"Forgive my audacity, Zaven, but who is that lovely girl?"

"One who will be my wife before I leave here," Zaven answered.

"Congratulations, then!" cried the policeman, jumping from his seat to shake Zaven's hand. "I'm glad that you told me. I'll keep that in mind. Is she from the orphanage?"

"No. I dragged her out of a Turkish house," replied Zaven without elaboration.

The policeman looked puzzled. "Zaven, will you trust me?"

"Of course, Melkon."

"That's all I wanted, Zaven," the policeman sighed.

When Zohra came to pick up the cups, Zaven introduced her to him. He looked at Zaven and smiled.

"I must leave now," Zaven said, standing. "I'll be back soon."

"We won't be here in the afternoon. I plan to take the girls shopping," said Mariam. "And I expect you and the boys for dinner."

"There will be just the two of us Mariam, me and Melkon."

Zohra walked them down. Zaven lingered behind and kissed her before she closed the door behind her. When they got back to the station, they were told the refugee train was on the way and should arrive before dark.

"That will give me enough time to see some people. By the way, who is governor, Melkon?" Zaven asked.

"You know him well, Zaven. Mr. Melikian," answered the policeman.

"Oh, yes," Zaven meditated, recalling the Chairman of the National Committee. "I'm glad it's him. I appreciate your assistance very much, Melkon, but I don't want to take advantage of your good nature. Please yourself until I get back."

"I will be happy if I could be of further help, Zaven. The man driving the Ford knows his way around. You will find me here when you return."

The Ford was parked in front of the station. Zaven walked to the car. The driver got out and held the door open for him.

"I'll sit in the front with you," Zaven said.

"As you like, sir," answered the driver meekly.

"You know my name," Zaven smiled. "Please feel free to use it."

"Yes ... er, Zaven."

"You handle this devil's contraption very well. How long have you been driving?"

"A long time. I used to drive for the Germans during the war. I know all about automobiles."

"Very good! Where are you from?"

"Antab."

"I know the town; I believe it's only two days' journey from Marash. We didn't get that far. But when the British evacuated Antab, many of the Armenians who were there came to Marash. I met many of them."

"Most of them came here," commented the driver.

"Did you find any of your relatives among them?"

"Yes."

"Good for you! Are you married?"

"Yes, I married a girl from my home town a couple of months ago."

"Do you like your job?"

"Yes, Erevant is good to me. This one is his personal automobile. He has three others for hire. I take care of all of them."

"I see you're quite indispensable to him. I'll speak to the rogue about your wages."

"Thank you, Zaven, please don't. He pays me well."

The large villa outside the city, once the residence of the Turkish Pasha, was chosen by the French Commandant as his quarters.

After a brief exchange of questions and answers, the security officer volunteered to direct Zaven personally to the Commandant. An impressive, keen-eyed general, whom Zaven had not seen before, acknowledged Zaven's salute from his chair and scrutinized the young officer of the scouts standing at attention.

"Come in, lieutenant," said the general. "We haven't met, but I know a great deal about you. You have my full commendation."

"Thank you, sir. We are grateful to France for giving us the opportunity."

"And France is appreciative of your services, lieutenant. Tell me, when did you leave Marash?"

"Four days ago, sir."

"Bad mess; maybe, we should never have gone there. How was the situation when you left?"

"Well in hand, sir. If you would allow me to express my opinion, we didn't have to leave."

The general looked sharply at Zaven. "I understand, lieutenant. We didn't leave Marash for military reasons. We who fight know little of politics, and have no voice but to follow orders." He rose and walked to the window. Zaven watched him and felt sorry for him. The general turned.

"Are the refugees here?" he asked.

"Some, but not all, sir. The rest will arrive within a few hours."

"I assume you want to get back and wait for them."

"Yes, sir."

"See that they have been taken care of well, and if I can be of any help, don't hesitate to report."

"Thank you, sir. The civilian authorities are well prepared."

"How long will you be here, lieutenant?"

"My papers say a week, sir."

"I don't anticipate any situation which will require you to be at your post, but keep in touch."

"Yes, sir. But I have a request, sir. It is personal. I hope it will be granted."

"Yes, lieutenant?"

"I wish to get your permission to be married, sir, before I leave."

The general rose, walked solemnly up to Zaven, and placed his hand warmly upon his shoulder.

"Permission granted, lieutenant. Who is the lucky girl?"

"A refugee, sir."

"I understand," smiled the general. "I, too, married under similar circumstances. She was a German girl. I have not regretted it for one minute. I wish the same luck to you, lieutenant."

"Thank you, sir."

When Zaven got into the car, the driver cast an inquiring glance at him.

"The Commandant is a good man. We're lucky to have him," he said to satisfy the driver's curiosity. "Now, take me to the governor."

The big, four-story capitol building occupied by the newly formed government looked impressive. Zaven felt proud when he saw the neatly uniformed guards. He entered the cavernous, marble-paved lobby with soaring pillars and walked up to the officer at the desk.

"I would like to see Mr. Melikian," he said casually.

The officer looked at him dubiously.

"My name is Zaven."

"Of course!" cried the officer. "The governor's office is right across the stairway on the second floor."

The floor of the governor's spacious office, with windows overlooking the courtyard, was covered with a Persian rug. The paneled walls, velvet armchairs, and the large walnut desk were tasteful but utilitarian. The one ostentation was a huge crystal chandelier. Three portraits and a map decorated the walls: the portrait of a renowned national hero Vahan Balian, who was instrumental in forming an Armenian unit early in the war to fight the Turks; next to it a portrait of a wealthy patriot, Vartan Kazarian, residing in Paris, pleading the Armenian cause before the Powers; and the third was an unauthentic picture of the Cilician King Levon the VI, who had played an important role in the crusades; the map was that of Cilicia, known as Little Armenia.

Mr. Melikian rose to shake Zaven's hand. "Sit down," he said. "You're a sight for sore eyes, my boy! How are things with you?"

"We're all right, but we lost some men," Zaven said quietly. "What concerns us most is our situation. It doesn't look good. That is why I am here."

"I know, Zaven. Despite our accomplishments, even here we are not secure until definite agreements are reached. France cannot do it by itself, and England won't let France get too big. Italy is siding with France, hoping that if France keeps what it wants, so can Italy. American is a benevolent neutral. Yes, President Wilson wants us to have Adana under the mandate of France. We set up this de facto government to strengthen Wilson's views. Our historic claim cannot be disputed.

"We have paid the price with over a million lives, but here is the challenge. England has what it wanted and is now handing back to the Turks the territory they had occupied. The cases of Marash and Antab are proof of that. The Turks demand that all occupying powers leave the country. The government in Constantinople is too weak, but this Mustafa Kemal, he is getting stronger each day. He has defied the government in Constantinople and the people are behind him. What do you know about him, Zaven?"

"Not much. So far I haven't come in contact with him, but this much I know because I happen to know some of the men who are with him. He is sincere and wise. His purpose is to salvage a new nation from the wreckage. He hasn't yet organized a military force, though the people are behind him. He will need help. Yes, help from those who are his enemies. With the condition the country is in at this time, four or five divisions could once and for all destroy Kemal's hopes. That's what we want, but those who have the means—do they think like us?"

The governor leaned back, staring at the ceiling. Seconds ticked away. "I'm aware that they don't," he said, looking at Zaven. "What will take the place of Turkey? And under whom? This is what has saved the Turks for the last two centuries. Kemal will find sympathizers. In the meantime all we can do is be discreet, be on guard, and pray that the Wilson's recommendation will be accepted. There are a hundred-fifty thousand of us in this city. I don't know how many more outside. In time, we can raise an army to defend ourselves.

"But for now, we depend on France. Should France make a deal with Kemal, all will be lost. In the meantime we cannot remain idle. We must bring here all the refugees who are outside the city so that at least they will be safe. I am sure of one thing: No matter what France does, it won't leave us to the mercy of the Turks. Do you understand that, Zaven? When the time comes, I will ask you to resign to help us directly. This is all I can say now, and I repeat: Let us pray."

"I'm glad that you mentioned my resignation. Everything is clear. We will bring the refugees here."

"We haven't many like you and Hagop, Zaven. Is he coming too?"

"He will, after I get back. By the way, I'm getting married today or the day after. It will be just a simple ceremony. I want you to be there if you can."

"I won't miss that, Zaven. And I won't even ask you who she is."

"But I shall tell you anyway. Her name is Zohra, and she is my life and my love."

CHAPTER 29

When Zaven returned to the station the refugee train had already arrived. Confusion prevailed. He saw Dio on the platform and elbowed his way toward him.

"Hi, Zaven," Dio shouted. "I didn't expect to find you here."

"You got here sooner than I expected," Zaven said.

"We were lucky. Didn't have to stop to repair the rails."

Zaven saw Eremia and Melkon approaching and turned towards them.

"Melkon would not let Hachik go with the other men," Eremia said with glee. "He put them in a carriage to go to his house."

"That's very decent of you, Melkon," complimented Zaven.

Melkon shrugged. "Why, back in the old days, Hachik and I played together. My house is big enough for both of us, until we have him settled, which won't be difficult. Besides, there isn't one good watchmaker in the city."

"Yes, he will be useful," Zaven agreed.

The policeman nodded. "All is set," he said. "It will be a short ten-minute walk to the barracks. You and the men need a little relaxation. Leave it to us. I'll report to you."

"Yes, Zaven, why don't you and Eremia go," Dio added. "I'll stick around."

"All right, Dio. When you finish go to Erevant's. We'll see you there sometime tonight, but don't forget, I want you fit for your last drink with me."

"I give my word. I'll be as sober as a monk until you come," Dio mumbled.

The two prospective bridegrooms got into the waiting Ford. Eremia looked nervous. Zaven put his hand on his shoulder.

"When I left Veronica and Zohra, they were so happy, Eremia. Mariam took them shopping. I know how you feel about Veronica, but for the first time I will ask you directly: Have you two decided? You can wait until things are more settled, but I cannot leave Zohra insecure. It is a serious step, Eremia, and I want you to be sure."

"Yes, Zaven, maybe Veronica's position is different, but I feel the same way as you. A double wedding is the way to go. I'll cherish this always."

They clasped hands.

"When will it be?" asked Eremia sheepishly.

"That's for the girls to decide," Zaven smiled. "Tomorrow suits me, to give us a week together with our brides."

As he was getting out of the car, Zaven said to the driver, "Thank you, I won't need you tonight."

"Do you want me to come in the morning?"

"No. We'll be in the hotel then," Zaven answered.

The door opened for them before they reached it. Mariam and the other women were busy cooking in the kitchen. Zaven stepped in and exchanged a few words with Mariam, then joined Zohra at the foot of the stairway. Veronica and Eremia were not in the parlor.

"Will I have you all to myself from now on?" she asked, clasping his hand between hers.

"Yes, my precious. I may visit the barracks before I see you tomorrow, then I hope that will be all."

"Will Dio and the others be here for dinner?"

"No. They will go to the hotel."

"Mariam is working very hard, preparing everything. I asked her not to, but she has her heart set on it."

Zaven kissed her.

"Do you want to see my wedding dress?" she asked. "It's white, pure white. But I don't want you to see me in it before the wedding. It's bad luck, they say, and I want it to be a surprise!"

"When do you want to wear it, Zohra?"

"I wish I could right at this moment, beloved."

"Wear it for me tomorrow evening, then, Zohra. It will be a simple wedding. There won't be more than a dozen guests. No ceremony. Just a priest to proclaim before God that we belong to each other."

Zaven opened his eyes. Though the room was in semidarkness because of the drawn blinds, he knew that it must be past noon. They were the last ones to leave Mariam's house after the wedding. It had been nice. Mariam hadn't overlooked a thing. He drank more than he ever had, as every one of the selected guests wanted a personal toast with him. But he seemed immune to liquor. Even the priest, who had cast aside his sacred cloak for the occasion, got tipsy and had to be taken home. Dio and Erevant between them had arranged that Erevant would be Zaven's best man and Dio would be Eremia's.

Erevant's wedding present to the happy couple was a week's stay in the sumptuous, two-room bridal suite—the best accommodations in his hotel. Zaven sat up gingerly in the regal bed. Zohra was still asleep. An angel from heaven could not look lovelier than her. He felt exhilarated; this exquisite creature was his wife! He didn't deserve her, but he would love and cherish her to the end. He drew his lips close to her cheek, but suppressed the temptation so he would not awaken her.

He quietly got out of the bed, tiptoed to the window, and looked outside through a chink in the blinds. Yes, it was after noon, a bright day, and the main street was bustling. He threw on his clothes and paused to gaze at Zohra's white silk wedding gown, draped carefully upon a sofa. He touched it as though it was a sacred object. She had looked so beautiful. The expression in her lovely brown eyes when the priest asked her, "Do you take this man as your lawful husband?" would forever live in his memory. She had gazed at him with eyes full of happiness.

He went to her and kissed her on the forehead. She threw her arms around him and drew him closer.

"I'll go down and have Erevant send something to eat," he whispered to Zohra.

"Yes, beloved. Just coffee and biscuits."

When Zaven returned Zohra met him in the parlor in a fashionable velvet gown.

"Erevant insisted on bringing our breakfast himself," he said and stood at a distance, watching her.

"Do you like this gown better, my husband, than the one I wore last night?" she asked, turning in a complete circle.

"To me, the one you wore last night is not of this world and will forever remain that way. But in that gown, you are ravishing—the loveliest wife in the world."

"And I exist for you alone, my beloved husband."

She took his arm and led him to the sofa. They watched the activities in the street for a while.

"Erevant is very close to you, Zaven," she reflected serenely. "Was he with you from the beginning?"

"No, Zohra. He, too, was an outlaw. When I came here, he had already established himself in business. He is doing well. Though it is not what he wants, he cannot get out of it. The way he sees it, I am doing what he wanted to do. You understand that, Zohra? He is a good man, but in his position he has to deal with all sorts. For the short time I will be away from you, I want you to know that you can trust him. Having him as my best man wasn't just a gesture. I want you to know that."

"Thank you, my husband, for letting me know these things."

There was a rap on the door. Zaven went to answer it. Erevant grabbed Zaven's arms and gave him a shake. A pageboy with a large tray of assorted dishes and coffee followed at his heels. Erevant walked over to Zohra. She bowed, took his hand, and brought it to her lips.

"It is the privilege of a sister to kiss her big brother's hand," she said softly.

Erevant smiled. "Thank you for accepting me, Zohra. There is nothing in my power that I wouldn't do for you two. Your husband knows that. I want you to know it, too."

"Come, you rogue," Zaven chimed in. "What are you up to?"

"Why, I just brought in your food, you ingrate, and I don't get a word of thanks!" Erevant jested.

"Are you going to join us?"

Erevant rubbed his ample paunch and said, "Haven't put a morsel in my mouth all morning."

Zaven laughed. "You could stand to lose a pound or two, my friend, but be our guest!" he said, arranging chairs around the table.

They ate in silence for a while before Erevant said, "Oh, yes, I almost forgot! Eremia and Veronica went to Melkon's. They are expecting you there."

Zaven nodded.

"I have plans for you when you get back," said the best man cagily.

"Better be good," smiled Zaven.

"It won't be anything new for you two soldiers, but it will make you blush in the presence of your wives."

"Well, I don't want to miss that," Zohra laughed.

Close to midnight, the Ford stopped at the hotel's front door. The honeymooners stepped out. Erevant met them in the lobby.

"I expected you earlier, but the night is still young," he said, leading the way.

They ascended a flight of steps covered with a fluffy rug. The muffled sound of the dance music was audible. Halfway down the hall a burly, hard-looking fellow stood outside a door.

"This isn't strictly private," Erevant commented, turning to his guests. "There are paying customers—a rowdy bunch that knows how to make merry. But for you, my friends, all libations are on the house. Come."

The big man opened the door as they approached and entered a large, dimly lit room. Through the dense haze of cigarette smoke Zaven could just make out a group of men and women sitting at tables around an elevated dance platform. The sensual undulations of an exotic dancer had the audience captivated.

Erevant led his guests to the head table. Dio and the others were there. Zaven looked around. He wasn't surprised to see so many familiar faces in French uniform. Dio nodded without diverting his eyes from the dancer. Eremia sat next to him. The brides sat side by side, Zaven next to Zohra with his best man beside him.

"She is marvelous, isn't she? She has danced before the Sultan," Erevant boasted. "I went through a great deal of trouble to bring her from Aleppo."

"What's her name?" Zaven asked.

"Bahria Hanum. Just between you and me, her father is an Armenian and her mother a Greek, but she is really a good girl."

Zohra pressed Zaven's arm when the waiter placed a glassful of aromatic cognac in front of her.

"You don't have to, love," Zaven whispered.

The waiter caught Erevant's glance, grinned sheepishly, and pushed the glass in front of Zaven.

"I have a bottle of rare Antab wine and have been saving it for a special occasion and special guests," announced Erevant. He turned to the waiter: "Go and fetch it, you fathead! It's in my closet."

The incomparable Bahria finished her dance in the midst of noisy applause. She bowed and wrapped herself in her embroidered robe and walked leisurely toward the head table. She stood facing Zaven. Up close she looked like any ordinary woman, with kind and understanding eyes beneath her mascara.

"My recollection of the dreaded name, Daly Mustafa, goes back to Constantinople," she said in a soft voice. "How much I wished then that I could dance for him. From the bottom of my heart, I wish you all happiness." To Zohra she said: "Take good care of him, my dear. He belongs to all of us."

Zohra pressed herself tightly against her celebrated husband. Bahria again bowed to the applause of her audience and made her graceful exit.

Zaven's eyes had become accustomed to the dim light. He straightened up and looked around. His eyes rested on a table in the opposite corner. Staring intently at the two occupants, he gradually recognized their faces—the two members of the Security Corps who had detained the Turks in fezzes on the train. Out of uniform now, the men were whooping and hollering and making great fools of themselves. Erevant noticed Zaven's intent concentration and patted his arm.

"Those two in the corner, Erevant," Zaven said in a hard voice, "do you know them?"

"Yes, Zaven, they have been regulars of late. Anything wrong?"

"I'm going over to speak to them," declared Zaven, standing up.

"No, Zaven, go to my room," Erevant whispered. "I'll bring them to you."

Zaven, with a gentle pat on Zohra's shoulder, left. Dio followed him. Eremia and the others looked at him, but made no move when they caught Zaven's glance.

"What's up, Zaven?" Dio asked, after closing the door behind them.

"We'll find out soon," Zaven answered curtly.

Erevant, with two of his men and the two loutish "security officers" who had spoiled the evening, walked into the room. The door was closed. Zaven measured the men; their automatic pistols bulged conspicuously under their jackets. They looked hard but uneasy.

"Do you remember me?" Zaven asked in a cold voice. "As I recall it, you were coming to see me."

It was the one who had so brazenly told Zaven on the train that they belonged to the Security Corps who spoke up. "We tried, Sivasly. Ask Erevant, if you won't believe us."

Erevant nodded. "They said they wanted to square themselves with you. Thought it was not my business to meddle."

"Yes, Zaven, we want to square ourselves with you," confirmed the man, speaking for his partner. He reached into his jacket and produced a bulky leather money sack. "This is what we got from the Turks. Share it as you wish." He laid the sack on the table.

Zaven stepped forward. Dio, with a lightning move, disarmed them.

"What did you do with them?" asked Zaven.

"They were Turks!" answered the spokesman in surprise.

"I know, but that doesn't explain everything." Zaven turned to Dio. "I saw the Commissar of police inside the room. Go and tell him that I want him."

He addressed the men again. "You scum! I would have dealt with you my own way if there had not been a higher authority to handle you. You would have killed them for this"—he threw the money sack at the men—"even if they had been Armenian."

"Zaven," interrupted Erevant before Dio was outside the room, "will you let me handle this thing?"

"You have a point there, Erevant. You seem to know them. They're your responsibility."

Erevant's bouncers dragged the men away. One of Zaven's men was waiting in the hallway. He told him that Eremia had taken the girls to their rooms.

"I must speak with them," said Zaven. "Tell Erevant I'll join him later."

The moment Zaven entered the room, Zohra stepped forward. "Those men in the dance club were the same men in uniform we saw on the train, weren't they?" she said. "Why were you so upset about them, my husband?"

"I want you to know this, Zohra," he said in a stern voice. "I have no use for scum, regardless of who and what they are. Do you want to go back? I promised Erevant that I'd join him."

"Why don't you two go?" Veronica suggested. "Eremia and I have so much to talk about. But don't stay too long."

The week went by too quickly. Zaven had to leave. For the first time, he fully experienced a peaceful life and liked it. During those quiet moments with Zohra, he had earnestly thought of ending his dubious pursuit. Now that he played more or less the part of persecutor rather than pursued, his view of right and wrong was not the same. To kill is to kill, regardless of motive. He remembered the words of an old philosopher who once had tried to stop him with the wise admonition, "Enemies cannot go on cutting each other's throats forever. Eventually, one of those throats must learn wisdom and demand that the bloodshed must stop!"

He had never completely believed in his vow to get revenge. Every time he had taken a life, he felt that part of his life was gone too. Yet, with all this realization and awakening, there was something stronger than his love for his wife, stronger than himself. There was no logic, no reason, but it was there, forcing him on, and against this force, everything else faded.

He had one hour before his train left. Dio and the others had already left. He and Eremia were going to join them at the station.

Zohra packed his clothes in the other room. She walked dejectedly toward him. Her eyes were red. He took her in his arms, placed his hand gently under her chin, and lifted her head. She could not suppress an emotional outburst.

"Do you feel better now?" whispered Zaven, kissing her. "I'll be away only a short while. You'll be safe with Mariam until I get back."

"You will resign, Zaven. That is definite?" she whispered.

"Yes, Zohra, and we will leave this land."

"That's all I want, my husband. I want a son like you, without the shadows."

She kissed him.

"Can I come to the station with you?"

"If you insist, but I would rather leave you here, knowing that you are safe."

She nodded, resting her head against his chest. There was a knock on the door. He knew who it was.

"Coming, Eremia!" he cried.

CHAPTER 30

As Zaven watched the countryside from the train, he realized how different the weather was at the higher altitude. North of Adana, winter had already arrived, whereas, when he boarded the train that morning, it looked like a pleasant, late summer day. This did not give him any comfort; his thoughts went back again to the room where he had left Zohra. He imagined her face before him. What would she be doing now? She must be with Mariam. That was better, much better. Mariam would be very nice to her.

Eremia was sitting beside him looking at a tiny gold locket attached to his watch chain. Zaven turned to him.

"Did Veronica give it to you?" he asked.

"Yes, Zaven," Eremia answered, fondling the locket. "It contains a lock of her hair."

Zaven smiled. "A happy thought."

"Zaven, are we going back to them soon?"

"I hope so ..."

Dio, who was sitting behind them, lifted his head over the seat between the two.

"You two lovebirds," he grunted. "And what does the future bode for me? Playing nursemaid to your broods of brats, no doubt! I'd better find a wife for myself."

"It will be a miracle," retorted Zaven, "if you could bring yourself to do it."

"I'll surprise you yet, Zaven. I, too, can become respectable," chuckled Dio as he reclined in his seat.

When Zaven stepped off the train at the little station of Bakcha, he sensed tension in the air. The troops posted were Algerians. This was not good. He did not expect to find any of his men there, as he had not let Hagop know which train he was taking. The town was nestled about two miles into the valley. Dusk was falling. They did not waste any time and took the narrow path in the snow. Zaven led the way; the others followed him in single file. He stopped now and then to look around. All was quiet, ominously quiet. Not a creature was moving.

They were at the edge of town when he saw four figures coming toward him. He recognized the one in front. Tovmas was one of the scouts who joined Zaven when he was commissioned by the French.

"Have you got a rooster tucked under your cloak, Tovmas?" he cried.

"There aren't any roosters left in the town, Zaven," answered the man in a somber voice.

Tovmas's glum behavior was out of character. Zaven always associated him with a humorous incident that brought a grin to his face whenever he looked upon his usually jocular companion. Once, while on patrol, Tovmas had spotted chickens perched high up in a tree in the courtyard of a Turkish house. Without explaining his intent, Tovmas climbed over the wall, secured a long pole, and started poking the fowl. His larcenous intention was too obvious to suit Zaven, but it was too late to do anything.

The ruckus that the molested roosters raised was loud enough to wake the whole neighborhood. Tovmas had opened the gate from the inside to make his exit easier. Zaven had walked into the courtyard when the owner of the purloined roosters appeared half-dressed with a shotgun in hand.

"You confounded ass, drop that shotgun!" Zaven had cried angrily. Tovmas, with the screeching roosters tucked under his arm, stepped out of the gate.

The Turk had obeyed the command and, after alternating his glances from the chicken thief to the commanding figure facing him, had stammered, "M-must have been the f-fox, Master."

"Go in, then," Zaven commanded, stifling his hilarity, "and don't let me catch you again getting so worked up because of a fox."

Back in the present, Zaven asked Tovmas, "How's everything?"

Tovmas hesitated. "The Captain is not here. He left behind thirty of us to wait for you."

"Where did he go?"

"To Hallow-Rock."

This was a small Armenian town tucked in the mountains about a day's march from Bakcha. Throughout many generations its inhabitants had established a reputation for bravery. The Turks had never completely subdued Hallow-Rock. They had survived the war and the deportation in their mountain hideouts and returned home when the French took over.

"When did he leave?" Zaven asked.

"Three days ago."

"Trouble?" groaned Zaven.

"We don't know. The Captain thought that the people there wouldn't be safe since the French withdrew all their forces from that section. He asked for a detachment of troops to go along with him, but he was refused. He told us that he should be back within three or four days.

"Even this town is partially surrounded, Zaven," Tovmas continued. "Only the Armenians are left. We won't go beyond the station. Yesterday a detachment of Algerians, under the command of a lieutenant, went out. Less than five miles away they were ambushed. We found the bodies of the French lieutenant and two noncoms. We don't know what became of the Algerians."

They passed by the schoolhouse that had once been their headquarters.

"The Algerians have taken it over," Tovmas declared in a resentful voice. "We're at an abandoned Turkish house at the other end of the town with a barn large enough for our horses."

They lumbered through streets knee-deep in snow. No one was in sight. Dim lights shimmering in windows here and there made the frigid night lonely and eerie. Tovmas's headquarters, a big, two-story house set well apart from the other buildings and surrounded by the conventional high walls forming a spacious courtyard, loomed welcomingly ahead of them.

Several men came out to greet Zaven. They went to the large room on the ground floor. An inviting fire blazed in the fireplace. Men with grim looks sat around it. Zaven's appearance had momentarily brightened their faces. The man in charge, a man named Grigor who was a veteran of many combats, came forward.

"We felt lost, Zaven, with the Captain gone and you not here," Grigor said. "My congratulations to you and Eremia." His words were echoed by all.

"Anything to report?" Zaven asked, settling down in front of the fire.

"I assume Tovmas told you where the Captain went," said Grigor.

"Yes. To Hallow-Rock."

Grigor sighed. "Things don't look good. We haven't done anything or gone anywhere—other than yesterday, when we ventured out to find out what happened to the Algerians."

"I know all about that, too," interrupted Zaven.

The chatter stopped. The faces were grim again.

"I'd better report to the officer in command," Zaven said.

"Don't you want to eat something first?" Grigor asked.

"Yes, you really should eat something," Tovmas chimed in. "The women who cook for us went home, but we have some choice portions left from the calf we slew today. The fire is perfect, and it won't take long."

"Maybe after I get back." Zaven turned to Dio and Eremia. "You two go ahead. Don't wait for me."

On the way to the headquarters, Zaven learned that the officer to whom he was to report was a new one, a captain. Although not hostile, he seemed unsympathetic toward those who were not directly under his command. The blow of losing two of his men had affected him badly.

With hesitating steps, Zaven ascended the stairs and paused in front of the door to the captain's private quarters for a moment to collect his thoughts. He tapped the door gently. A harsh, guttural voice commanded him to enter.

Clad in a rumpled dressing gown, the captain sat in an armchair with a bottle in front of him. He stared with glassy eyes at Zaven, who was standing by the door waiting to be invited in.

"Take a chair, lieutenant," mumbled the captain. "We haven't met. I am pleased to have you back."

Zaven sat down in a chair several feet away.

"Get closer, lieutenant. Drinking alone is not a habit of mine."

"You have my heartfelt sympathy, captain," Zaven said in a solemn voice.

The captain filled a glass, handed it to Zaven, and looked straight into his eyes. Without a word, Zaven emptied the glass. The captain's eyes seemed clearer.

"I'm wondering," he muttered, "would it have happened if you were here, so that I could have sent you along ..."

"May I ask the nature of the mission, captain?" Zaven asked.

"Oh, yes, the mission," mumbled the captain. "Your commanding officer asked me if I would assign some troops to go along with him. I refused, because I didn't want him to go. But, I knew that it wouldn't be right to stop him. This is no longer a case of restoring order, but a case of kill or be killed. The whole damned Mohammedan world is out for Christian blood, and we Christians are trying to win them over."

He emptied his glass. "What a farce!" he growled. "Yes, we evacuated other Armenian villages, but these were fairly close, and the Turks did not ask for trouble. As for Hallow-Rock, I don't know."

He reached for the bottle and refilled his glass.

"However, after Hagop left, my conscience started bothering me. The lieutenant involved reprimanded me for sending him alone. I ordered the lieutenant to take two platoons and follow him. He was ambushed a few miles from here. My information is that the whole affair lasted less than fifteen minutes. We found only the bodies of Frenchmen, three of them. As for what became of the Algerians, your guess is as good as mine."

Suddenly he slammed his glass on the table and cried, "How can I trust those bastards under me?"

Zaven remained silent.

"My job is to guard the railway," continued the captain. "If it becomes necessary, I'll evacuate this town and set up my post at the station."

"There are more than a thousand people in Hallow-Rock," said Zaven. "We cannot leave them to the mercy of the enemy. If Captain Hagop is not back by tomorrow, I will go."

"How many men do you have?"

"That is immaterial."

"I cannot give you troop support."

"I don't want any," answered Zaven defiantly.

"Very well. You may go without my consent, but I'll not bring charges of insubordination against you. All I want you to know is that I, too, would have done the same thing if I were you."

Zaven left the captain with the feeling that something tragic was in the air. Did Hagop reach Hallow-Rock? If so, would he take the far riskier chance of the journey back, hampered by the presence of women and children? The moment he entered the room, the men gathered around him.

"If I had my way, I would start for Hallow-Rock without delay," he said solemnly.

The men looked at each other, but no one spoke. There were long moments of silence.

"While you were away, one of the local villagers, whose name is Arshag, dropped in," Dio spoke somberly. "He wanted to wait until you got back, but I told him that it would be better if he sees you in the morning."

"How long has he been here?" Zaven asked pointedly.

"Several days, since his village was evacuated. They had a few skirmishes with the Turks, but Hagop went there at the right time to evacuate them. He said he has a dozen dependable men who would like to come along. Zaven rose and glanced at his watch. "Two hours before midnight," he muttered. "That will give us enough time."

"Feel like eating something?"

"No, Dio, I'm going up to rest, and I advise you all to do the same. We're leaving shortly after midnight. Send someone after Arshag. I want to see him immediately."

He turned to the man in charge of arms and ammunition. "Have you got enough?"

"Yes, Zaven, all we can carry, including grenades and several portable machine guns."

"Good, we'll take all we can. I want to make this move in secrecy, and tonight is the night. Oh, yes, every one of us will be clad in a white sheet when we get in the open."

"We haven't enough white sheets to go around, Zaven," answered the man whimsically, "but we can round some up."

"See to it!" Zaven said as he mounted the stairs to the second floor.

Dio stood a few paces away from him and wavered but decided to stay where he was. Zaven walked into a small room in the rear of the house. There were two homemade wooden cots. Which one was Hagop's? That didn't matter. He stretched down on one of them and closed his eyes. A nap, regardless of how short, would do him good. But, it was useless to try. His eyes were wide open, staring at the dark ceiling. Irrelevant thoughts, questions without answers, whirled around and around in his mind. The tapping on the door stirred him awake. He sat up, lit the candle, and went to the door. Dio and Arshag walked in.

Arshag was a short, stocky fellow in his late thirties with cold eyes, bushy eyebrows, and a weather-beaten face that hadn't seen a razor for at least two weeks. He was fully armed and carried a white sheet under his arm. Zaven knew a great deal about him. He had been an outlaw since his teens. No one knew the section of the country they were to travel better than he did. Zaven smiled and extended his hand.

"I should have waited," Arshag said apologetically.

"They told me of your offer, Arshag."

"Yes, Zaven, I'm ready."

Zaven placed his hand upon Arshag's shoulder. "We must leave—every moment counts," Zaven said calmly.

"I know, Zaven," answered the man grimly.

"How many are coming along?"

"Some of them are already downstairs. Others will be here soon. The number of your volunteers, I believe, will be around forty. Good men, Zaven, take my word for it."

"I have no doubt of that, Arshag. I want you to map a course in your mind that will take us there without touching the regular road, and at the same time will be close enough to have our eyes on it at all times."

"That won't be hard, Zaven."

"All right, let's go."

It was a clear, brisk, moonlit night. About eighty armed men, half of them in uniform, waited for the signal that would bring them out. The whole town slept. Not a glimmer of light was visible. A solitary figure, partially sheltered by a tree, stood at the fringe of the road, where he had a clear view of the surroundings. He walked slowly to the gate and opened it.

"All right, men, proceed two by two," Zaven ordered them. "Count to thirty before following the pair ahead of you."

A short, stocky figure enveloped loosely in a white sheet stepped forward.

"No, no, Arshag," Zaven scolded him. "We don't put that on until after we get out of the town."

A mile out of town, Zaven stopped along the banks of a swiftly running stream at the bottom of a ravine. All had gone well so far. No one, except the native who guarded the town, knew what was going on.

"This is a good place to regroup, Arshag," he said. "From here on you lead. Take four men; keep your distance between each other. We'll follow you. Keep on moving; if you have anything to report, just let one of the men fall behind. Don't lose sight of the road. Now, put on your sheets. They will make us virtually invisible in the snow. No one will notice you until you walk up to him."

They did not stop once throughout the night. The course at times was difficult. They had to circle wide around the villages and farms. On the whole, all had gone well, but the eerily glowing eyes of wolves watching them annoyed and even frightened them a little. Had these beasts been bold enough to challenge them, it would have been embarrassing, as Zaven's order was not to shoot. Presumably wary of ghostly white figures stalking the night, the wolves thankfully kept their distance.

The sun was up. They were on a pine-covered ridge overlooking the main road a mile below. It was a good place to rest. Zaven had dispatched the sentinels at vantage points in all directions. He selected a sheltered rock and sat on it. Arshag came over to him.

"How much ground did we cover?" Zaven asked.

"More than I expected," answered the guide.

"When can we get there?"

"After nightfall."

"Are we going to move by daylight?"

"Of course—from here on it doesn't matter. We know what lies ahead."

He noticed one of the sentinels hurrying toward him, and rose to meet him halfway.

"Zaven, we saw three men in the woods not far from the road heading in this direction," said the man excitedly.

"Sure they weren't peasants?"

"Not likely—they were moving too clumsily. Like someone lost ... or wounded."

"Let's see," said Zaven.

Dio followed them. They stopped and the sentinel pointed in the direction where he had seen the stragglers, but no one was in sight.

"They must be in the ravine," explained the sentinel." They headed that way."

Zaven moved forward to a point that offered a better view. He could see clearly with the aid of his binoculars. Dio and the sentinel, standing several paces away, noticed his concentration.

"You're right," Zaven mumbled. "They are in the ravine. If they follow the course they seem to be taking, it will bring them directly to where we stand."

He was still watching when he cried suddenly, "Come here, Dio!" and handed him the binoculars.

Dio gasped. "Why, Zaven, they're in uniform."

"Yes, like ours. And the one in the lead, if he's the one I think he is ..." He paused, and when he spoke again, his voice rang with hope. "Keep your fingers crossed, Dio. Hagop might not be far away."

He looked again, placed the binoculars in their case, and moved forward.

"I have a good idea who they are, but we have to be careful."

Crouched behind a rock, Zaven watched the stragglers moving toward him. They were less than a hundred yards away. Their identity was now beyond a doubt. The one leading was Sarkis. As the ragtag trio got closer, Zaven observed how pitiful they looked. Their hats were gone, their unforms torn and bloodied. They had rifles, but the cartridge belts crisscrossing their torsos were empty. Sarkis's head was bandaged; the other two were limping. The way they shuffled on, every step they took seemed to be an effort.

Zaven was shocked; the sight before him was evidence of a tragic outcome. His immediate problem was not to startle them. He lay low and motioned the others to do likewise. When they were within earshot, Zaven cried, "Sarkis!"

The men, stunned, mechanically threw themselves on the ground.

"This is Zaven, Sarkis!"

It took some time for his words to penetrate into the men's brains. They stood up. A weak, plaintive voice stammered, "I-is that r-really you, Zaven?"

Zaven advanced toward them. With newfound energy they dashed forward and took Zaven in their embrace. He uttered a few reassuring words. What a welcome sight he was!

"What happened?" he whispered.

"Trapped," Sarkis answered.

"When and how?"

"The same day, toward sundown," Sarkis declared, in a low hesitant voice. "It was a well planned trap, prepared long before we got there."

He paused; Zaven stared at him, tense, tight-lipped.

"There must have been a thousand of them," he continued. "The Captain was one of the first to fall. From then on it was every man for himself, but we held them."

Zaven felt his heart leap to his throat. He didn't want to accept what he had heard: Hagop wad dead.

"At dark we tried to break through," Sarkis was saying. "How many of us, that I don't know. We met later and have been wandering in the mountains ever since. Traveling at night, hiding at daylight ..."

The story was over. There was nothing else that Zaven cared to know. He bit his lips, stood erect, and gazed at the sky. Was he trying to hide his eyes? He tapped Sarkis's shoulder.

"Let's go," he said. "You three must be starving, and these wounds need to be looked at. You've done a lousy job binding yours, Sarkis."

Dio got closer to him, as if he wanted to say something, but then changed his mind when he caught Zaven's eyes. Hagop was gone, as well as the rest of them. But, Hallow-Rock was still there. Had others survived and reached it? It might be only wishful thinking, but Zaven and Dio held onto that hope.

Zaven glanced at his watch. It showed half an hour past noon. The day was cloudy, not too cold, and snow was in the air. They had just forded a waist-deep river. Their breeches were soaked, but they managed to keep their ammunition dry.

Earlier, before they had reached the river, while scanning the distant ridges, Zaven had seen figures scattered here and there. It was not his inclination to ignore them, but there was nothing he could do except move on cautiously, prepared for any eventuality.

He sent the vanguard far ahead, extended the flanks of his force, placed a strong unit to act as rear guard, and went down to the plains lying ahead. He knew that the enemy was close. He heard the distant echo of a single shot. Stopping, he took out his binoculars and looked around. He felt certain that the shot was a signal.

Two minutes later he heard another, this one a little closer. The men around him were tense, expecting orders from him. But Zaven merely moved on with clenched fists, with his head low, raising it now and then to look around.

Arshag, who was in the lead, had fallen behind.

"I think they're ahead of us, Zaven," he said. "Not too many. And my guess is that they're falling back."

Zaven nodded. There came another shot. "How far are we from Hallow-Rock?"

"Less than ten miles, Zaven."

"We'll make it," he said confidently. "I would like to follow the river upstream. That will give us good flanking position. Will that throw us far off our course?"

"Not much, Zaven. And it will take us within a mile of Hallow-Rock."

"Good. That way we can defend our flanks and move. What we've been hearing are signal shots. It will take time for the Turks muster a force large enough to stop us. Let's hurry!"

It was getting dark, though there still remained a couple of hours of daylight. Fine snowflakes danced lazily in the air. Zaven with Dio and a few others behind them cleared the summit of a towering hill that started its rise from the bank of the river. It dominated the surrounding terrain. Arshag was there waiting for him.

"The Turks are straight ahead, Zaven," he said. "My guess is that they are aiming for this hill."

Zaven nodded. "Did they see you?"

"I don't think so. Some of them are halfway down the hill," revealed the guide.

"We will stay here to observe them." Zaven turned to Dio. "Deploy the men around the hill," he instructed. "I want them to come at us."

In a half-crouched position, Zaven surveyed the surroundings, listened, and sniffed the air. In his long career, Zaven's nose had become a reconnaissance tool nearly as keen as his other senses.

"Do you hear gunfire?" he asked nonchalantly.

The guide concentrated and listened for a moment, then shook his head.

"Maybe not the noise, but the vibration is in the air," Zaven remarked. "Had it been clearer, you would have seen smoke rising over the mountains ahead of us. What's behind it?"

"Hallow-Rock, Zaven," Arshag answered.

"Hope I'm wrong, but the way I see it, we have to break through a siege to get to Hallow-Rock."

"You're likely right, Zaven. They have tasted blood," said the guide.

They didn't have to wait long; the enemy was in sight and climbing the hill. Zaven ordered his men not to fire at the vanguard. He let them pass by in order to catch the main force.

The strategy worked better than Zaven hoped. The vanguard was less than a hundred feet away from him. The main force already was halfway to the hill. They outnumbered his men at least three to one. That didn't disturb him. To him, they looked more like a mob than an organized fighting unit.

Dio, who was beside him manning a submachine gun, was getting restless. Zaven sneered. It was the sneer of a beast on the verge of pouncing upon his prey. He let them come still closer. Then he raised his arm and dropped it. The machine gun rang out. Men tumbled down. The grim saga of life and death had begun.

Zaven was not worried about those who were on the hill. In time he would get rid of them, too. But how many were behind them? He was not sure of his next move. Should he move on after this was finished? If the Turks had really besieged Hallow-Rock, the better plan would be to direct their attention toward him. He could defend his position as long as he wanted. Then, when he broke out and got close to the town, he would receive help from the defenders of Hallow-Rock.

The battle of the hill lasted less than two hours. As darkness fell, everything was still. Zaven was aware that half the enemy had escaped and joined a much stronger force around the hill, waiting for his next move. The clear sky and the stillness of the night had confirmed his conjecture that Hallow-Rock was under siege. The enemy was concentrating its forces around him.

Now he was ready for the second phase. He regrouped his men in a small circle that could not be penetrated, and instructed them not to fire a single shot unless they had a target.

At dawn there was a furious assault, but they forced the enemy back. The enemy did not try again. During the day, the enemy completed a maneuver and encircled Hallow-Rock. That didn't worry Zaven nor did the enemy's strategy.

Zaven knelt upon one knee, and gazed at the eastern horizon. The time had come. He must break through the surrounding enemy chain before sunrise. Everyone was thoroughly familiar with his own part. Once they were in the open, the situation would be under control. From then on they had to go through slow, orderly, rear guard action that would bring them closer and closer to Hallow-Rock. Then the defenders there would play their part. The enemy would be caught between their crossfire and would have to yield.

In a straight line ten feet apart from one another, six of Zaven's men began creeping down. The snow in the background hid their white forms, helping them to get closer than they had expected. Suddenly, the whole region reverberated with the blasts of grenades and the rat-a-tat chatter of machine guns. This was followed by a brief interval of hand-to-hand skirmishing. Zaven received a gash on his arm, a nuisance that didn't hinder him. His strategy worked; they broke through. Then, he divided the men into three groups. Dio was in charge of the hindmost one.

All of Zaven's strategies s had worked. The defenders of the town warmly greeted him. Dio arrived, but not on his feet—two men carried him. Zaven rushed forward. They laid him down. His face was white, his eyes closed. Zaven kneeled beside him and raised his eyelids. There was no life. Dio's lips curved to form a smile as though, even in death, he had become conscious of his dear friend's touch. With great tenderness Zaven closed Dio's eyes, pressed his fingertips to the lips that would never speak again, and walked away. Later he learned Sarkis and the other survivor had also fallen in the battle.

At the narrow entrance of the town formed by twin rocky precipices, he saw two of the men who had been with Hagop. His face brightened in spite of everything. He walked over to them.

"How many of you made it here safely?" he asked.

"Eight of us, Zaven," came the answer.

Zaven had nothing else to say. Had she spared them for one more battle? Such was the ironic hand of fate.

CHAPTER 31

Hallow-Rock was a proud little town of two hundred families. The stone, two-storied huts were clustered together within the inaccessible towering precipice. It was a natural fortress with only one entrance—the narrow passageway through which Zaven had entered. Those who had lived there generation after generation were a resilient and resourceful people, as strong and indomitable as the rocky face that surrounded them.

Though the aid that arrived was not what they expected, it restored hope for the town. It meant that they were not totally forgotten and would not fight alone the grim battle of life or death. The price paid by those who had come to their aid was heavy. Twenty were killed; more than half who had reached there were wounded. After the battle, it was hoped that things would be quiet for a while. No doubt the enemy would still concentrate on the town, but it did not matter. In the minds of the town folk, the legendary Zaven was as mighty as a hundred men, with or without the scanty force he had brought with him.

The men were housed among the families. Zaven, Eremia, and Arshag were houseguests of the man who had extended the official welcome. His name was Avak, and to all, young and old, he was the Keha, or leader, and he was addressed as such. He was a soft-spoken man in his early sixties, gray-haired but strong and heathy. He led his guests to his home, the best one in the town, centrally located next to the church. Zaven casually observed the chickens cackling in the courtyard, and the barn in the back of the house seemed well stocked.

The room where the Keha received his guests was on the second floor.

A small wood stove in the center made the room warm and comfortable. There were no chairs, but wide, plush carpet-covered ottomans lined the wall. Zaven wasn't cold, but it was a pleasant feeling to stand by the hot stove with his arms outstretched. An elderly woman with a careworn countenance walked in with a bottle and several glasses.

"I know you're hungry, but relaxing your nerves comes first," said the host, as he handed Zaven a glass. He then gazed at Zaven's bandaged, blood-soaked arm and cried, "Sara, you'd better attend to that!" Turning back to Zaven, he said, "My wife is very good at taking care of nasty wounds like that."

"Oh, it's just a cut," Zaven shrugged. "It isn't as bad as it looks. There are others who need attention more than I do."

"Don't worry about them. They'll be looked after," said the Keha. "We have a man here who is the best around these parts when it comes to wounds."

The old woman walked out and was back soon with her first-aid kit in a tin box. She removed the bandages and examined the wound for a moment.

"Even though it looks a bit messy, you're done the right thing, son," she said, "by applying hot ashes. We must clean it first; it might hurt a bit."

Zaven smiled. She gently pressed his arm and went to work. The job was done well and Sara left.

"Does it feel better now?" the Keha asked, refilling Zaven's glass.

"Much better, thanks to your wife," Zaven smiled.

"Sara is a good wife; the best a man could wish for."

A brawny, vigorous man in his mid-thirties, who was fully armed, opened the door and walked straight up to Zaven.

"He's my eldest son, Vahan," said the Keha in a proud manner. "He is in command, but from now on you take charge. I am sure you'll find him very cooperative."

"If you hadn't come, we would have had a very hard time defending the town, Zaven," Vahan said, extending his hand.

"Better men than me tried to come, Vahan," said Zaven solemnly.

"Yes; we know about Captain Hagop. It hurts to think of it. I know you understand our feelings."

Zaven nodded. "We're here to do what we can. How does the situation look, Vahan?" Zaven asked calmly.

Vahan hesitated and looked at his father, thinking perhaps that the old man should answer. But the Keha remained silent.

"You have been through it, Zaven," Vahan answered. "You know more than we do. But if you want to know how we are set to defend ourselves, I believe I can answer that. We have enough men and arms to fight an army for a year, if we need to. Hallow-Rock has never been taken by force. We will not mar that tradition."

Zaven felt small and uneasy. His thoughts ran in a different direction. He had come to save the people by evacuating them, which from his point of view was the surest way. But could he do that under the existing conditions? Would those who thought like Vahan accept his views? The old man's keen eyes were upon him. He held his head high, proud of the words spoken by his flesh and blood.

"The brave will think like you, and I want you to know that I understand, Vahan," Zaven said in a sincere manner, "but I'm here to save lives. It is said discretion is the better part of valor. I believe that proverb to be true in this case, and I would prefer to begin evacuating the town tonight."

"That is a noble thought. I would have been disappointed if you had spoken otherwise, Zaven," declared the old man. "But isn't it a bit too late for that? And the French, whose uniform you wear to save your own people, let you come here all by yourself. We know how things are. If we wanted to leave our homes, we could have done that safely right after the French handed back Marash to the Turks. They sent some troops here to evacuate us." He stood up straight. "We refused. If Adana will become the Small Armenia, Hallow-Rock will be a part of it!" he cried.

Silence engulfed the rustic, hospitable room. Zaven looked down; he had nothing to say. An unexpected volley of shots dispelled the tenseness. Vahan went to the window. The shooting stopped as suddenly as it began.

"Just routine," Vahan commented indifferently. "They won't let us forget that they are there."

"And we cannot afford to forget it either," Zaven commented, "but I won't be too concerned unless they really do mean business."

"Right. We don't waste ammunition. Of course, you may want to go around and see the situation for yourself. Anytime, you're ready, Zaven."

"We'll do that after we have eaten, my son," interjected the Keha. "A competent commander is half the battle won, and God sent one to us." He turned to Zaven. "We know little of what's happening outside, Zaven. Will you tell us about it?"

Zaven thought for a while. "I don't know much, Keha, even though I left Adana three days ago. However, I did not like what I saw and heard. The prospect of Adana becoming an Armenian colony under the mandate of France is not yet settled. All the Armenians outside the big city have been evacuated. French troops are stationed along the railway; that's why Bakcha and other outposts are still held. My conversation with an officer before I left led me to believe that soon Bakcha, too, will be evacuated.

"However, I'm sure of one thing: France will never leave those who are in Adana to the mercy of the Turks. That's why I thought of getting out of here while the French are still around."

The Keha could not hide his irritation. "Very well, Zaven. Suppose I'm in accord with your views, which I'm not. Where would you have us go? To Bakcha, which by the time we get there could be in the hands of the enemy? And how many of us do you suppose will reach there? Or you would have to go all the way to Adana, five days' journey under normal conditions. Under these war-torn conditions, we would be lucky if we could make it in fifteen days."

Zaven looked sharply at the old man. "I thought you credited me with a bit more sense than that, Keha," he retorted. "When there's no alternative left, a short and favorable route to the railway can be found."

"Please forgive my impudence," the Keha replied. "If some hundred fifty-thousand Armenians in Adana and the French troops within twenty miles of us would neglect us, the shame would be on their heads. We will last to the bitter end."

Months went by. Spring was in the air, bringing hope and vitality. During the long winter months, Hallow-Rock had stood up defiantly against the forbidding odds. Everything in the town had become common property. Whatever food left had to be rationed, but ammunition was more of a problem. Every shell fired was saved and refilled.

Recently there had been a marked change outside the enemy camp. Regular troops in uniform had replaced the motley bands. The chain that surrounded the town had been pulled back a half mile from the defensive walls, eliminating continuous contact and making a breakthrough almost impossible. That night the town was shelled by long-range guns. This was the first time, and the defenders were worried.

Two weeks earlier, a messenger who had miraculously slipped into the town brought news that French troops no longer guarded the railway, and France would definitely not dispatch troops to Hallow-Rock.

But, the people in Adana, with the blessing of France, which had supplied the arms, had organized a large, well-equipped force to rescue Hallow-Rock. The question was, how long could Hallow-Rock hold out against this new threat?

Zaven was at his observation post. Eremia and Vahan were with him. Zaven saw a lone uniformed figure holding a white flag on his way to the town. He turned to his companions.

"Did you see him?" he asked. Both men nodded. "I know why he's coming. Meet him outside, Eremia. Don't let him get too close. Take the message. If he demands a direct answer, tell him where to go. If it is a note, take it, and tell him that they will receive an answer within twenty-four hours."

Eremia, with Vahan following close behind him, was in the open and headed toward the approaching messenger. He came close enough to recognize him, and suddenly froze in his tracks. The man with the white flag wavered momentarily. Then he, too, was stunned.

"Osman!" cried Eremia.

"Eremia!" responded the messenger, who threw down the white flag and dashed forward to put his arms around his old friend. Vahan watched them in amazement from a safe distance. The former comrades, now sworn enemies, gazed at each other for a moment in silence. Osman was the first to recover from the sentimental interlude.

"I have a message for Mustafa, Eremia," he blurted out. "It's from Badjad." He fished into his inside pocket, produced a sealed envelope, and handed it to Eremia.

"Badjad—so he's in command," Eremia mumbled.

"Yes, Eremia. He wants to see Mustafa. I want to see him, too, very much ..."

Eremia hesitated. "I cannot take you to him. But I know that he will come out to meet you. Wait here." He turned to Vahan. "Will you stay with him while I get Zaven?"

"As you wish," said Vahan, looking none too pleased.

When Eremia arrived back at the observation post, Zaven took just one look at him and knew exactly what he was about to say. "You saw one of the boys, and the message is from Badjad," Zaven reflected calmly.

Eremia was astonished and a mite embarrassed. "Yes. The messenger was Osman."

Zaven gave no reaction to the familiar name and simply said, "Let's see the note."

Eremia handed it to him. The envelope was not addressed. He tore it open. He did not need to examine the signature; he would recognize the handwriting anywhere. It was a note made up of two short sentences. "Must see you tonight, Mustafa. Please designate the place."

Zaven paced back and forth, massaging his forehead. Had the note been worded differently, he would have a ready answer. But he knew and understood Badjad well. In spite of their disparate origins and backgrounds, they were alike. Their personal feelings, regardless of how sincere and true, would not cause either one to compromise his principles.

Zaven tore out a sheet from his notebook and scribbled a few lines, folded it, then turned to Eremia. "Let's go. I want to see Osman."

Standing face to face with his old leader, Osman was at a loss for words. He thought quickly of the incident when Mustafa had let him live. Mechanically, his hand went to his forehead in a poor semblance of a salute. Zaven laughed.

"I see, Osman, Badjad has trained you well, and you're a top sergeant. How is he?"

"Very well, Mustafa, and he wishes you well."

"Thank you, Osman. When you hand him my note, tell him that I, too, wish him well."

The rendezvous Zaven had chosen was an orchard situated on a hill on the southern outskirts of the town. It was no man's land. A secret tunnel dug through the rocky precipice led there. Zaven found the night air refreshing and savored the quiet. The fragrance of newly sprouted blossoms filled the air. Everything was peaceful here.

Under the faint moonlight, Zaven noticed five figures climbing the slope. He advanced to meet them halfway. Several paces apart, the two one-time outlaws stopped and looked at each other. Badjad wore a long military cloak displaying the gold-braided epaulettes of a colonel upon his shoulders. Next to him stood another former follower of Daly Mustafa, who was wearing a captain's insignia. It was Hazim, the Albanian. Osman stood in the rear, and two of Zaven's former men, who had escorted the commander of the besieging forces, stood at a safe distance.

"It is good to see you, Badjad," Zaven said, and moved forward.

Overcome with emotion, Hazim rushed forward and threw his arms around Zaven.

Badjad hesitated a moment, then moved closer. "It is good to see you. Oh, Mustafa!" he cried.

They walked away arm in arm in search of privacy. Memories of the past flooded back upon the two leaders. They faced each other.

"I thought you'd have Dio with you, Mustafa," said Badjad. "Is Eremia the only one left?"

"Yes, the only one left," answered Zaven, grimly. "I lost Dio on my way here."

"You lost another one whom I had not seen, but heard about."

Zaven looked surprised. Badjad continued. "Had you not been so clever, you wouldn't have reached here either, Mustafa."

"Hagop was betrayed, then," Zaven grunted.

"The same thing would have happened to you, only the intelligence arrived a bit too late."

"Who supplied the intelligence, may I ask, Badjad?"

"Some of those in French uniform whose heart is in the Muslim cause."

There was an interval of silence. Eremia and Hazim were sitting together a short distance away.

"This war has been my nightmare ever since we parted, Mustafa," said Badjad in a soft voice. "I know each of your moves, and what you have done. You are married, Mustafa. That was the last thing I expected of you. And I know who she is. You killed her foster father. Not that I hold this against you—I would have done the same thing. Men like him have no place in our plan. He and a few others like him caused the loss of thousands of lives, and the destruction of a city. Had they been patient, the French would have handed Marash back to us with their compliments.

"You don't do things halfway, do you, Mustafa? When you love, it is just that simple. Or perhaps it was she who loved you—I can understand that. Why did you leave her, Mustafa? Haven't you had enough? I still think of you as a brother. If this had been personal between us, you know how we would have settled it. What are you thinking, Mustafa? Be honest with me."

"My aim is the same as yours, Badjad: to serve my own people," Zaven answered curtly.

"I understand that and admire you for it. But you cannot do that anymore, not in this country. 'Not to harm the innocent, to defend the helpless, and to die with honor.' Those were your words, Mustafa, and I've tried to live up to them."

Badjad supplied the cigarettes, offered a light, and then continued. "Adana will not become an Armenian colony. It's already been evacuated. The force that was to come to your rescue has been disarmed and exiled by the French upon our demand. England would not let France have Adana. We gave Syria to France as her prize. She is satisfied. Now she is our ally, arming us so that we can kick the Greeks out of Smyrna. England does not like that, but they will not start a new war. First, we will get rid of rogues in Istanbul* and establish ourselves as the de facto government and force the withdrawal of all occupying forces from Turkish territory."

Badjad paused again, thinkng, and took a long drag at his cigarette. "So you see, Mustafa, your cause ends here. If you intend to pick up where you left off, you will go against your own convictions, and I swear I will be the one to stop you. I didn't come here to demand your surrender because I know you too well. I sincerely want to spare the people—and you, for your wife's sake. Tell me, what would you do if you were in my place?"

Zaven had thought of this very question over and over again since he had received Badjad's note, but he was not sure how to answer.

"You would have made it easier for me if you had given your terms and told me to take it or leave it, Badjad," Zaven answered gravely. "To save those who cannot or will not fight comes first. But I will not surrender."

"I know that. I'll be putting myself at a disadvantage, Mustafa. But I'll tell you what I'll do. Send the women and children—and the men who will

**Turkish name for Constantinople*

not fight—to me unarmed, and I'll have Hazim, the Albanian, personally escort them to the Syrian border and hand them over to France. If you want to fight against me to the bitter end, I will accept that. I would kill you, but I will not let you be humiliated."

"I accept," Zaven replied curtly.

"Just one more thing. I have too much respect for your courage and ingenuity, Mustafa. What will you do if you succeed? I want to know that."

Zaven rose and placed his hand upon Badjad's shoulder. "Try to find my wife, Badjad," he whispered.

"Then I'll be wishing for your escape more than my own triumph."

"I believe it, Badjad, but I warn you I won't be generous."

Badjad smiled. "I see you are still carrying my gift," he said, gazing at the Luger at Zaven's side.

"Yes, Badjad, should the time come when I can no longer carry it, my wish is that you get it back."

They stood there for a moment, grasped each other's hand, and then moved slowly away.

"Tomorrow, then, after sunrise, you send the women and children out, and the men who would not stand with you. They will be turned over to France unharmed, I promise," said Badjad coldly.

"I know they will be safe," Zaven responded. "Thank you for making it possible, Badjad. May I suggest a period of cease-fire until Hazim is back?"

"As you wish, Mustafa. You will be calling the shots. It would be unwise for you to start anything before the refugees are in safe hands."

Badjad moved away without glancing back. Zaven stood there and watched him until he was out of sight.

Vahan, who had heard the end of the conversation, asked anxiously, "What's up, Zaven?"

Zaven's answer was curt. "The force that was coming to Hallow-Rock's rescue no longer exists. Adana has been evacuated. All of this territory has been turned over to the Turks. My purpose is to save you, and it's been arranged. There will be no massacre of women and children."

Vahan looked at him with surprise. "What about you and the rest?" he asked.

"We will fight it out. Only those without families and willing to sacrifice their lives will stay with me. You have a wife and three children; you're out, Vahan. You will go with the rest."

"Aren't you in the same situation as me?" Vahan asked slyly.

Zaven laughed. "Not quite, Vahan. What I am in is of my own making."

CHAPTER 32

Five days, quiet yet full of suspense, had passed since Zaven had evacuated the people of Hallow-Rock from their homes, never to return again. It was heartbreaking. It was difficult for Zaven to convince the Keha and his son that they needed to leave. Only fifty men remained with him within the rocky walls of the town. Most of them had started with him from Bakcha. Eremia and Arshag were among them. He had finally received a message from Badjad stating that all the refugees were safely in the hands of the French at the Syrian border.

During this lull Zaven thought of several ways to break through, but it came down to one option: He had to blast his way out. What made it even more difficult was that Badjad was familiar with his maneuvers. Zaven's forces were not large enough to defend the town and make Badjad take the initiative. Every hour of delay would go against him. There would never be an opportune moment to surprise Badjad. The orchard where the two had met and the secret passageway leading straight to it were the best outlet, in spite of the fact that the enemy was entrenched just above it. It would be suicidal to force his way out of the main entrance.

He stood up impulsively, like someone who has suddenly made up his mind. Within an hour the sun would fade below the horizon. He would have light not too much longer—just enough for the initial phase. Then darkness would help. Besides, there was the chance that Badjad wouldn't expect action so soon and at that particular hour.

He walked over to Eremia and instructed him curtly, "Group the men! We're getting out."

Eremia looked at him, somewhat surprised, but moved on without comment to carry out the order.

He decided on a simple strategy of forming two groups, but he had to act fast. While one group fired, the other moved. If the enemy rushed them, that would suit him. But it was unlikely. Badjad knew better. He would try to wear them down.

Zaven's hope that they might slip out into the open unobserved did not materialize. He and four others had hardly emerged from the trenches, when the alarm was given. They crouched down behind the trees and started shooting to cover the others coming out. The first group was out and in position.

Then the battle began with a fury. The enemy seemed very well prepared. They were using machine guns and were about two hundred yards away. It was a long distance to cover. The second group came out and crept forward with Eremia in charge. When they had advanced about fifty yards, they stopped and began firing to cover the movement of the first group. It was a slow, laborious process but it was the only way. Yet, the enemy declined to meet them at close quarters. They also employed somewhat similar tactics and added an encircling maneuver.

It was growing darker by the moment. The enemy had surrounded them. The pressure from their rear was more threatening than the blockade in front of them. Many of Zaven's men had already fallen. Zaven crept forward. Eremia, about fifty feet ahead, had dropped. Blood flowed from his chest. Zaven lifted his head; his eyes were glazed over.

"Don't let them get me. Finish it," Eremia whispered weakly.

Zaven signaled the men around him to move on. Then he picked up Eremia, defying the bullets whizzing by.

"If you love me as a brother, do what I ask," Eremia implored. "I'm finished. You still have a chance."

Zaven ignored his plea. It was a miracle that he was not yet hit. He was alone. The enemy was closing in. There was no escape. A horrible thought flashed through his mind, and brought him quickly to his senses. He, too, must not be caught alive. He used his last grenade. This momentarily stopped the rushing enemy. His rifle was several feet away from him. He had no time to reach it. He set Eremia down, drew his Luger and fired at the enemy, then placed the muzzle of the gun on Eremia's temple and pulled the trigger. He fell to the ground with the Luger pointing at his own temple, but it was not a bullet that numbed him: It was a blow on his head.

When he opened his eyes, it was bright daylight. The room and the objects around him seemed familiar. In fact, he was lying on the same ottoman that he had slept on many nights before. Supporting himself on his elbow he tried to sit up, but his head was heavy and his arms too weak. Badjad was sitting across the room and rushed to his side. He gently laid Zaven's head on the pillow.

"Take it easy," he said, sitting on the edge of the ottoman. "I knew that you would pull through."

Zaven stared at him with mixed affection and hatred. He lay quietly for a while. Then, he made another attempt to sit up.

"If you insist, let me, then, Mustafa," said Badjad and walked across the room with a couple of hard pillows. Zaven sat up. Badjad placed the pillows behind him.

"I'm all right now, but why did you do it?"

"Isn't that obvious, Mustafa?" answered Badjad serenely.

They were both silent for a few moments.

"It would have been better to end it then and there," Zaven mumbled.

"Maybe, but you made a mistake. Probably the first time in your life." Badjad's eyes roved over the wicked purple bruise on Zaven's temple. "Mustafa, wouldn't it be better for you to rest? We'll have plenty of time to talk later."

"I may not be quite up to grappling with you for your gun, but I can talk, Badjad."

"I suppose even the devil can't keep you down," Badjad jested as he rose, walked to the closet, and returned with a bottle and glasses.

"This may help if you're in a talkative mood," he said, and handed a glass of wine to Zaven.

"What time is it?" Zaven asked.

"The afternoon of the following day. I had no intention of hitting you so damned hard, but I had to knock you down, for your own stubborn good. We might have saved Eremia if ..."

Zaven shook his head. "I remember squeezing the trigger. Why didn't it go off?"

Badjad walked to the closet again. This time he returned with Zaven's Luger. He pulled out the magazine.

"You had fired the last bullet, Mustafa. You wouldn't be here if there had been one left."

"I am glad that it's back in your hands. I didn't want anyone else to have that gun."

"I don't take back a gift, Mustafa."

Zaven laughed.

"I mean what I say. It's yours—but without the bullets in it."

Badjad read the question in Zaven's sad eyes. "I know what you're thinking, Mustafa," he said. "I buried thirty-two of them, including Eremia That might give you an idea of how many got away."

"What are you going to do with me?" Zaven asked calmly.

"You will know in time. For the moment, I want to enjoy your company. I have only my personal squadron with me. As soon as you are strong enough to ride, we will go to Adana."

"For a ceremonial hanging?"

Badjad smiled. "Don't tempt me! You have done enough damage. If I have to, I will kill you, but I will not let anyone touch you. Will that make you feel better? This was a personal assignment. I will answer to Mustafa Kemal, the Pasha, alone. Before going to Adana, I intend to inspect the border. By the way, I have another prisoner. He was not with you, but he says he knows you. I am sure you would like to meet him."

"Is he from Adana?" Zaven asked.

"Yes. The men, too, want to see you. But that can wait." He went to the door. "Osman, bring in the prisoner," he commanded.

He turned to Zaven. "I'm leaving for a while. Take it easy. I've gone to the trouble of having your favorite dish prepared—wild boar steak."

Zaven was alone. He looked around the room. Everything he had observed when he came here months ago, tired and downhearted as Keha's guest, was in its place. Then it had looked warm and hospitable. Now it seemed cold and uninviting. He wanted to test his legs. They were rubbery, but he stood up and hobbled to the window. The scenery was as quiet as a graveyard.

He heard the door open and turned toward it. A familiar face stood in the half-opened door. He rubbed his eyes to try and clear his vision, and to make sure it was not an illusion. Yes, he was sure! Unshaven, weary, looking twenty years older, but he was the same!

"Melkon!" he cried, but instead of rushing at him, he sank onto the ottoman.

"I was told that you were hurt, Zaven," Melkon blurted out, sitting on the floor in front of him.

"Tell me what happened," Zaven said.

Melkon told the tale eagerly. "It's a long story, but I'll try to make it short. A day before we were to take off, about four thousand of us, well equipped and full of spirit, found ourselves surrounded by the French troops. An armored car drove right to the command post. Mr. Melikian, another high official, and a French colonel stepped out. Erevant and others in command came out to meet the unexpected visitors. The colonel was very curt. Adana, he said, would be turned over to the Turks, and he demanded that we immediately disarm—otherwise we would jeopardize the lives of a hundred and fifty thousand in the city.

"It was not his threat that subdued us, but the plea of Mr. Melikian. Most of the men were taken to the train on their way to the nearest port to be exiled to Armenia. Erevant and some of us who could be of help were sent to the city to aid the evacuation. But we had other ideas. A few hours before the last group of troops was to be evacuated, seventy of us went to the hills to reach you, Zaven. We got far, but not far enough. The day before yesterday we were caught in a trap less than ten miles away. Erevant and most of them were killed. I was captured."

Zaven stared at Melkon. He could find no words.

"I know," Melkon continued, "you want to know what became of your wife. She is in Beirut with Veronica and Mariam. Erevant arranged it; they will be all right."

"That is a great consolation," said Zaven in a hushed voice, as though talking to himself. "The last time you saw her, how was she?"

"She looked unhappy, but not despondent, Zaven. These were her words: 'God will send my husband back to me.' She's pregnant, Zaven. Mariam told me."

He rose, circled the room, returned to Zaven, and this time took his place beside him. "Who is this colonel, Zaven?" he asked in a whisper. "He wanted to know all about you and your wife. I had the feeling that he can be trusted. I told him everything that I know."

Zaven looked calmly at the former policeman. "The two of us once fought side by side," he said. "He has convictions and purpose. He isn't vicious and wouldn't spill innocent blood, unless he had to. He has already proven that. But he would not tolerate anything or anyone standing between him and his cause."

"I understand," Melkon mumbled.

Badjad walked in. Melkon jumped to his feet.

"Sit down," Badjad commanded. "I am holding Zaven responsible for you." He spoke to Zaven. "Now that the picture is clear, Mustafa," he said seriously, "the future and the welfare of your wife concern me most. Do we understand each other?"

"We do, Badjad," Zaven replied solemnly. "You have a monumental cause. I have none but a wife who needs me."

"You are the lucky one, Mustafa."

Zaven, Badjad and Melkon had been riding the whole day, determined to reach their destination before sundown. The territory they had traveled through was familiar to Zaven. At midday they passed through Bakcha. The sight of that little town brought back memories that he wanted to forget. They had not stopped there, which pleased him.

Zaven and Badjad rode side by side at the front. Neither said a word for a long time. Each was buried in their own thoughts. Badjad might have been thinking about anything or nothing; Zaven's thoughts were obvious. The prospect of seeing Zohra and holding her in his arms was all he could think about. How did she look? How would she act? Would she cry?

The faces of two great men he had lost abruptly dismissed this warm vision. What could he say to Veronica and Mariam, now widows? Zaven was glad Mariam had a son and daughter to give her comfort and security, but they would be no substitute for the love of a good husband. As a young wife, Veronica's pain and loneliness would be even more profound.

Badjad guided his mount closer to Zaven's.

"Have you been there, Mustafa?" he asked, pointing to a cluster of reddish huts ahead.

"Yes," Zaven answered.

"It is a French border post. We'll move past our border guards and get to a safe distance where you can go ahead without trouble. I have taken the pains to bring you this far; I won't have anything go wrong. You still have your uniform. That will help. Who knows, you may even be recognized."

"You have been generous, Badjad."

The colonel laughed. "Did I thank you when you let me live, Mustafa? But I'm not taking any chances. What a pity that someone like you belongs to the other side."

"It is a shame, Badjad. We have no control over where we are born. The day may come when there will be no barriers between people."

"Your words have always mirrored my feelings, Mustafa. How I wish that I could see your wife. Soon you will have a child. I hope it will be a boy. Will you tell him about me?"

"Not only that, but what's more fitting than to name him after you?"

"Thank you, Mustafa. That's the nicest thing you could have said to me." He hesitated a moment, pulled back on the reins, and stopped his mount across from Zaven's. "Do you have any plans?" he said softly.

"No, Badjad. No plans, but a promise to my wife that our child will not grow up under the shadow of the past. Somewhere in this world there may be a place where the people will accept us as we are, not for what we have been."

Bedjad dismounted; Zaven followed his example. A hundred yards away, two soldiers in French uniform crouched and pointed their rifles at them.

"You're on your own from here, Mustafa," Badjad said. "Do you want to take your horse?"

"I won't need it, Badjad."

They all dismounted.

"It was good to see you once more," Zaven said.

"And you, as well," Badjad replied.

Hazim handed Melkon a white flag. Badjad reached in his saddlebag, took out the Luger, and gave it to Zaven. "This is yours; it's empty. I want your promise that you will keep it empty, Mustafa."

"Yes, I will, Badjad," said Zaven. They hugged and parted.

Hoisting the white flag, Zaven and Melkon slowly advanced toward the guards. Zaven looked back. Badjad was still there, watching. He turned to his companion.

"Are you sure Zohra and the others are in Beirut, Melkon?" he asked.

"Positive, Zaven. I have been there. I even know the hotel where they're staying."

Zaven smiled and pressed Melkon's arm. "After seven years it is finally over," he whispered. "I was never meant to be the person I have become, but maybe it was my destiny."
